Vargas Llosa and Latin American Politics

VARGAS LLOSA AND
LATIN AMERICAN POLITICS

Edited by Juan E. De Castro and Nicholas Birns

palgrave
macmillan

VARGAS LLOSA AND LATIN AMERICAN POLITICS
Copyright © Juan De Castro and Nicholas Birns, 2010.

First published in 2010 by PALGRAVE MACMILLAN® in the United States—a division of St. Martin's Press LLC, 175 Fifth Avenue, New York, NY 10010

Where this book is distributed in the UK, Europe, and the rest of the world, this is by Palgrave Macmillan, a division of Macmillan Publishers Limited, registered in England, company number 785998, of Houndmills, Basingstoke, Hampshire RG21 6XS.

Palgrave Macmillan is the global academic imprint of the above companies and has companies and representatives throughout the world.

Palgrave® and Macmillan® are registered trademarks in the United States, the United Kingdom, Europe and other countries.

ISBN: 978-0-230-10529-4

Library of Congress Cataloging-in-Publication Data

Vargas Llosa and Latin American politics / edited by Juan E. De Castro and Nicholas Birns.
  p. cm.
  Includes index.
  ISBN 978-0-230-10529-4 (alk. paper)
  1. Vargas Llosa, Mario, 1936—Criticism and interpretation. 2. Vargas Llosa, Mario, 1936—Political and social views. 3. Latin America—Politics and government. I. Castro, Juan E. De, 1959- II. Birns, Nicholas.

PQ8498.32.A65Z945 2010
863'.64—dc22   2010011095

Design by Scribe Inc.

First edition: October 2010

10 9 8 7 6 5 4 3 2 1

Printed in the United States of America.

Transferred to Digital Printing in 2011

CONTENTS

ACKNOWLEDGMENTS

We want to thank our colleagues at Eugene Lang College, Professor Laura Frost and Dean Neil Gordon, for their encouragement and for creating an environment that promotes research and scholarly production.

Salmagundi and *Revista de Estudios Hispánicos* generously permitted the inclusion of revised versions of essays they had previously published.[1]

Nicholas Birns thanks Larry Birns, his father, and Margaret Boe Birns, his mother, for their affection and support and for having introduced him to Latin America. Juan De Castro is grateful for the support of his wife, Magdalena, during the writing and editing of this book.

We both thank the colleagues who kindly contributed their essays. Without their enthusiasm, dedication, and patience, this book would not have been possible.

1. An early draft of Chapter 5, "Mario Vargas Llosa, the Fabulist of Queer Cleansing," by Paul Allatson, was first published as "*Historia de Mayta*: A Fable of Queer Cleansing" in *Revista de Estudios Hispanicos* 32.3 (Oct. 98): 511–35. An early version of Chapter 8, "Sex, Politics, and High Art: Vargas Llosa's Long Road to *The Feast of the Goat*," by Gene H. Bell-Villada, was published as "The Inventions and Reinventions of Mario Vargas Llosa," in *Salmagundi* 153/154 (Winter 2007): 148–57.

TIMELINE

1936   Jorge Mario Pedro Vargas Llosa is born in Arequipa, Peru on March 28.

1957   His short story "El desafío" ("The Challenge") wins a literary competition organized by *La Revue Française*. The award is a trip to Paris.

1959   Wins the scholarship Javier Prado at the Universidad Complutense in Madrid. His short story collection *Los jefes* (*The Chiefs*) wins the Leopoldo Alas award.

1963   *La ciudad y los perros* (*The Time of the Hero*) is published.

1966   Publishes *La casa verde* (*The Green House*).

1967   Publishes *Los cachorros* (*The Cubs*). *La casa verde* receives Rómulo Gallegos Award given to the best Spanish-language novel written during the previous five-year period. His reception speech "La literatura es fuego" ("Literature Is Fire") is widely disseminated.

1969   Publishes *Conversación en La Catedral* (*Conversation in the Cathedral*).

1971   His PhD dissertation at the Universidad Complutense is published as *García Márquez: Historia de un deicidio*. Also publishes *Historia secreta de una novela*, on the writing of *La casa verde*. The "Padilla affair"—the jailing of dissident Cuban poet Heberto Padilla and some of his collaborators—leads to Vargas Llosa's permanent break with the Cuban Revolution.

1973   Publishes *Pantaleón y las visitadoras* (*Captain Pantoja and the Special Service*).

1975   Publishes *La orgía perpetua: Flaubert y Madame Bovary* (*The Perpetual Orgy: Flaubert and* Madame Bovary).

1977   *La tía Julia y el escribidor* (*Aunt Julia and the Scriptwriter*) is published. Begins writing biweekly essays in a section called Piedra de toque (Keystone) for the Peruvian magazine *Caretas*. These are currently syndicated by the Spanish newspaper *El País*.

1981   Publishes *La guerra del fin del mundo* (*The War of the End of the World*). Publishes his first play *La señorita de Tacna* (*The Young Lady from Tacna*). Publishes *Entre Sartre y Camus*, a collection of essays. Broadcasts a TV series in Peru's Panamericana TV: *La torre de Babel.*

1983 Publishes first volume of *Contra viento y marea,* a collection of his political and cultural articles. He will update the collection throughout the decades. Publishes the play *Kathie y el hipopótamo* (*Kathie and the Hippopotamus*). Accepts to head a commission investigating the murder of journalists in the Andean town of Uchuraccay. The commission publishes the "Informe sobre Uchuraccay" ("Report on Uchuraccay"). A revised version of his section of the "Informe" was published in the *New York Times* under the title "Inquest in the Andes" and in *Granta* as "Story of a Massacre."

1984 Publishes *La historia de Mayta* (*The Real Life of Alejandro Mayta*).

1986 Publishes *¿Quién mató a Palomino Molero?* (*Who Killed Palomino Molero?*). The play *La chunga* is published. Writes the "Foreword" to Hernando de Soto's economic study of the Peruvian informal economy, *El otro sendero* (*The Other Path*). It is widely reprinted under the title, "La revolución silenciosa" ("The Silent Revolution").

1987 Publishes *El hablador* (*The Storyteller*). Founds a political movement—Movimiento contra la estatización de la banca en el Perú (Movement Against the Nationalization of Banks in Peru)—against the planned state takeover of banking in Peru.

1988 Publishes *Elogio de la madrastra* (*In Praise of the Stemother*). Founds the political party Movimiento Libertad (Liberty Movement), which allies itself with conservative parties in the Frente Democrático (Democratic Front), also known as FREDEMO.

1989 Becomes the FREDEMO's presidential candidate.

1990 Loses in a second electoral round to Alberto Fujimori. Publishes collection of literary essays *La verdad de las mentiras;* republished in an expanded version in 2002.

1991 Publishes *A Writer's Reality,* based on a series of lectures. *Carta de batalla por Tirant lo Blanc,* which collects all his essays on that novel of chivalry, dating back to 1969, is published.

1993 Publishes *El pez en el agua* (*A Fish in the Water*), a books of memoirs, the novel *Lituma en los Andes* (*Death in the Andes*), and the play *El loco de los balcones.* Threatened by members of the Fujimori government with having his passport taken away, the government of Spain grants him Spanish citizenship.

1994 Publishes *Desafíos de la libertad*. Writes a radio play for the BBC, *Ojos bonitos, cuadros feos*. Receives the Cervantes Award, the highest literary award in the Hispanic world.

1996 Publishes *La utopía arcaica. José María Arguedas y las ficciones del indigenismo* (*The Archaic Utopia: José María Arguedas and the Fictions of Indigenismo*). A selection of his essays is translated into English as *Making Waves*.

1997 Publishes *Los cuadernos de don Rigoberto* (*The Notebooks of Don Rigoberto*) and *Cartas a un joven novelista* (*Letters to a Young Novelist*).

2000 Publishes *La fiesta del chivo* (*The Feast of the Goat*).

2001 Publishes the essay collection *El lenguaje de la pasión* (*The Language of Passion*).

2003 Publishes *El paraíso en la otra esquina* (*The Way to Paradise*) and *Diario de Irak*, a journalistic study of the war in Iraq.

2004 Publishes *La tentación de lo imposible. Víctor Hugo y Los misérables* (*The Temptation of the Impossible: Victor Hugo and* Les Misérables).

2005 Publishes in France *Dictionnaire Amoureux de l'Amérique Latine* (in Spanish *Diccionario del amante de América Latina*), which organizes alphabetically texts written over fifty years on Latin America.

2006 Publishes *Travesuras de la niña mala* (*The Bad Girl*) and *Israel/Palestina. Paz o guerra santa*, essays on Israel and Palestine.

2007 Publishes the play *Odiseo y Penélope*. Publishes *Touchstones*, a collection of essays.

2008 Publishes *Wellsprings*, a collection of his lectures, the play *Al pie del Támesis*, and the monograph *El viaje a la ficción. El mundo de Juan Carlos Onetti* (*Journey into Fiction: The world of Juan Carlos Onetti*).

2009 Publishes *Sables y utopías. Visiones de América latina*, a collection of his political essays.

INTRODUCTION

JUAN E. DE CASTRO AND NICHOLAS BIRNS

AMONG THE MANY REVOLUTIONS OF THE 1960S, ONE MUST count the surprising irruption of the Latin American novel into Western literary consciousness. Until then Latin America had been seen as, at best, a backwater at the margins of the turbulent currents that flowed throughout literature, at worst, merely as a source for topics and settings mined by European and U.S. writers such as Graham Greene, Malcolm Lowry, Ernest Hemingway, and Thornton Wilder. While this view from the cultural center was myopic, to say the least, the fact is that, for instance, a critic of the importance of Edmund Wilson could boast about never having been interested in a Latin American novel.[1]

This situation changed with the publication and relatively rapid translation into English and French of a series of brilliant novels by a group of young Latin American novelists.[2] As was the case in music with the Beatles, four were Latin American novelists who captured the reading public's imagination: the Mexican Carlos Fuentes; the Argentine Julio Cortázar, the oldest of the group; the Colombian Gabriel García Márquez, up to now the only Nobel Prize recipient; and the Peruvian Mario Vargas Llosa, the youngest and the subject of these essays. Just like the Cuban Revolution brought Latin America to the mainstream of international political discussion and reflection, as well as to the front pages of the major newspapers throughout the West, the literary revolution known as the 'Boom,' permitted the region's novel to win critical consideration and the preferences of many readers throughout Europe, the United States, and the rest of the world. As evidenced by the statements and writings of authors as diverse as John Barth, John Updike, or Salman Rushdie, the Latin American novel became during this period a major influence on both established and beginning writers.[3]

The previous reference to the Cuban Revolution is not arbitrary. In fact, public interest in anti-imperial struggles, exemplified by Cuba and

Vietnam, played a major role in creating an environment favorable to the reception of the Boom novels. Despite being written by sophisticated authors who had, without exception, fully incorporated the high modernist innovations of earlier Western masters such as James Joyce or William Faulkner, many saw these texts as representing the views of Latin Americans oppressed by the international political and economic system. Moreover, in addition to helping shape their reception, the Cuban Revolution was actually a central event in the lives of these writers. All were committed supporters of Castro's government, a fact that helped make these four writers from very different countries in the region into a coherent group that collaborated and supported each other. Political and artistic revolution seemed, for once, to go hand in hand. But what the Cuban Revolution joined, the Cuban Revolution would separate.

BIOGRAPHY

Perhaps the one Boom writer closest to the Cuban Revolution, Mario Vargas Llosa, was a member of the governing committee of its main cultural institution, Casa de las Américas, and participated actively throughout the 1960s in the island's cultural life. While born in the Andean Peruvian city of Arequipa in 1936, Vargas Llosa had, thanks to a fellowship, moved first to Spain, then to Paris. (Later in the decade he would move to London). He became a pan-Hispanic celebrity in 1962, when his *La ciudad y los perros* (known in English as *The Time of the Hero*) won an award given by the Barcelona-based press Seix Barral. His formally innovative novels of the 1960s were characterized by political and social topics—patriarchy in the military, in *Time of the Hero*, the imperfect and discriminatory modernization of the Amazonia in *The Green House* (1967), the social corrosion occasioned by the Odría dictatorship in Peru in the 1950s, in *Conversation in The Cathedral* (1969)—that seemed to warrant his reputation as a leftist.

In 1967, *The Green House* received the first Rómulo Gallegos International Novel Prize, one the most prestigious literary awards in the Spanish speaking world. His reception speech "Literature Is Fire" has been frequently interpreted as the clearest statement of his 1960s radicalism. With characteristic passion, Vargas Llosa states, "Literature is fire, that it means nonconformity and rebellion . . . the raison d'etre of a writer is protest, disagreement, and criticism . . . society must either suppress for ever that human faculty which is artistic creation and eliminate once and for all that unruly social element, the writer, or else embrace literature, in which case it has no alternative but to accept a perpetual torrent of attacks" (72). Vargas Llosa then adds the following: "Literature is a form of permanent insurrection and cannot accept straight jackets" (72). The anticonformist ethos of the 1960s, which played such a major role in the reception of the Boom, is here eloquently presented by the Peruvian novelist. Aesthetic, political, and moral insurrection are presented as interrelated.

However, the case can be made that Vargas Llosa's speech already reflects his burgeoning malaise regarding the direction that the Cuban Revolution was taking. According to Vargas Llosa, after the award was made public, Haydée Santamaría, the director of the principal Cuban cultural institution, Casa de las Américas, proposed that he publicly donate the money to Che Guevara's guerrilla, while privately the Cuban government would reimburse him. He reacted with indignation to the Cuban novelist and diplomat Alejo Carpentier, who had served as mediator: "Alejo, what Haydée is suggesting is an offensive farce . . . This is not the way to treat a writer who respects his own work" (Setti 149). This emphasis in "Literature Is Fire" on a writer's moral obligation as unaffected by social or political considerations could be seen as expressing his nascent doubts about the Cuban Revolution.

Thus, rather than expressing a belief in the dissonance between literary creation and capitalism, as one would expect from a left-winger of the 1960s, "Literature Is Fire" describes a perpetual tension between true literary creation and society. In fact, Vargas Llosa goes out of his way to emphasize the fact that a writer's divorce from the mainstream of society is not exclusive to capitalism but would also continue under a socialism that he still considered necessary "for Latin America to enter, once and for all, a world of dignity and modernity" (73). He, in fact, concludes, "But when social injustices disappear, this will not mean that the hour of consent, subordination and official complicity will have arrived for the writer. His mission will continue, must continue, to be the same: any compromise in this area will be a betrayal. Within the new society, and along the road that our personal ghosts and demons drive us, we will continue as before, as now, saying no, rebelling, demanding recognition for our right to dissent, showing . . . that dogma, censorship and arbitrary acts are also mortal enemies of progress and human dignity" (73). Although one can see in Vargas Llosa's words a statement of the (at least apparent) universal tension between communal needs and individual desire, implied in his reference to "personal ghosts and demons," this passage responds directly to the "arbitrary" proposal by Santamaría that Vargas Llosa convert the Rómulo Gallegos award ceremony into propaganda for the Cuban Revolution. Instead Vargas Llosa, implicitly criticizing the incipient political hardening that would soon be exhibited in the Padilla affair, vindicates freedom as the essence of literary activity: a position still central to his novelistic practice.

THE PADILLA AFFAIR

In 1968, the censoring of Heberto Padilla's poetry collection *Fuera del juego*, despite having received an award from the Cuban Writer's Union, led to the first major fissure between progressive intellectuals, including the Boom authors, and the Cuban Revolution. A second, more dramatic stage of what would be known as "The Padilla affair" was reached in 1971, when, after being jailed, Padilla, his wife Belkis Cuza Malé, Pablo Armando Fernández, Manuel Díaz Martínez, and Cesar López, published what were obviously forced self-criticisms and confessions. In response to burgeoning international criticism, Fidel Castro made a speech in which he defied international pressure and implicitly included the Boom writers among his targets, upbraiding them as "brazen Latin Americans, who instead of being here in the trenches live in the bourgeois salons 10,000 miles from the problems" ("Discurso").

It had until then been possible to interpret Castro's famous 1961 speech "Words to the Intellectuals," especially his statement, "within the Revolution, everything goes; against the Revolution, nothing," as implying the toleration, even the fostering, of artistic experimentation and freedom as long as it was not explicitly antisocialist ("Palabras a los intelectuales").[4] However, Castro's 1971 speech made it clear that intellectual "freedom" was now to be determined from a purely instrumental perspective by the Cuban government and that rigorous alignment with the revolution and subordination to its political dictates was a precondition for intellectual activity.

In an April public letter addressed to Santamaría, Vargas Llosa resigned from his position in Casa de las Américas and criticized in the strongest words the "affair," which reminded him of "the Stalinist trials in the 1930s" ("Letter to Haydée Santamaría" 105). In September of that year, many liberal and radical intellectuals, including the four major Boom novelists, signed an open letter, written by Vargas Llosa, criticizing the treatment of Padilla and the other writers. (Other signatories were Jean-Paul Sartre Sartre, Simone de Beauvoir, Susan Sontag, and Italo Calvino).

For reasons beyond the scope of this essay, Cortázar and García Márquez recanted from their criticisms of the Cuban Revolution. In fact, Cortázar famously addressed Castro admitting, "You're right Fidel, only in the struggle is there a right to dissidence, only from inside can there come criticism" (Ubilluz 333). García Márquez, despite serious misgivings at the time, would ultimately become a friend and confidant of Fidel Castro.[5] The Boom writers, who had once been a united literary front, went each their own way—in the case of Vargas Llosa and García Márquez, becoming political and personal adversaries. Moreover, given the progressive loss of interest in anti-imperial and radical politics, as the 1970s went on, no longer were the Boom writers primarily read as representing a unified expression of Latin America, even if their individual reputation as writers did not suffer.

AFTER THE BOOM

In the case of Vargas Llosa, the post-Boom novels—*Captain Pantoja and the Special Service* (1973), about the unintended consequences of establishing an official military prostitution service in the Peruvian jungle for the isolated servicemen, and *Aunt Julia and the Scriptwriter* (1977), a semiautobiographical narration of the author's own courtship of his first wife, his aunt by marriage—are characterized by what Raymond L. Williams has called "the discovery of humor" (*Mario Vargas Llosa* 93). Of equal importance, in these novels Vargas Llosa used a much less complex narrative style and seemed, at least superficially, to embrace popular culture: *Aunt Julia*, for instance, is indebted to radio soap operas.[6] While Vargas Llosa would rediscover the ambition to create "total"—that is, self-sufficient—narrative worlds, in his 1983 masterpiece *The War of the End of the World*, about the peasant rebellion of Canudos in late nineteenth-century Brazil and in 2000, and in *The Feast of the Goat*, a novel about the brutal Trujillo dictatorship, Vargas Llosa's narrative style nonetheless became much more accessible after the 1960s.

When Vargas Llosa returned to live Peru in 1979, he was no longer part of the Left and, instead, began associating with those attempting to renovate free market ideas. And by the mid-1980s, Vargas Llosa had become the main face of antistate activism in Peru and Latin America, opposing Peruvian President Alan García's attempted nationalization of the banks and, as we will see, writing the foreword, to his then-friend Hernando de Soto's free-market analyses of Peruvian and Latin American black markets, *The Other Path: The Invisible Revolution in the Third World* (1986), which has frequently been considered a neoliberal manifesto. In 1990 he became a candidate for the Presidency of Peru on a free-market platform. He was defeated by a nearly unknown university professor and engineer, Alberto Fujimori, whereupon he returned to Europe.

Despite this setback, his political influence has grown. While Vargas Llosa has, on occasion, taken political positions discordant with those that characterize the Peruvian and international Right—such as vocally supporting the candidacy of Barack Obama in the United States—today he is as well known as a supporter and propagandist for free-market policies, as he is as a novelist.[7] Vargas Llosa, who once defended socialist revolutions, has become a proponent of neoliberal "invisible" revolutions.

UNDERSTANDING THE "NEW" VARGAS LLOSA

This new orientation of Vargas Llosa not only startled some of his long-time admirers but also posed a vexing set of questions for his academic readers. Although the default position of most intellectuals is assumed to be the democratic Left—it is the assumed political strand that "great writers" have been on since at least the time of Victor Hugo—the authoritarian Left (Sartre, for a time W. H. Auden, Pablo Neruda, and Theodore Dreiser) and the authoritarian Right (Pound, Heidegger, in a different way T. S. Eliot) have attracted their adherents, the democratic Right is the (Of course in a Latin America long ruled by rightist dictatorships, it was not nearly as easy to be on the democratic Left as it was in the U.K., Sweden, or even France). The democratic Right is so unusual an affiliation for the traditional intellectual that Vargas Llosa's adherence to it was itself attention getting, given his status as an internationally known writer very close to being a literary household name. The general emergence of the neoliberal intellectual, if not necessarily tethered to the democratic-right party of his or her nation at least willing to entertain endorsing it, was a new phenomenon. It was not a new phenomenon for parties of the democratic Right to be in power in Western countries. But it was a new phenomenon for intellectuals of world renown to attach themselves to those parties or to the ideologies they represented, with the enthusiasm and brio that had characterized the engagement of intellectual with the Left.

A notable aspect is that intellectuals who attached themselves to these ideologies did so without the expectation of receiving government posts or perquisites. In one of the rare previous incidents of a prominent center-right literary intellectual, André Malraux had supported de Gaulle after his return to politics in the late 1950s and received a cabinet post for it. The tradition of Latin American and French writers being appointed to diplomatic posts by their governments, such as Octavio Paz (who himself moved to the Center-Right in his last decades) being named to the Mexican ambassadorship to India, is well known, although this was often less an instance of political affiliation than of providing a kind of honorarium to prominent writers and also letting their nation put its best cultural foot forward internationally. Though Vargas Llosa sought the presidency of Peru, he did not otherwise accept any government sinecure. His public engagement has not been publicly patronized or sanctioned.

But it has been conducted through a web of private institutions, from the Spanish newspaper *El País* to, as Juan De Castro points out in his essay for this volume, such U.S. think tanks as the American Enterprise Institute. Vargas Llosa's public engagements could be seen thus not under the lens of government but of what Michel Foucault, in his later work, called "governmentality"—the web of paragovernmental institutions that do not formally exercise political authority but that in their operations cement and ramify the hold of reigning mentalities. In an era of what Zygmunt Bauman calls "liquid modernity"—where not only the form but also the substrate behind the form is perpetually morphing and being revalued—having one's intellectual identity anchored in governmentality rather than in government or governance not only is in tune with the antistatism of free-market ideology but also is the only way to be portable, flexible, and intellectually on the move. This is not to say that Vargas Llosa's particular positions are the only ones that can be taken in a neoliberal era—there are many possible positions, including many fiercely critical of both Vargas Llosa and neoliberalism. Yet most intellectuals of the early twenty-first century are likelier to gain their authority from "govermentality" rather than "government." And no serious thinker of this era can avoid confrontation, for good or for ill, with neoliberal beliefs and dogmas.

A link between the free market and democracy is endemic to Vargas Llosa's post-1980 intellectual self-presentation. There is a tacit and sometimes explicit argument here that this is not "conservatism" as such but a return to nineteenth-century liberalism, when a zeal for opening new markets and securing unfettered economic exchange was linked to extension of the franchise and social and national liberation in Europe. Vargas Llosa and his defenders are correct to say that this was the original meaning of "liberalism" and that the term did not at first possess the implications of social welfare and collectivism that, at least in North America, it eventually acquired and that mandate the "neo'" prefix. On the other hand, though, one of the hallmarks of the neoliberal era has been for authoritarian governments to try to sever economic from political liberalism in a way that would have horrified Richard Cobden, John Bright, and other exponents of the "Manchester liberalism" to which contemporary neoliberalism often harkens back. From that of Augusto Pinochet in 1970s Chile to Hu Jintao in 2000s China, to use the rhetoric of free markets and open borders while discouraging that of political pluralism and the free flow of information was a prominent tactic. And there is another valence for the "neo": neoliberalism's insistence on presenting itself as a self-sufficient ideology that is on the rise, that is the coming thing, and that is comprehensive. Thus Roland Forgues, in his essay in this volume demonstrates that, even though Vargas Llosa rejects Sartre's revolutionary absolutism for Camus's sage skepticism, it is the Sartrean model of the engaged intellectual superstar that the Peruvian writer tailors to a very different political style. Fabiola Escárzaga also demonstrates that Vargas Llosa seeks to present his political affiliation as a token of moral and intellectual virtue, as was common in the days when a leftist ideological attachment was to a writer what a knighthood, or the patronage of a titled aristocrat or merchant prince, was in the seventeenth or eighteenth centuries.

Vargas Llosa, though, is, even in his latter work, not totally a creature or a manifestation of neoliberalism. In his criticism, the novelist continues to defend the autonomy of the literary. Leftists might think this is simply a code word for defending bourgeois interests. We all know, and to some extent have misinterpreted, Walter Benjamin's distinction between Marxism making the aesthetic political and Fascism aestheticizing politics. By thinking their only enemy is simply political disengagement, by presuming that all political affiliations that are not unspeakably Fascist must be on the Left or "progressive"; intellectuals have been blindsided by the very existence of a forceful, trenchant body of work affiliating itself with center-Right viewpoints and ready to provide a comprehensive alternative to leftist pieties. Some writers who have turned away from radical causes become "aesthetes" or talk about the autonomy of art, wish to distance art from politics. Vargas Llosa is not like that at all. Although he speaks eloquently on behalf of the independence of art, he is really speaking of the writer's own unfettered ability to create. He does not see art as inherently apolitical or ravished by politics. In this way, he is "path dependent" on the leftist tradition of the engaged intellectual. The leftist-engaged intellectual endorses politicians, supports causes, attacks dictators, and announces epochal changes of mind on pivotal issues—so does Vargas Llosa. In general, the renascent Right has changed the content of political debate. But it has not altered the formal definition, or the procedural contexts, of the field of the political. This is so even despite the vast changes in technology and communication that neoliberalism has seen and with which it has interacted.

After reading Sergio Franco's discussion of *A Fish in the Water*, though, we might reflect that leftist intellectuals, though, seldom ever ran for public office, especially the president to their country. Perhaps this is because so few of the people agreed with them. Vargas Llosa at least had the Peruvian upper middle class on his side. Vargas Llosa also was linked with the example of Václav Havel, and this link gave him the moral authority of anticommunism on his side, even though Alan García, for all his haplessness was hardly Gustav Husak. (Indeed, not even General Velasco was this). Vargas Llosa associates his personal moral virtue with what he sees as the terminal paralysis and misjudgment of the Left at the end of what

Eric Hobsbawm has termed "the short twentieth century" from 1914 to 1989—a century that, for leftist political ideals, was disastrous. If history had simply neatly rounded back to form with the fall of Communism, Vargas Llosa's election might have been the feather in the cap of this temporal rerouting. Alberto Fujimori's election and the subsequent tragedy of his administration illustrates that history still had other detours to make and that one of the problems with Vargas Llosa's candidacy was that its implied rationale was an intellectual one rather than one that resonated with the overall Peruvian electorate.

Vargas Llosa, as candidate, thus might have had overly simple or categorical assumptions about the way things would go. But there is indeed a difference between Vargas Llosa and some other intellectuals who leant rightward during the twentieth century's last decades. The American neoconservative Norman Podhoretz, who started out as a literary critic—he studied with Lionel Trilling and F. R. Leavis—has written very little literary criticism since 1980. But what he has written has been more or less in the service of neoconservatism, defending those writers whose beliefs or practices are thought conservative and attacking those who are clearly outside the fold. Vargas Llosa, on the other hand, has continued to admire just those writers he had admired from the beginning, such as Flaubert, who necessarily would at once outsoar and deride any political affiliation. Vargas Llosa has not just critiqued the Left but affiliated himself with a counter agenda often possessing its own revolutionary aspirations, as the popularity of the phrase "the Reagan Revolution" in the United States demonstrated. But in his criticism, he has made clear his own judgments of art and taste are what matters.

This position has also, perhaps surprisingly, been true in his fiction. Although Jean O'Bryan-Knight, in her essay in this volume, refutes the assertion of other criticism that Vargas Llosa, while exalting the entrepreneur in his nonfiction, has not represented businessmen in his fiction, he certainly does not propagandize for them or situate them as virtuous heroes the way a hypothetical neoliberal inversion of socialist realism might. Nor is Vargas Llosa scathingly critical of leftists or revolutionaries in his post-1980 novels that concern politics. As Birns asserts in his essay for this volume, the reader of *The War of the End of the World* uninstructed in Vargas Llosa's politics might see him as possessing a grain of sympathy for the rebels of Canudos, or at least refraining from editorializing about them. Similarly, as Forgues shows, *The Way to Paradise* is not scornful of Flora Tristán's utopian and feminist hopes. Though the novel neither shares Tristán's perspective nor propagandizes for it, it nonetheless shows that her hopes were worthy and emancipatory ones and that she is a figure of historical importance and value, not just a fatuous naïf. And as Gene H. Bell-Villada shows in his exploration of *The Feast of the Goat*, there seems no particular political bias in that novel except a hatred of dictatorship. Though one could construct an allegory in which the monstrous Rafael Trujillo (and his ghoulish entourage) either stands for what the Chilean commentator Claudio Véliz has termed "the centralist tradition in Latin America" or is the model of a caudillo such as Vargas Llosa has long accused Fidel Castro and later Hugo Chávez of being, the historical truth that Trujillo was a right-wing dictator supported by the United States is incontestable. Moreover, Vargas Llosa shows no particular sympathy for Joaquín Balaguer, who, far more than Trujillo, became the acceptable face of U.S. influence in the Dominican Republic in the decades after Trujillo's violent demise. Vargas Llosa's portrait of Balaguer—the calculating, methodical sidekick who slickly moves into the Number One slot after the overweening tyrant has gone down in flames—has the impartiality and fascinated contempt that Shakespeare might well have exerted if the English playwright had found such a subject available to him. In calling *The Feast of the Goat* a return to Vargas Llosa's old form, Bell-Villada is noting this artistic impartiality, which can use the political but not be bound by it.

As Sabine Köllmann considers at the beginning of her essay, this split may be convenient in terms of reception for Vargas Llosa. The nimble formula Köllmann cites as commonplace about Vargas Llosa—"love his fiction, hate his politics"—provides a handy way for Vargas Llosa to not lose the reading public for his fiction, most of whom will at least have maintained nominal allegiance to left-wing identities, without compromising the deeply felt political beliefs he has come to have. Furthermore, even in a political climate, extending at least from 1980 to 2008, friendly to the Right, aesthetic purity still had, to use the terms of Pierre Bourdieu, more "cultural capital" than an explicitly rightist linkage. But Köllmann provides a more satisfying answer when she points to the sheer heterogeneity of Vargas Llosa's oeuvre, in which, if politics does impinge on aesthetics it does so in so many multifarious ways as to prevent the generation of one predetermining formula. Vargas Llosa seems to encourage this sense of plurality, as Franco points out in his analysis of *A Fish in the Water*. The novelist will not write a "straight" memoir of his 1990 campaign for the Peruvian presidency. Rather, it has to be braided with a memoir of his childhood and maturation, as if to show where the mature public man came from and that he must be considered in the light of his sources, not on his own, on the basis solely of his manifest platform. The biographical trajectory of *The Bad Girl*, where the malevolently enchanting lady comes

INTRODUCTION 11

to personify various states of mind from sixties leftism to, arguably, neo-liberalism itself, insists on a similarly genetic survey of the character of its protagonist Ricardo Somocurcio. Context, and therefore heterogeneity, rules all.

But other essays in the volume show there can be dark turns amid these heterogeneities. For Ignacio López-Calvo, Vargas Llosa, in *The Storyteller* and *Death in the Andes*, is at least ostensibly not against the indigenous people of the Andes. But the novelist is opposed to the left-wing myth of the indigenous because the Left has, in his view, infused indigenous discourse with a lot of romantic absolutes designed to foil bourgeois modernity. Vargas Llosa says he is hostile to most iterations of the indigenous not out of racism or Eurocentrism (though there are hints that López-Calvo himself does not totally buy the novelist's position here) but because the Left has taken sympathy for the indigenous as one of its major talking points. Therefore proindigenous rhetoric must be disempowered as part of the comprehensive counterideology of neoliberalism requires with respect to leftist discourses. It is like, in aerial bombardment, hitting the enemy's oil refineries not out of environmental motives but merely to take away one of the enemy's logistical assets. Vargas Llosa indeed had a point. Too often the Left has assumed that any person of color, or women, or indigenous person who does not commit themselves to identity-based liberation in the terms defined by the Left is a traitor to their kind. Vargas Llosa can thus claim to be defending a genuine indigenous identity against the fiction of such imposed by the intelligentsia. There are two issues here, though, that complicate matters. One is that Vargas Llosa accepts the basic model of identity being something that has to assert itself in the face of prejudice; the difference being whereas the Left asserts the subaltern identity in the face of Eurocentrism, neoconservatives asserts it in the face of univocal assumptions about the coincidence of identity and politics. The fundamental association of progress or the socially desirable with the vindication of the subaltern identity is not questioned.

The second issue is that this neoliberal counterargument seizes on an opening in the secondary reverberation of a rhetorical argument, a syllogism that does not follow through on its premise. But Vargas Llosa and neoliberalism in general try then to base their major argument about indigenous and other identities on the occasional hypocrisies of leftist identity politics. They make a general argument about the oppression of the indigenous, which they nonetheless assume, and therefore leave that ground in the hands of the Left after all. Of course López-Calvo implies that this may all be rodomontade, that Vargas Llosa may in fact be Euro-centric (certainly he quotes statements that imply a sense of European cultural superiority on the par of the novelist—to which one could add Vargas Llosa's description of pre-Columbian cultures in *Wellsprings* as "the antlike societies" [127]), and that all the vindication of an "actual" identity corrupted by leftist misappropriation may be a counterargument mounted to tactically outflank an argument and not something the novelist is ultimately willing to stand on as a bedrock first principle.

Paul Allatson focuses on the revelation by the narrator of *The Real Life of Alejandro Mayta* to the "real" Alejandro Mayta that the Mayta the narrator has concocted for his tale is a homosexual. Allatson considers the gap between the rhetorical appearance and the pragmatic reverberations of this ascribed identity. The novelist embraces the cosmopolitan panache and worldliness that a tolerance of homosexuality indicates. Yet this tolerance is tinged with a bit of existential pathologizing—the Queer subject as the "other," just as, in existentialist embraces of the thought of Frantz Fanon in the 1960s, it was so convenient to have the African be the perpetual other, the nonnegotiable figure of alienation. Even more fundamentally, it satisfies the need to have an outsider, somebody to keep out of the economy, somebody who is alienated and unincorporated, as the darker-skinned or hued female was so often kept out of the marriage plots of Sir Walter Scott and James Fenimore Cooper. There is sympathy for the Queer subject but not a sense that they can ever become representative or typical.

Fabiola Escárzaga analyzes Vargas Llosa's political ideas not as a set of disparate opinions or even as a purely political identity—as an ordinary partisan columnist with no literary affiliations might have—but as part of a comprehensive identity. Not pretending to intellectual originality as he might in creative terms in his fiction, Vargas Llosa, for Escárzaga, anchors his stake in politics to an identity as a public intellectual, whose willingness to pronounce on issues and organize ideas for mainstream consumption is not just product but substantive anchor of his virtue. Vargas Llosa also tries to use the intellectual ground to make up for more worldly losses, such as his loss to Albert Fujimori in the 1990 election. Playing unabashedly to the light-skinned elites of prosperous urbanized areas, Vargas Llosa in a sense becomes president of the Latin American neoliberal movement. From this lofty vantage point, Vargas Llosa can decide what leaders and personalities are to his liking, so that Michelle Bachelet made the grade whereas Rafael Correa did not. But Escárzaga implies that Vargas Llosa's true antagonist is not any politician, not Hugo Chávez, not even Fujimori (who was in any event not sufficiently to the left of the novelist's ideologically), but the left-wing intelligentsia. As in López-Calvo's essay, for Escárzaga the leftist intelligentsia is the true source of all evil in the eyes of the novelist; other entities, from politicians to group identity affiliations, are but pawns of the lettered elite. If Vargas Llosa thus assumes a role that gives him great honor and stature it is not without cost, according to Escárzaga. As Vargas Llosa voices opinions of moneyed, white elites, most of them lacking both the novelist's argumentative subtlety, his creative genius, and his genuine dedication to what seems to him morally right, there arises the unpleasant conundrum as to who is using who.

Yet for all the sarcasm implicit in Escárzaga's title, there is a sense that, as errant a knight as Vargas Llosa may be from the point of view of the democratic Left, he is not truly a knave either. Notably Vargas Llosa has not at all caved or capitulates to the market by writing strictly out of commercial motivations to cater to perceived public taste. Even when he has written books in popular genres or alluded to such (e.g. *Who Killed Palomino Molero?* or *Death in the Andes*), one senses he is following his muses, not looking for a quick payout. Moreover, this interest in the popular preceded the explicit neoliberal turn and can be seen in *Captain Pantoja and the Special Service* and the much acclaimed *Aunt Julia and the Scriptwriter*, Vargas Llosa has had no more a commercial a career as those Boom peers of his who have remained on the Left such as Gabriel García Márquez or anchored somewhere in the center such as Carlos Fuentes. Those skeptical of the Boom could see the entire paraphernalia of the movement—the denigration of previous Latin American fiction, the marketing of the Boom outlook to the world as consummately representative of Latin America—as inclined toward garnering commercial reward. But it would be the generation and movement as a whole—not Vargas Llosa and not his politics—that would be so accused.

Indeed, as Wilfrido Corral argues, Vargas Llosa, for all his love of the contrivance of fiction, its capacity to render the invisible real, has always been a man of ideas and a writer who sees literature as having a responsibility, not to tow a particular political line, but to unfurl what Vargas Llosa forthrightly calls its "lies" in order to disseminate a more skeptical and plural idea of truth than any ideology, Left or Right, can give. As Corral notes, Vargas Llosa touches many issues that inevitably excited journalistic reaction and counterreaction, occasioning a play of interpretive responses that are apt to degenerate into sterile polemics. Corral couples this, though, with a plea to regard Vargas Llosa with the intellectual seriousness that his achievement warrants, to separate assessment of the writer's work from a merely polemical, journalistic milieu in which the prejudices and contests of the moment obscure more lasting values. This is, in general, the goal of this book as well. Composed of contributions that take various individual perspectives on the wisdom of neoliberalism, none doubt its importance as a historical phenomenon, or treat Vargas Llosa's enmeshment with it as merely casual. As anthropological as argumentative in method, these essays, taken in sum, provide a composite portrait not only of a single individual but also of a global society coping with both a new ideological terrain and the more-than-incidental adjustments in intellectual perspective that change in terrain insists on. The rationale for this book is not just that Vargas Llosa's recent work needs to be scrutinized but that it is important to braid together abstract assertions of neoliberalism and the career and trctory of a particular writer, to see how precept and actuality connect across several political and geographical contexts. In *Wellsprings*, Vargas Llosa praises Sir Isaiah Berlin for evoking the past of ideological conflicts that "we wrongly considered to be specific to our age" (135). Though perhaps less universally minded than either Vargas Llosa or Berlin, the essays in this volume similarly try to look outside of entrenched positions and navigate a longer perspective.

VARGAS LLOSA AS NEOLIBERAL

The essays included in this book have been grouped into four sections that attempt to look at Vargas Llosa's writings after his neoliberal turn from both analytical and chronological perspectives. The first section, comprising the essays of De Castro, Escárzaga, and O'Bryan-Knight, emphasizes Vargas Llosa's overall presentation of himself since 1980—the way in which his intellectual and professional context is conveyed in relation to specific political allegiances and identities. Is neoliberalism an affiliation for Vargas Llosa? An ideological affinity? A cause? What kind of personal image is Vargas Llosa striving for? When he states to the American Enterprise Institute that they have seen him as "a unified being," he implies that the existing moral judgments of him are partial, fragmentary, and even schizoid and that they rend the literary from the political. Yet at other times, particularly in his criticism of postmodern theory, he acts as if he is a defender of the aesthetic against the intrusions of politicization. Vargas Llosa's philosophical liberalism does not mean he is a corporate gun for hire, or a propagandist for the entrepreneur. His identification with certain liberal or even libertarian sociopolitical positions is a way of negotiating the interstices where the private and the public, the polemical and the introspective, meet. Though the contributors have different perspectives on the merits of Vargas Llosa's cumulative public positions, they present a fairly concordant picture of what these positions have been. It could also be argued that Vargas Llosa's public manifestation is in a way a move within neoliberalism, a brake against the atomizing or individualistic tendencies, a continuation of the role of the intellectual as a rallying point and a bonding agent of what might otherwise wither in fragmented anarchy.

Vargas Llosa in the 1980s and 1990s is addressed by the essays by Birns, Allatson, López-Calvo, and Franco. The essays in this section examine those decades when Vargas Llosa became openly identified as a neoliberal, or someone who was no longer a proponent of leftist, revolutionary ideas, but as their adversary. Often this awareness was slow to dawn—at least until Vargas Llosa's run for the Peruvian presidency in 1990, it was generally assumed that Vargas Llosa was writing as much from a leftist-humanist standpoint as from a pro-free-market one. It took a while for readers to understand that Vargas Llosa was no longer just a skeptic about the extreme Left—as Camus or George Orwell had been—but someone who was actually endorsing free-market alternatives to socialist presuppositions. Thus novels like *The War of the End of the World* or *The Storyteller* received very different notices in the English-speaking journalistic press than the treatment in this section, not so much because the treatments here are more skeptical or academic but because they have had the benefit of contextualizing Vargas Llosa via thirty years of his journalistic commentary whereas the reviews were still vaguely operating out of an assumption that all Boom generation writers must be leftists of one stripe of another. The essays, though, also show how Vargas Llosa's political development is not simply linear, that he changes from book to book, that the treatment if indigeneity in *The Storyteller* and *Death in the Andes* can be very different, and that utopianism in both *The War of the End of the World* and a much later novel like *The Way to Paradise* exerts an ambivalent siren's call but is centered more around community identity in the former and social hope in the latter. Vargas Llosa at times seems both for and against homosexuals, leftist communitarians, and indigenous people, though one type he has consistent scorn for is the urban, elite intellectual seeking validation amid the subaltern's desire for social justice. Part of the task here is determining just where the writer stands. In his autobiography, Vargas Llosa depicts himself as a literary man willing to enter the political arena because he is the only man willing to save his country. But this reluctance may be a product of defeat. Would he feel so uneasy with politics had he won the election, which, after all, was a close loss to a dark-horse candidate?

The third section, which includes the essays of Bell-Villada and Forgues, looks at Vargas Llosa in the twenty-first century. This is a very different time for Vargas Llosa not so much literarily—his books continue to reinvent himself from volume to volume, with *The Feast of the Goat* winning worldwide accolades while *The Bad Girl* generally received a less-than-glowing response—than from the different political climate. In the 1980s and 1990s, the world saw the final stages of the Cold War and then the seeming triumph of unipolar neoliberalism and what in Latin America was termed 'The Washington Consensus.' The 2000s saw the rise of the "Pink Tide" of populist movements—in particular that of Hugo Chávez of Venezuela, who becomes Vargas Llosa's *bête noire*, a man with the rabble-rousing skills of Antonio Conselheiro but slicker; telegenic; equipped with oil wealth; wielding alliances with Russia, China, and Iran; and having managed to secure some form of popular consent. By the time Chávez looms into view, Vargas Llosa has been firmly identified with a strand of the political Right for virtually half of his literary career. He is a known quantity even if he has new reactions to new challenges and even if some of his gestures, like the not-so-veiled reference to Fujimori in the Japanese suitor of the title character in *The Bad Girl*, seem more personal than political. Vargas Llosa also emerges in this era as a defender of Western values against Islamic terrorism, which calls to mind his persistent criticism of religion and of moral intolerance throughout his fictional oeuvre. As he becomes an elder statesman of the world republic of letters, Vargas Llosa crops up in multiple guises: debating Chavistas along with his son Álvaro at a Caracas symposium; being feted by bilingual literary audiences at New York readings; writing widely read biweekly opinion pieces syndicated by a Madrid newspaper; confronting *piqueteros* in the Argentine city of Rosario. The essays in this section take account of the most recent engagements in Vargas Llosa's dual public life and how they differ from the first decades of the neoliberal era.

The final section, which includes the essays by Kohlmann and Corral, returns Vargas Llosa to the world where he would arguably most want to be placed: the sphere of a man of letters, whose political views are incidental to his conduct as a writer and an intellectual. Vargas Llosa is a widely read man and his intellectual roots are complicated, involving multiple European and American ramifications. Vargas Llosa insists that the Americas cannot relinquish their European inheritance—that for all the delights of indigenism and cultural nationalism, it would be an illusion to suppose that renouncing European, humanistic values would be desirable or conceptually even possible. The essays in the final section see Vargas Llosa's politics as a way of illustrating his literary positions, reversing the emphasis in the other parts of the volume. Future generations may see Vargas Llosa's continued production of novels and criticism as more important than the concrete political interventions he has launched. At least this is what the essays in the final section suggest. They reveal Vargas Llosa as a thoughtful, erudite man whose variety and voracity of interest may veer every which way on occasion, but they remain firmly concentrated on the rare intellectual contribution he has made to contemporary culture.

NOTES

1. Vargas Llosa concludes his "The Latin American Novel Today," first published in English in 1970 and one of the main critical texts that helped introduce the Boom novels to the U.S. reading public, by claiming "Edmund Wilson boasted several years ago of never having been interested in the Latin American novel. I wonder if he would repeat today with the same conviction this somewhat abrupt remark" (16).

2. For instance, Carlos Fuentes's main novel of the period, *The Death of Artemio Cruz*, published in Spanish in 1962, was translated into English in 1964 and into French in 1966. Julio Cortázar's *Hopscotch*, originally published in 1963, was translated into English and French in 1966. Mario Vargas Llosa's *Time of the Hero*, published in 1963, was also translated into English and French in 1966. García Márquez's *One Hundred Years of Solitude*, the bestseller of the group, which was first published in Spanish in 1967, was translated into French in 1968 and into English in 1970.

3. According to John Updike, already a established writer by the time the Boom novels became known in the United States, "I have read a lot of García Márquez—and Vargas Llosa and Machado de Assis [sic]. I think Latin Americans are in some way where Americans were in the nineteenth century. They have really a whole continent to say; suddenly they've found their voice; they are excited about being themselves and their continent and their history. And that's a great weapon in the armory of an artist, to be excited by your subject" (201). Also see John Barth's significantly titled "Literature of Replenishment" and Rushdie's essays "Gabriel García Márquez" and "Mario Vargas Llosa" in his *Imaginary Homelands*.

4. Vargas Llosa had interpreted "Words to the Intellectuals" as implying a defense of artistic freedom: "The recognition of Marxism as the official philosophy of the revolution does not exclude . . . other ideological viewpoints . . . Castro's statement to the Congress of Cuban Writers—'Within the revolution, everything; against the revolution, nothing'—is being put into practice in a rigorous manner. In art and literature this is very obvious: there is no official aesthetic" ("Chronicle of the Cuban Revolution" 21–22).

5. In a press release provided by García Marquez at the time, the Colombian novelist argued about his relation with the Cuban revolution, "The only pending matter is that of the poet Heberto Padilla. Personally, I haven't succeeded in convincing myself that Padilla's self-criticism was spontaneous and sincere . . . The tone of his confession is so exaggerated, so abject, that it seems to have been obtained by ignominious means" ("Gabriel García Márquez" 54).

6. According to Raymond L. Williams, "A love affair—and soap operas, in fact—provide the anecdotal material for Vargas Llosa's sixth novel *Aunt Julia and the Scriptwriter*" (*Mario Vargas Llosa* 2). In fact, Williams designates both novels of the 1970s as "Vargas Llosa's entertainments" (94). Also see Castro-Klarén, 15–16.

7. On Vargas Llosa's support for Barack Obama, see his articles "Obama y las primarias," "Obama en los infiernos," and "Obama y el sueño americano."

PART I

MARIO VARGAS LLOSA AND THE NEOLIBERAL TURN

CHAPTER 1

MR. VARGAS LLOSA GOES TO WASHINGTON

JUAN E. DE CASTRO

IN MARCH 2005 MARIO VARGAS LLOSA RECEIVED THE IRVING Kristol Award. This award is granted by the American Enterprise Institute (AEI), the influential probusiness think tank that then had close ties to the administration of President Bush. The symbiosis between the AEI and the Republican administration is evidenced by the fact that former President George W. Bush made public his decision to invade Iraq during the ceremony for the first of these awards in 2003. In fact, among those present at the award dinner and reception in 2005 were then–vice president Richard B. Cheney and then–deputy secretary of defense Paul Wolfowitz, two of the architects of the Iraq war.

Granted to "an individual who has made notable intellectual or practical contributions to improved public policy and social welfare" ("Annual Dinner and Lecture"), the Irving Kristol Award implies the recognition of Vargas Llosa's political actions and writings by the U.S. Right.[1] It can thus be seen as a defining moment in the novelist's public ideological evolution since his break with the Left during the Padilla affair, as well as the acknowledgment of Vargas Llosa as a member of the international elite of the political Right. However, the speech, which implicitly criticizes many of the central tenets held by the U.S. conservative political establishment, also shows the contradictions that exist between Vargas Llosa's version of neoliberalism and the dominant intellectual tendencies of the U.S. Right.

Latin American neoliberalism and North American neoconservatism are frequently seen as identical. For instance, in *The Other Path*, de Soto briefly states, "Neoliberalism—called 'neoconservatism' in the United States" (242). There is obviously a significant convergence evidenced by the awarding of the Irving Kristol Award to Vargas Llosa and the latter's acceptance of the prize. However, as David Harvey makes clear, despite sharing common core beliefs with neoliberalism, neoconservatism also exhibits significant differences: "U.S. neoconservatives favor corporate power, private enterprise, and restoration of class power. Neoconservatism is therefore entirely consistent with the neoliberal agenda of elite governance, mistrust of democracy, and the maintenance of market freedoms. But it veers away from the principles of pure neoliberalism . . . in two fundamental respects: first, in its concern for order as an answer to the chaos of individual interests, and second, in its concern for an overweening morality as the necessary social glue to keep the body politic secure in the face of external and internal dangers" (82). Thus, according to Harvey, both neoliberalism and neoconservatism are elitist, antidemocratic, free market ideologies, diverging only in the latter's concern with order and conventional morality. Neoconservatism's emphases on political order and a return to putative traditional moral values "can best be understood as products of a particular coalition that was built in the 1970s, between elite class and business interests . . . on the one hand, and an electoral base among 'the moral majority' of disaffected white working class on the other" (84). Irving Kristol, after whom the AEI award is named, describes this coalition as "united on issues concerning the quality of education, the relations of Church and State, the regulation of pornography, and the like, all of which they regard as proper candidates for the government's attention" (35). Other values shared by the neoconservative coalition are, as Harvey notes, a strident nationalism, an embrace of conservative evangelical Christianity, opposition to abortion and "new social movements such as feminism, gay rights, affirmative action, and environmentalism" (84).

Vargas Llosa's Irving Kristol speech "Confessions of a Liberal," as well as his other recent essays, contradicts the moral positions characteristic of neoconservatism, as well as its opposition to (some) "new social movements."[2] Vargas Llosa declares that "with regard to religion, gay marriage, abortion and such, liberals like me, who are agnostics as well as supporters of the separation between church and state and defenders of the decriminalization of abortion and gay marriage, are sometimes harshly criticized by other liberals who have opposite views on these issues. ("Confessions of a Liberal").

While Vargas Llosa here, with excessive diplomacy, admits the existence of "liberals" who do not believe in the separation of church and state, he nevertheless makes clear his stance against the political implementation of religiously based moral codes.

Vargas Llosa in other writings is explicitly critical of the influence of religion in North American politics. Thus, in an article published soon after the 2004 reelection of George W. Bush, Vargas Llosa argued,

This [the links with the Christian Right], in practical terms, implies that the Bush administration will increase its legal actions against abortion, gay marriage, euthanasia, stem cell research, and its support for campaigns to infiltrate religion in the public schools, authorizing school prayer and the teaching of a science made compatible with the Biblical word. This is a dangerous path that can gradually deteriorate the culture of freedom and reestablish different forms of censorship in the cultural and social life of the United States, as well as restrict and abolish individual rights that are the clearest expression of a free society. ("Los próximos cuatro años" 20).

In "Confessions of a Liberal," Vargas Llosa defines liberalism as "political democracy, the market economy and the defense of individual interests over those of the state." However, as the previous quotation makes clear, the encroachment of religion on the political sphere can be seen as threatening political democracy and individual interests. Only the market economy would be (at least at first) relatively untouched by the growing power of the alliance between neoconservatives and the Christian Right.

Thus Vargas Llosa's extension of the term "liberal" in his Irving Kristol speech to those who propose the hegemony of religion contradicts what he states are his core beliefs. And this apparent contradiction may well serve as an indication that in reality freedom of the market is valued by Vargas Llosa over the other liberal principles. Even at his most critical Vargas Llosa only exhibits a partial opposition to Republican policies. Not surprisingly, he is very sympathetic to what he identified as the economic core of the Bush program: privatization of social security and free trade in the Americas ("Los próximos cuatro años" 20).

Vargas Llosa's rebuttal of the neoconservative embrace of religious morality is rooted in his belief in "the dogmatic and intransigent nature of religion" ("The Sign of the Cross" 85). For him, and in this he is a classic liberal, "the basic principles of democratic life" are "pluralism, relativism, the coexistence of contradictory truths, the constant mutual concessions required to arrive at social consensus" (85). And in "Confessions of a Liberal," he adds that "liberalism . . . is tolerance and respect for others, and especially for those who think differently from ourselves, who practice other customs and worship another god or who are non-believers."

"Confessions of a Liberal," however, demonstrates that Vargas Llosa, like neoconservatives, is concerned about the social and moral dissolving effects of the free market: "The free market is the best mechanism in existence for producing riches. But it is also a relentless instrument, which, without the spiritual and intellectual component that culture represents, can reduce life to a ferocious, selfish struggle in which only the fittest survive" ("Confessions of a Liberal"). But if North American neoconservatives pose religion and nationalism as solutions to social anomie, Vargas Llosa sees "culture" as the antidote to the dark side of capitalism.

Vargas Llosa's emphasis on culture as the necessary supplement to capitalism has well-known precedents. In late nineteenth-century England, Matthew Arnold, faced with the destruction of communal social bonds by the long first major wave of unfettered free market policies proposed "culture"—literature, especially poetry—as "the most resolute enemy of anarchy" (197). Like Vargas Llosa today, Arnold saw in the arts and literature the ballast necessary to survive the individualistic storm that had led to the economic and political hegemony of England.

It has been argued that democracy is not a central value for both neoliberals and neoconservatives. Harvey argues that "democracy is viewed as a luxury [by neoliberals], only possible under conditions of relative affluence coupled with a strong middle-class presence to guarantee political stability" (66). However, in perfect congruence with classical liberalism, Vargas Llosa emphasizes the importance of political democracy and individual rights. In "Confessions of a Liberal," after criticizing the belief that only a "firm hand" could implement free market reforms, Vargas Llosa argues, "This explains why all the so-called "free market" Latin American dictatorships have failed. No free economy functions without an independent, efficient justice system and no reforms are successful if they are implemented without control and the criticism that only democracy permits. Those who believed that General Pinochet was the exception to the rule because his regime enjoyed economic success have now discovered, with the revelations of murder and torture, secret accounts and millions of dollars abroad, that the Chilean dictator, like all of his Latin American counterparts, was a murderer and a thief" ("Confessions of a Liberal"). In contrast, during the 1970s, Margaret Thatcher's Tory and neoliberal government had friendly relations with the Pinochet regime, which, in fact was the first to apply radical free market policies consistently.[3] Moreover, in a 1981 interview for the Chilean newspaper *El Mercurio*, Hayek admitted that if forced to choose between formal democracy and (neo) liberal economic policy, his "preference is for a liberal dictator and not for a democratic government lacking in liberalism" (Bowles and Gintis 12).

Vargas Llosa's defense of democracy, which he understands in a traditional liberal sense as based on equal representation and countervailing institutional powers, again distances him from sectors in the Latin and North American Right. Nevertheless, it is necessary to point out that Vargas Llosa's consistent emphasis on the importance of democratic institutions, which has characterized his discourse from the 1970s to the present, may simply have been prescient. After all, as the Bush Administration's designation of the promotion of democracy as the central value of the country's foreign policy demonstrates, the U.S. Right has also evolved from political pragmatism to what, at least in appearance, seems to be idealism. However, this adoption of democracy has also implied an identification of the term not only with radical free market policies but also with the forced export of North American political institutions. Internationally, democracy has been used as a cover for the execution of policies that in last resort exclusively reflected the interests of the Bush administration and allied social groups. And internally it has been presented as compatible with the undermining of the protections and rights that have traditionally been seen as constitutive of a democratic legal system.

In "Confessions of a Liberal," Vargas Llosa celebrates cultural difference and Latin American immigration to the United States. Contradicting Samuel Huntington (1927–2008), a member of the committee of academic advisors that selected him for the Irving Kristol Award, Vargas Llosa argues,

> In my opinion, the presence in the United States of almost 40 million people of Latin American heritage does not threaten the social cohesion or integrity of the country. To the contrary, it bolsters the nation by contributing a cultural and vital current of great energy in which the family is sacred. With its desire for progress, capacity for work and aspirations for success, this Latin American influence will greatly benefit the open society. Without denouncing its origins, this community is integrating with loyalty and affection into its new country and forging strong ties between the two Americas. ("Confessions of a Liberal")

Unlike Vargas Llosa, many neoconservatives believe, in Huntington's words, that "there is only the American dream created by an Anglo-Protestant society," and they are therefore resistant to any significant modification of North American identity (45). Given the stress placed by many neoconservatives on nationalism and unity, immigration is one of the most feared social solvents unleashed by the market forces they otherwise celebrate.[4]

Vargas Llosa's defense of immigration is linked to his opposition to any restrictive vision of national (and other) identity. Thus in stark difference with neoconservative emphasis on the centrality of a clearly defined U.S. identity, Vargas Llosa argues the following in his 2001 article "The Culture of Liberty": "The concept of identity . . . is inherently reductionist and dehumanizing, a collectivist and ideological abstraction of all that is original and creative in the human being . . . true identity springs from the capacity of human beings to resist these influences and counter them with free acts of their own invention" (68). Moreover, "the notion of collective identity is an 'ideological fiction' and the foundation of nationalism" (68). According to Vargas Llosa, globalization and modernization, for him the latter a near synonym of the former, are leading to the dissolving of rigid national identities: "Thanks to the weakening of the nation state, we are seeing forgotten, marginalized, and silent local cultures reemerging and displaying dynamic signs of life in the great concert of this globalized planet" (71). Thus Vargas Llosa's positive view of Latino contributions to the United States—his emphasis on the possibility of plural changing identities, his advocacy of multiculturalism—is perfectly consistent with his promotion of the free market.[5]

Vargas Llosa's speech at the AEI is a clear example of the points of contact between his brand of neoliberalism and the neoconservative Right in the United States. Vargas Llosa, like other neoliberals and neoconservatives, has a near-religious faith in the efficacy of the free market not only as the central tool for the allocation of resources but also, even more importantly, as the necessary foundation for what he calls the culture of freedom. In fact, it is not farfetched to see his political evolution as merely substituting the free market for socialism as the basis on which all individuals would be granted a fair access at material and cultural resources. However, unlike neoconservatives, Vargas Llosa exhibits concern with the distribution of income, opposes traditional religious moral and nationalist values, emphasizes the importance of pluralism for democracy, and considers multiculturalism as contributing to the culture of freedom.

However, these differences with the neoconservative mainstream have not in the least soured Vargas Llosa's relationship with them. The fact that Vargas Llosa downplays his divergence with neoconservatives is surprising given the acrid tone he frequently uses when criticizing those who even minutely diverge from free market policies. Vargas Llosa has subjected those who defend the "cultural exception"—that is, those who propose that cultural products should be excluded from free trade agreements or those who oppose the privatizing of the water supply or other essential services—to vitriolic attacks. One can only conclude that for Vargas Llosa positions such as these are more dangerous to the "culture of freedom" than the implicit authoritarianism, exacerbated nationalism, and penchant for foreign interventions that characterize the neoconservative Right.

But if Vargas Llosa's "Confessions of a Liberal" and other political writings lead to doubts about the Peruvian author's coherence, they also have a surprising resemblance to contemporary progressive ideas. At the end of the speech, Vargas Llosa describes the utopia that underlies his political thought: "We dream, as novelists tend to do: a world stripped of fanatics, terrorists and dictators, a world of different cultures, races, creeds and traditions, co-existing in peace thanks to the culture of freedom, in which borders have become bridges that men and women can cross in pursuit of their goals with no other obstacle than their supreme free will" ("Confessions of a Liberal").

Even if the underlying theoretical bases are significantly different, this description reminds one of a progressive multicultural and hybrid borderland. However, Vargas Llosa's utopia is grounded on a strict celebration of the free market. It is presented not as contradicting neoliberal policies but rather as their culmination. The fact that it closely resembles many liberal (in the North American sense) as well as progressive utopias raises the question whether these are also not compatible with the economic and cultural policies they frequently decry.

NOTES

1. Other award winners have been political commentator Charles Krauthammer, former Australian Prime Minister John Howard, and former head of the Multi-National Force in Iraq (and later head of the U.S. Central Command) General David Petraeus.

2. Mario Vargas Llosa has published an abridged version of this essay titled "Confessions of an Old-Fashioned Liberal" in *The American Enterprise Magazine*, which, as the title indicates, waters down his differences with the U.S. neoconservative mainstream.

3. According to Perry Anderson: "One must note that the Chilean experience of the 1970s interested profoundly certain British advisers of importance to Thatcher, and that there were always excellent relations between both regimes during the 1980s" (19).

4. Vargas Llosa explicitly addresses Huntington in "Confessions of a Liberal": "It [the United States] is a democracy which I admire for what Professor Samuel Huntington fears: that formidable mixture of races, cultures, traditions and customs, which have succeeded in co-existing without killing each other, thanks to that equality before the law and the flexibility of the system that makes room for diversity at its core, within the common denominator of respect for the law and for others."

5. However, Vargas Llosa has, on several occasions, expressed doubts about the compatibility of indigenous cultures with modernity. Thus in "Questions of Conquest: What Columbus Brought and What He Did Not," he laments: "If forced to choose between the preservation of Indian cultures and their complete assimilation, with great sadness I would choose modernization of the Indian population, because there are priorities, and the first priority is, of course, to fight hunger and misery" (52–53).

CHAPTER 2

THE WARS OF AN OLD-FASHIONED (NEOLIBERAL) GENTLEMAN

FABIOLA ESCÁRZAGA

BEGINNING IN THE 1970S, THE PERUVIAN WRITER MARIO VARGAS Llosa took up the titanic struggle of defending the neoliberal cause both in his native country and in the Hispanic world at large. He believes that his activity as a proponent of neoliberalism and his public interventions as a prestigious intellectual in its favor are necessary in order to sway public opinion to his cause. This belief springs from what he perceives as the absence—or ineptitude—of committed local politicians who ought to be fulfilling this mission and the indifference of international institutions that should have the capacity of intervening in a more active and coherent manner in national processes, in order to prevent Latin American countries from ending up at the mercy of corrupt and demagogical populist strongmen. Instead of analyzing the theoretical bases of Vargas Llosa's discourse, or their contradictory character, I will expose the systematic manner in which he has fulfilled his mission as an ideologue of neoliberalism.

Vargas Llosa does not develop new ideas or original interpretations. Instead he translates, for the lay public, arguments that are of a technical or philosophical nature, that originate in the social sciences, or that deal with complex realities, making them coherent and easy to understand. He presents them to the general, or at least educated, public, so that they can be repeated by others who will then disseminate them on radio and television. The writer intervenes in representation of universal values in political situations and especially elections where the future of the countries in the region is at risk. The ubiquitous and opportune presence of Vargas Llosa and his political analyses has intensified since the end of the 1990s.

This is the time when political movements, composed by the social sectors affected, began to question neoliberalism in the form of popular mass demonstrations, in elections, or by a combination of both. In all of these political conjunctions, Vargas Llosa has participated using his prestige as a world-class intellectual against the emergent leaders, questioning their programs, strategies, leadership, personal weaknesses, contradictions, or at least what the novelist considers as such. The aggressive tone of his discourse, which frequently resorts to pejorative imagery and epithets, underlines the social distance that separates him from these leaders, even as they evidence his implicit racism. They do not come from the traditional elites of their countries, nor do they belong to the *criollo* (Euro-American) elites. They all come from the peripheries of the system, from the middle or poor classes and evidence the phenotype one associates with that background: Venezuelan President Hugo Chávez is a mulatto, Bolivian President Evo Morales is an Indian, Peruvian political figure Ollanta Humala is a mestizo, as are the Presidents of Nicaragua and Ecuador Daniel Ortega and Rafael Correa. And they emphasize this fact by their explicit vindication of their ethnicities, professions, and socioeconomic origins; by their clothes, manner of speech, and body language; by their disregard for conventional etiquette—all of which evidently favors the identification of the majorities of their respective countries with them.

Vargas Llosa's ideological analyses generally conclude by also raising negative questions about the citizens who with their votes have favored these leaders, helping them gain, or come close to gaining, power. Lack of historical memory or political awareness, ignorance, and so on are some of words and phrases used by Vargas Llosa to describe the masses that identify with and feel represented by these leaders.

THE ELECTORAL DEFEAT OF 1990 AND LATER IDEOLOGICAL VICTORIES

Three years before the Peruvian elections of 1990, and indeed up until a few weeks before the vote was taken, Vargas Llosa was the heavy favorite in all polls.[1] However, he was surprisingly defeated by a complete unknown, Alberto Fujimori, an engineer of Japanese origin, who, as the head of an improvised political party, Cambio 90, had few resources but much ingenuity.[2] This humiliating defeat caused Vargas Llosa to promise to retire from "professional politics" and to abstain from criticizing the government (*A Fish in the Water* 529). Moreover, he took up Spanish citizenship, thus emphasizing his increasing distance from his native country, not returning to Peru for seven years. Nevertheless, Fujimori's auto-coup of April 1992 awakened Vargas Llosa's sense of moral obligation to denounce the dictatorship, and he continued criticizing it systematically until its collapse in 2000. He also condemned the international community, financial institutions, the U.S. government, and the Organization of American States for adopting a double standard when evaluating Fujimori's government: implicitly supporting it by accepting its authoritarianism and corruption as the price to be paid for its successful counterinsurgency and its implacable and efficient implementation of neoliberal policies.[3]

Disappointed with politics, Vargas Llosa returned to literature and published, among others, two books that expressed in different degrees his coming to terms with his traumatic electoral defeat: *A Fish in the Water* (1993) and *La utopía arcaica. José María Arguedas y las ficciones del indigenismo* (*The Archaic Utopia: José María Arguedas and the Fictions of Indigenismo*) (1996). Both texts offer rich and intense material that can be used to analyze his profound misencounter with his country and with the popular sectors that he had not been able to seduce, as well as of his complete alignment with neoliberalism.

In his memoirs, *A Fish in the Water*, Vargas Llosa writes as if his introduction to professional politics in 1987 constituted an unexpected, radical change in his life, by means of which he sacrificed his successful writing career and his position as a permanent candidate for the Nobel Prize all for the good of Peruvian society. He also presents his candidacy as if it were his political baptism, blaming his deficient performance as presidential candidate and his defeat at the hands of Fujimori on his supposed condition as an improvised politician.

In reality, Vargas Llosa has been participating constantly in Peruvian and Latin American political life from 1971 to the present, taking advantage of his condition as a prestigious, charismatic, and influential writer to promote the neoliberal and conservative view of the world by means of his literary writings, newspaper articles,[4] lectures, and university courses throughout the world, television programs, meetings with political leaders, and so on. These political interventions have not negatively affected his career as a writer. On the contrary, they have increased his public visibility, thus contributing to the commercial success of his novels and other literary writings; neither have they hampered his great productivity.

In *La utopía arcaica*, he undertakes to analyze "what there is of reality and fiction in indigenist literature and ideology" (10) through the writings of the Peruvian novelist José María Arguedas (1911–1969), the only Peruvian writer who Vargas Llosa admits as having literary merit and who, in fact, is the literary hero of the Left and of popular sectors since his suicide.

In the book there is no self-criticism regarding the main reason behind his earlier electoral defeat: his incomprehension and mis-encounter with the "Peru *profundo*" ("real Peru"). Far from it, what he does is to develop a theory about the ethnic problems of Peru that refutes Arguedas and disqualifies as utopian and archaic—that is, as inexistent—the rural Andean and urban marginal worlds that Arguedas attempted to express and explain in his writings. The interpretation of Peru's ethnic and popular problematics developed by Vargas Llosa is as subjective as the one he criticizes in Arguedas but is ideologically its opposite: (neo)liberal, modernizing, and mestizophilic. It constitutes a version of Peruvian reality according to his desires, in an unconscious exercise that excises, destroys, and nullifies the world to which he does not belong, that he does not understand, and that voted against him. It is a similar operation to the one that takes place in his memoirs, which elude any admission of his role in his electoral defeat.

The archaic utopia, a concept constructed by Vargas Llosa in order to devalue and nullify the indigenous Peruvians, not only represents Peru's subaltern culture and movements that caused his electoral defeat but also includes all types of cultural, political, economic, or social popular action and resistance, whether peaceful or violent, that oppose or question capitalist globalization, the hegemony of the market, the centrality of individual liberty, and the expansion of Western democracy to all the world and, in particular, Latin America. He disqualifies these social causes as utopian, archaic, antidemocratic, totalitarian, nationalistic, and as representing obstacles to overcoming poverty in third-world countries. As we see below, these are arguments he will develop in his more recent participation in politics.

In *A Fish in the Water*, Vargas Llosa emphatically declares that he is not a racist because he does not believe in natural human inequality based on race. He says he unsuccessfully attempted to eliminate from the presidential campaign references to race, in particular, to Fujimori's Japanese origin, brought up by his supporters. (However, Fujimori used race—especially the question of Vargas Llosa's whiteness—with great success).[5] Vargas Llosa only sees the other side of racism, that which he claims victimizes whites in Peru. This reverse racism is presented as the product of the social resentment of Indians or mestizos toward the criollo elite, and of the lower toward the upper classes. This reverse racism would make victims of the criollo elite, and is presented as having affected his presidential candidacy. Vargas Llosa argues that this racism is "the national disease by antonomasia, the one that infests every stratum and every family in the country and leaves them all with a bad aftertaste of hatred, poisoning the lives of Peruvians in the form of resentments and social complexes . . . an effervescent structure of prejudices and sentiments—disdain, scorn, envy, bitterness, admiration and emulation—which, many times, beneath ideologies, values and contempt for values, is the deep-seated explanation for the conflicts and frustrations of Peruvian life" (*A Fish in the Water* 5–6). Thus, instead of being the consequence of the people's rejection of his political platform, according to him, his defeat was due to the the the leftwing intelligentsia's envy and resentment toward him and the antipathy against him of the mediocre, which had originated with his first literary successes. This conclusion avoids taking into account that the weaknesses of his campaign and of himself as a candidate are the consequence of a still-unresolved problem: the political and ideological inconsistency of the Peruvian Right. The Right has shown an inability to appeal to the masses, which are ethnically different from the elite and a lack of will to incorporate their historical demands into its programs. This refusal to incorporate popular demands is due to the oligarchic origin and continuing colonial tradition of the Peruvian Right, which maintains an abyss between government and those governed based on the ethnic, social, and regional differences between Indians and mestizos and criollos, between poor and rich, and between the Andean highlands and the urban coast. The absence of channels that permit the incorporation into the elite of those from a popular background persists and has become accentuated due to neoliberalism's closing of the few previously existing means for social improvement, such as public education.[6] Vargas Llosa's presidential candidacy was a symptom of the Right's inability to produce legitimate political leaders with the capacity of appealing to a nonelite electorate. His defeat was a consequence of the inability to change this situation.[7]

LITERATURE AND POLITICS: A PERSONAL FORMULA

In the myth about himself concocted in his novels and memoir, Vargas Llosa vindicates a leftist past, which, in reality, in his Peruvian period only lasted a few months more than a year. It began in 1954 when he entered San Marcos University to study letters and law and concluded in 1955, when he joined the Christian Democratic Party. In 1959, already settled in Paris, he experiences another period of identification with the Left, when he becomes part of the Latin American literary 'Boom.' These authors combined the defense of the Cuban Revolution with the writing of a progressive literature that attempted to represent the complex social reality of the region, its struggles, and its cultural heterogeneity. As a journalist, Vargas Llosa visited Cuba, wrote articles about the Revolution, and between 1965 and 1971, belonged to the editorial committee of the *Casa de las Américas* journal and was a member of its yearly eponymous award. However, Vargas Llosa likes now to point out that he always held his distance from Fidel Castro's government to a greater degree than Cortázar, Fuentes, or García Márquez and that his initial identification with the Revolution was not as a Marxist but as an embryonic liberal attracted to the frustrated democratic project defended by sectors of its vanguard. In 1971 he abandoned his left-wing militancy, joining other writers in criticizing the Cuban government for having imprisoned the dissident writer Heberto Padilla, though he has stated that it was Castro's support for the Soviet invasion of Czechoslovakia in 1968 that led to the beginning of his distancing from the Cuban Revolution.

DIAGNOSIS OF PERUVIAN SOCIETY

Beginning in the early 1970s, the novelist argued in articles and polemics for the need to apply liberal reforms in order to save Peru. In the 1980s, his pronouncements, his authority, and his political presence in his country increased.[8] The center-right president, Fernándo Belaúnde, of the Acción Popular party, offered him several governmental positions during the former's second government (1980–1985): the position of ambassador in London and Washington, the Ministries of Education and of Foreign Relations, even that of prime minister. The only position he accepted was that of head the commission investigating the murder of eight journalists in 1983 in a remote community in the department of Ayacucho, Uchuraccay. In fulfillment of his mission, he constructed a plausible explanation for the murders that had been executed by members of the indigenous community. Vargas Llosa's report exonerated the police forces and local authorities of any responsibility in the murders. Belaúnde even suggested that Vargas Llosa become a candidate in 1985 for an alliance between Acción Popular and Partido Popular Cristiano that the parties ultimately did not accept.[9]

At the start of his social-democratic government (1985–1990), President Alan García proposed to Vargas Llosa that he become ambassador to Spain. Vargas Llosa did not accept the position.[10] Not long after, Vargas Llosa started a campaign against the government, criticizing the massacre of *senderistas* (members of the guerrilla group Sendero Luminoso, or Shining Path) in Lima's prisons in June 1986 (Vargas Llosa, "Una montaña de cadavers"). According to Raymond L. Williams, the foreword to Hernando de Soto's *The Other Path* was Vargas Llosa's first explicitly political text: an economic essay that argues for political solutions (*Otra historia de un deicidio* 70). Afterward came the electoral campaign of 1990, with the results noted previously.

In what remains of this chapter, we will look at Vargas Llosa's political interventions in Peru and other Latin American countries from 1999 to 2007, giving special emphasis to the period between 2005 and 2007, when there were elections in several Latin American countries, including Peru, which placed two alternatives face to face: the continuance or rejection of neoliberalism. We will also analyze the reconstruction of Latin American reality in the writer's texts.

THE RETURN OF THE PRODIGAL SON

In August 1997, the writer returned to Peru, for the first time after his electoral failure, in order to receive an honorary degree from the private Universidad de Lima. Three months later he received another honorary doctorate from the public Universidad de San Agustín, in his natal Arequipa. Again, as was the case ten years earlier, there was the implication he could become a unity candidate of the anti-Fujimori front for the 2000 elections. The idea was for him to continue Fujimori's economic program while rebuilding the democratic institutions that the latter had destroyed. A public poll was taken in order to see what was the public approval of the writer's potential candidacy. The result was negative. Only five percent supported Vargas Llosa. Public opinion had not forgiving him taking up Spanish nationality ("El pez vuelve al agua").

Like 1990, the elections of April 2000 had a surprising result. Alejandro Toledo, one of the candidates with the lowest support in the polls, ended up in first place.[11] In a fraudulent manner the electoral board gave the plurality of the votes to Fujimori, thereby forcing a runoff (Pajuelo Teves 57). In protest over the lack of conditions for a fair election, Toledo decided not to participate. On July 27, 2000, one day before Fujimori was sworn in for his third term, two hundred and fifty thousand anti-governmental demonstrators came to Lima from all over the country in what was called La Marcha de los Cuatro Suyos (Vich). This demonstration, named after the four provinces (*suyos*) of the Inca empire, marked the beginning of the end of the Fujimori regime. On November 19, Fujimori, then visiting Japan, sent his resignation from the presidency, being impeached by Congress the following day.[12] Then the newly elected President of the Congress, Valentín Paniagua, from Acción Popular was named president.[13] Paniagua called for new election in April, 2001.

Not long before the elections of 2000, the still skeptical writer expressed his support for Toledo, the candidate for the Peru Posible party, who, a year earlier, had named Álvaro Vargas Llosa, the writer's son and former spokesperson of Mario's 1990 campaign, as one of his advisers.[14] Toledo, son of Andean migrants to the coast, had a Ph.D. in economics from

Stanford University and had become a bureaucrat in the World Bank and the United Nations. His political platform was neoliberal, and he was married to a Belgian-born anthropologist fluent in Quechua.[15] According to the writer, he had "a splendid Indian face," he was called a *cholo* (mestizo) from Harvard, the racist epithet used by his adversaries.[16] Both qualities—Indian origin, Ivy League education—were highly valued by Vargas Llosa, and permitted Toledo win the presidency after the runoff in 2001.

By supporting Toledo, Vargas Llosa was able to make his presence felt in Peruvian politics again without running the risks associated with being a candidate. The attempts by Toledo and his administration to reestablish democracy after ten years of authoritarianism without significantly modifying the neoliberal policies applied by Fujimori and without being able to remove the former president's allies from the political scene, again manifested the weakness of the Peruvian Right and its inability to defend its interests by means of democratic institutions. Toledo's performance was increasingly questioned and at the end of his government he only had 5 percent approval. By early 2004, the writer rescinded his support of Toledo and began to question his misgovernment, enormous mistakes, incoherence, and irresponsibility.[17]

THE WARS OF THE SCRIBBLER

Recently the main target of Vargas Llosa's criticisms has been President Hugo Chávez and, with him, all the presidents and candidates who propose rejecting neoliberalism and who, because of this, have been seen by their adversaries as followers of the Venezuelan colonel: Evo Morales, Rafael Correa, Ollanta Humala, Daniel Ortega, Manuel López Obrador, and Néstor Kirchner. Vargas Llosa's battle against Chávez began 1999, less than a year after the latter came to power. On August 8, after Chávez was successful in elections of the new Constitutional Assembly, the novelist published an article titled "El suicidio de una nación" ("The Suicide of a Nation"), in which he questioned Venezuela's democracy and described Chávez as ignorant and as a demagogue: "That a large number of Venezuelans have supported the populist and autocratic deliria of that laughable character Lieutenant Colonel Hugo Chávez does not transform him into a democrat; it only reveals the extreme desperation, frustration and lack of civic culture of Venezuelan society" ("El suicidio de una nación").

Late November of the same year, two weeks before the referendum on the new constitution scheduled for December 15, the writer gave a conference in Caracas titled "Corrupción y estado de derecho en una sociedad libre" ("Corruption and Rule of Law in a Free Society"). In the conference and the interviews given to the mass media, Vargas Llosa asked Venezuelans to vote against the new constitution. President Chávez, in his weekly Sunday program "Aló Presidente," described the writer as an "ex-Peruvian" and criticized his statements on the Venezuelan political process. Vargas Llosa answered by noting that he had never renounced his Peruvian nationality and that Fujimori's threat of stripping him of his citizenship forced him to ask the Spanish government to grant him double nationality. He also expressed his concern that Venezuelan democracy was threatened by the growing closeness between Chávez and Fidel Castro and by seeing in the Cuban Revolution a model for Venezuela, positions that were incongruent with the democratic origins of Chávez's government ("Vargas Llosa pide lucidez a los venezolanos"). Probably the attacks of September 11 in New York and Washington distracted the attention of the novelist from Latin American issues; instead he wrote about the dangers of nationalist conflicts in the West. He wrote about these in the essay "La amenaza de los nacionalismos" ("The Threats of Nationalisms") published in October 2001. There he argued that socialism was no longer a threat to democracy and that the true danger was now constituted by nationalism. He refers exclusively to the nationalist conflicts in Europe—in particular Spain and Great Britain, with their separatist movements—and to the violence in the Balkans, but there are no references to Latin America, with the exception of the mention of Mexican nationalism under the PRI regime.

> The socialism that exists . . . fortunately for democratic culture, is socialist by name only. It accepts that private enterprise generates more jobs and wealth than public enterprises, especially in a market economy, and is convinced on the need for political pluralism, elections, freedom and the rule of law. This socialism . . . has become ethical. Instead of preparing for the revolution it is committed to the defense of the welfare state . . . and to the redistribution of income through taxes as the means of correcting what it calls market inequalities. Frequently, these policies in the economic and social fields are barely distinguishable from those defended by liberals or conservatives. ("La amenaza de los nacionalismos")

Meanwhile, "all nationalist doctrine is an act of faith, not a rational and pragmatic conception of history and society. It is a collectivist act of faith that grants a mythical entity—the nation—transcendental attributes: It is able to survive unchanged through time, unaffected by circumstance and historical events; it is coherent, homogeneous, and possesses a unity of substance among its member and constitutive elements, even if due to contingence that unity is invisible and belongs to the realm of fiction" ("La amenaza de los nacionalismos").

He argues that there is in nationalist ideology, in its conception of humanity, society and of history, the seed of violence that necessarily develops when it becomes governmental action. According to Vargas Llosa, nationalism always leads to totalitarianism. He makes no explicit reference to George W. Bush's argument that terrorism was the central concern of humanity.

The growth of Chávez's influence in the region, his electoral success, the radicalization of his government's policies, his references to a socialism of the twenty-first century, and the emergence of popular candidates in the region who looked for his political protection led to an intensification of Vargas Llosa's attacks, which declared the Venezuelan president a bad example for the region. On November 10, 2003, during the Miami Book Fair, the writer again attackedthe government of Venezuela as populist and corrupt. He also criticizedthe people of that country for having exhibited "monumental irresponsibility" when they reelected Comandante Chávez and gave him "powers of an almost absolute master." Additionally, he directed his barbs against the corrupt governments of Mexico (before 2000) and Argentina ("El escritor Vargas Llosa acusa a Chávez").

THE BATTLE AGAINST OLLANTA HUMALA

In December 2005, the writer arrived at Lima when the electoral process was beginning. On January 3, 2006, in Caracas, during a press conference, Hugo Chávez and Evo Morales presented Peruvian presidential candidate Ollanta Humala as a surprise guest, expressing in eloquent speeches their complete support for the candidate. President Toledo criticized Chávez's interference in Peru's internal affairs and called home his ambassador in Venezuela.

Within this context, on January 15, Vargas Llosa published an article "Raza, botas y nacionalismo" ("Race, Boots, and Nationalism") in which he attacks Chávez, Morales and Humala with equal virulence. The article makes similar arguments to those made in "La amenaza de los nacionalismos," though now applied to Latin America, proposing that socialism is no longer a danger, but that instead it is the nationalism of Chávez, Morales, and Humala that threatens the region. He accuses these leaders of promoting racism "as a value that determines the good or evil of people, their political correction or lack of correction" (A4). He points out that "to propose the Latin American problem in racial terms is irresponsible, only substituting the prejudices against Indians of those Latin Americans who consider themselves whites, with those, equally absurd, of Indians against whites" (A4). He considers that "by reason of basic justice and equality, racial prejudice must be eradicated as a source of discrimination and violence" (A4). He returned to the argument he had earlier made in *La utopía arcaica* of the existence of of a reverse racism of which whites are victims. He also questions the nationalism these leaders promote describing it as "the culture of the uncultivated, an ideological entelechy constructed in as obtuse and primitive manner as racism (and is its unavoidable correlation) which makes belonging to a collectivist abstraction—the nation—the supreme value and the privileged trait of an individual" (A4). He argues that "if there is a continent where national-ism has had negative consequences, it is Latin America" (A4). However, he admits the existence of "another more responsible and modern Left"—that of Ricardo Lagos, Tabaré Vásquez or Lula da Silva—which he clearly differentiates from that represented by Chávez, Morales, or Humala. However, in his opinion, this Left is unfortunately less influential.

In March 2006, the nationalist candidate Humala was first in the Peru-vian polls with 32 percent, followed by Lourdes Flores with 28 percent and Alan García with 21 percent. The strategy of ex-president García, who began his campaign with few supporters, concentrated on attack-ing Lourdes Flores, questioning her right-wing platform, while abstaining from attacking Humala. On April 6, three days before the first electoral round, the Defensoría del Pueblo (the Human Rights Government Office) gave the novelist the medal for the Defense of Human Rights. This was the perfect moment to "break his silence" and pronounce him-self in favor of his former archenemy Alan García. And the reason was that the gravity of the situation merited his intervention, because what was in play was "not only a change in administration, but a change in regime" ("Vargas Llosa afirma que los peruanos se arrepentirán"). The support of the writer, as well as other factors,[18] helped García, who placed second with 24.4 percent, while Humala was first with 30.6 percent of the votes. Flores, the candidate of the Right, who had received 23.8 per-cent, just 0.6 percent less than García, was left out of the runoff elec-tions. She, with less experience than García and proposing a right-wing platform, was, according to experts, a sure loser against Humala. García had an additional advantage: he represented the only mass party that had survived all the political vicissitudes that the country had gone through and, therefore, had great electoral experience.

It was a similar result to that of 2001, when Flores, then also the favor-ite, lost in the first round to Toledo and García. On that occasion, Vargas Llosa had been asked about García's second place showing, and he replied, "This shows that countries have a short memory because Alan García's government was a disaster economically, from the point of view of human rights and institutions, so one would have expected that the electorate would have remembered it and that he would have paid the price, but no, a fourth of the electorate has supported him" ("Vargas Llosa: 'se cancela la dictadura'").

In his article of April 23, titled "Razones para una alianza" ("Reasons for an Alliance"), the writer warned that "the triumph of Ollanta Humala would be a catastrophe for Peru and Latin America, a brutal regression, in a continent that seemed to be in the process of democratization, to the worst plagues of our past: caudillismo, militarism, populism, and authoritarianism." He argued that García was "the lesser evil" compared with Humala, and he called for an alliance of Flores' right-wing party with García, as the only possibility of defeating Humala in the runoff: "I say it with no joy, as all know my criticism of Alan García's disastrous government between 1985 and 1990. But now what must be given priority is not personal political sympathy or antipathy, but the defense of democracy in Peru, which, if Ollanta Humala becomes president, runs the risk of being destroyed by an act of force (as with Fujimori) or of being slowly degraded until it disappears, as is happening in the Venezuela of Hugo Chávez" ("Razones para una alianza").

He proposed "a great concentration of all democratic forces, even if, in order to achieve it, one has to overcome scruples, forget offenses and vote holding one's nose." He asked not only for an electoral alliance but also for a platform that was, in fact, that of the neoliberal Right: "A long-term program in which, in addition to the strengthening of democracy, helps preserve certain institutions characteristic of open societies, which both Christian democrats and Apristas claim to respect: free market policies, support for free enterprise and foreign investment, and the promotion of property acquisition among those sectors that still havenot had access to it" ("Razones para una alianza"). On May 23, after the presentation of *The Bad Girl*, Vargas Llosa reaffirmed that García was the "lesser evil" and that faced with the risk of a dictatorship, it was necessary to vote for him. He argued in García's favor by noting that during his government there was freedom of the press and that he had respected the results of the 1990 elections ("Vargas Llosa: Alán García es el mal menor").

García took distance from Vargas Llosa's support by calling these statements "opinions that have not been consulted or requested"; and he recalled that during the first electoral round he had rejected Vargas Llosa's proposal for an alliance of all political forces to defeat Humala. He emphasized that he would not follow "his [Vargas Llosa's] suggestions" ("Vargas Llosa: Alán García es el mal menor"). García complained publicly against the statements of his new ally, but his support was invaluable. García's strategy, which astutely took implicit advantage of Vargas Llosa's support, was central to his surprise win. In the runoff elections on June 4, the alliance between the center and the Right, under the slogan "all against Humala," led to García's victory with –52.6 percent of the votes.

The neoliberal program proposed by the writer as the basis for the alliance has been followed faithfully by García, as a satisfied Vargas Llosa admits in an interview on May 10, 2007: "It is of interest to me to see how the ideas I have defended and which were originally received with great hostility have today achieved general consensus, because, with the exception of a small and anachronistic Left, no one in Peru today argues for the nationalization of enterprises or the restriction of foreign investment. It seems that Peruvians have finally learned the lesson" ("El PSOE se ha vuelto en caballo de Troya" 11).

Finally, President García and the writer met in January, 2008, at the Peruvian National Palace, thus sealing their political pact. The writer stated, "Today Alan García is a responsible politician, his policies are those I've been defending for years . . . He defends the free market, private enterprise, democracy. I'm glad to know that there is a more solid consensus about these than 20 years ago" (Nuñez). Another aspect of García's policies praised by Vargas Llosa was the correct handling of the differences with Chile over maritime borders.[19] According to the novelist, the solution was in the right place: the International Court of Justice at the Hague; adding that this "should not be an obstacle to continuing the collaboration between Peru and Chile in all fields, especially in the economy, in which there are shared interests"; denying the possibility of a military conflict between both countries, which is "pure demagogic and chauvinist speculation, since there is no reason for our southern neighbor to dismiss an institution to which it belongs . . . We have to wait for the verdict, but I am confident that both sides are going to respect it. I believe that the law is on the side of Peru, and if I am correct, I am sure the Chilean government will respect the verdict" ("Vargas Llosa: El derecho asiste a Perú"). He also admitted that the court case against Alberto Fujimori was being handled properly and in strict adherence to the legal norms "and that the process was an example for the country and for Latin America" (Nuñez).

Vargas Llosa continued his attacks on Chávez in a March 9, 2008, article "Tambores de guerra" ("War Drums"). Here, the writer accuses Chávez of "stomping on the sovereignty of the other Latin American countries, helping finance extremist movements and candidates, underwriting strikes and armed strikes." More specifically, Vargas Llosa rejects the Venezuelan President interference in Colombia by supporting the FARC, and in Peru, where

> his long arm and his money are behind the social violence—which only serves to postpone development—that small extremist groups have unleashed in Peru with strikes demonstrations, taking over of establishments and factories. [He achieves this] by manipulating marginal and less favored sectors. The ALBA [Alianza Bolivariana para los Pueblos de Nuestra America/ Bolivarian Alliance for the People of Our America] houses, which Chavez's government has sown all over the Peruvian Andes. are far from being the humanitarian institutions they pretend to be. In truth, they are sources of revolutionary propaganda with the objective of undermining in peasantand marginal sectors any form of allegiance to the democratic system and tocreatesupporters for the forces that are attempting to overthrow it. (A4)

In this manner, popular dissatisfaction and the demonstrations against García's government do not have for the writer a valid basis, nor do the local actors make autonomous decisions, have the ability to decide on their demands, or have legitimacy. Everything comes from outside, from the perverse will of Chávez or Humala.

FINAL WORDS

The distinction proposed in the January 2006 article "Raza, botas y nacionalismo" between the acceptable liberal-leaning socialism of Brazil's Lula da Silva, Uruguay's Tabaré Vázquez, and Chile's Michelle Bachelet and the dangerous nationalist socialism of Chávez and his allies was repeated and expanded as the basis for several later articles written between 2006 and 2008. These articles generated angry replies from several intellectuals of the Left, such as the Argentine Atilio Borón, who pointed out that this differentiation was not an original idea of the writer but Washington's new official doctrine on democracy. Behind this doctrine we can identify clear material and political interests: the strategic alliance established between Bush and Lula in March 2006 on the basis of their common interest in promoting the production of ethanol in the Americas. This doctrine would lead to a deepening of social inequality, the destitution of the majority from their control of natural resources, greater earnings for multinational corporations, and greater social tensions.

The approach to the interpretation of Latin American reality proposed by Vargas Llosa is repeated in his articles from 1971 to the present, without contributing to the understanding of the existing problems in the different countries or helping to find feasible and just solutions to these. It is a circular discourse that is repeated and recycled according to the new circumstances of a confrontation that is always the same. On the one hand, there are the interests of the popular sectors of Latin America—Indians, mestizos or poor whites. They are represented by programs and leaders who, having adapted to the new circumstances of the loss of the relevance of the socialist referent, attempt to face and eliminate the conditions of oppression and exploitation imposed by the internationally dominant economic forces. On the other hand, these forces restructure productive processes in order to maintain their economic hegemony and attempt to preserve, renew, and increase the processes of exploitation and expropriation of the wealth generated throughout the world.

The representative democracy that the writer vindicates as the optimum form of the social compact constitutes the political framework that has permitted the neoliberal restructuration and the containment of popular discontent since the 1980s. However, the latter has manifested itself by taking advantage of the democratic framework or surpassing its limits. Despite what had been argued, representative democracy has not necessarily contributed to the achievement of social justice or equity in Latin America. In the twenty-first century, most social mobilization has been channeled into electoral strategies by the popular sectors themselves, guided by leaders who have come from outside the system. However, these processes have shown their limitations when it comes to reverting and transforming neoliberal policies. The conclusion of the current confrontation is impossible to predict.

Discourse like that of Vargas Llosa does not attempt to reach a solution to this confrontation through a negotiation in which both sides compromise. Instead it mask the elites' intolerance and closed mindedness; their unwillingness to in practice implement social and civil rights that have been formally recognized; or sacrifice a small percentage of their earnings in order to improve, even marginally, the well-being of the majority and the governability of dependent Latin American societies. As always, they want to keep it all. The shortsightedness of the elites is the shortsightedness of our famous writer who demonizes as fanaticism, chauvinism, and ignorance the opinions and causes of the Left, without noticing his own fanaticism and that of the sectors he represents, which are heightening social tensions in an irresponsible manner. The ideological battle will not stop, emotions will become frayed, and the groups struggling will become further polarized. Vargas Llosa has chosen his side.

NOTES

1. Vargas Llosa was the candidate of the Frente Democrático (Democratic Front), better known as FREDEMO, an electoral alliance of his Movimiento Libertad (Liberty Movement), Acción Popular (Popular Action) and the Partido Popular Cristiano (Popular Christian Party).
2. The results of the first voting round on April 8, 1990, were as follows: Vargas Llosa 27.6 percent, Fujimori 24.5 percent, Alva Castro 19.17 percent, and Barrantes 6.97 percent. Since none achieved an absolute majority, there was a second round with the candidates with the highest votes. In this second round Fujimori received 56.53 percent and Vargas Llosa 33.92 percent. Fujimori defeated Vargas Llosa because he received the votes from sympathizers of the APRA and the Left.
3. These neoliberal policies were, in fact, Vargas Llosa's platform. In order to implement it, Fujimori turned to Hernando de Soto, who had once been the novelist's friend and advisor.
4. "Piedra de toque," a biweekly column that has appeared since 1980 in the Madrid newspaper *El País* and is now syndicated to publications in twenty countries of America and Europe, many of them owned by the Prisa corporation, which owns *El Pais*. He has published six anthologies of his chronicles, essays, and articles from 1962 to the present, in which can be read his ideological evolution, his economic, philosophical and political background, and his neoliberal vision of the world (Escárzaga "La utopía liberal de Vargas Llosa").
5. The writer's supporters questioned Fujimori's participation in the election because as the son of Japanese immigrants, he was a first generation Peruvian. Fujimori, on the other hand, emphasized Vargas Llosa's social and cultural distance, as a white man, member of the oligarchy, and cosmopolite, from the Indian, mestizo, black, and Asian majority. Fujimori promoted their identification with him emphasizing his condition as an outsider from the traditional elites. This strategy led to his electoral success (*A Fish in the Water* 316–17, 500–503).
6. Probably the period in which public education best helped the social mobility of middle and lower class individuals, as well as those from the provinces, was during Vargas Llosa's youth. As Morote points out and as Vargas Llosa notes in *A Fish in the Water*, the fact that the novelist went to high school at the public Colegio Militar Leoncio Prado, where he came into contact with the ethnic plurality of his country, and to college at a state university, were decisions imposed by his father who wanted to distance him from the elitist circles of the Llosa family and, at the same time, discourage his son's literary vocation. This youthful contact with classes and groups beyond his provincial experience as a child of the oligarchy was traumatic, but it also contributed significant topics to his literary corpus.
7. One must remember that universal suffrage, which incorporated the indigenous population to the electoral process, was introduced only with the Constitution of 1979, and first put into practice during the election of 1980.
8. Between 1974 and 1990, Vargas Llosa's official residence was Lima, but he only lived there sporadically since his academic obligations forced him to constantly travel to Europe and the United States.

9. Vargas Llosa does not mention this possible candidacy in his memoirs, *A Fish in the Water.*

10. García put into effect a populist and anti-imperialist program, which included measures that attempted to increase internal demand: raise in wages, price control, fixed exchange rates with the dollar, increase in the monetary mass, and so on. This increased the macroeconomic disequilibrium and led to hyperinflation.

11. On the Peruvian elections of 2000, the fall of Fujimori, the interim presidency of Valentín Paniagua (2000–2001), and the elections of 2001, see my "Venciendo el miedo" and Pajuelo Teves's "Perú. Crisis política permanente y nuevas protestas sociales." ("Venciendo el miedo" also deals with the Peruvian elections of 2006). Due to his apparent lack of support, Toledo had not been subjected to the attacks of the media aligned with Fujimori's regime.

12. In addition to the demonstrations, the determining factor in the fall of Fujimori was the loss of North American support. The United States had also been a victim of the corruption surrounding Fujimori. Valdimiro Montesinos, Fujimori's intelligence czar and one of the most powerful men in the regime, had sold ten thousand AK-47 automatic rifles to the Fuerzas Armadas Revolucionarias de Colombia (FARC).

13. The crisis of the regime did not permit Fernando Tudela, Fujimori's first Vice-President, or Martha Hildebrandt, a member of Fujimori's party, and until November 15, 2000, President of the Congress, to assume the provisional presidency.

14. Vargas Llosa, "¿Una Luz en el Túnel?"

15. The title of the José María Arguedas's novel Todas las sangres (*All the Bloods*; 1964) was used as Toledo's campaign slogan in 2001, and during the first year of his administration, his wife, Eliane Karp de Toledo, was in charge of the strategy that attempted to co-opt indigenous leaders in order to help legitimize it.

16. A few days before the first electoral round, the father of the conservative candidate Lourdes Flores called Toledo an *auquénido* (cameloid) from Harvard in an interview. The use of this racist epithet probably cost Flores the presidency.

17. Álvaro Vargas Llosa, Mario's son, had become distanced from Toledo since the first electoral round in 2001, accusing him of "ethical and moral incapacity" due to his refusal to acknowledge a daughter born out of wedlock. The writer supported Toledo and argued that he was the victim of a "dirty war" in favor of his rival, the ex-President García. This disagreement led to a temporary distancing between father and son. On Mario Vargas Llosa's criticisms of Toledo, see Puertas.

18. There was speculation about possible manipulation of the results in favor of García and that Lourdes Flores was convinced of not protesting about the fraud against her (Monereo 25).

19. The relationship with Chile has represented a historical trauma in Peru since the loss of the territories of Arica and Tarapacá during the War of the Pacific in 1879. This historical trauma has been central to Peruvian nationalism since then.

CHAPTER 3

"LET'S MAKE OWNERS AND ENTREPRENEURS"

GLIMPSES OF FREE MARKETEERS IN VARGAS LLOSA'S NOVELS

JEAN O'BRYAN-KNIGHT

THAT PERUVIAN WRITER MARIO VARGAS LLOSA ABANDONED HIS EARLY socialist convictions in favor of neoliberal values is certainly not news. Thanks in large part to the author's own reflections on this transformation, we know when and how it took place. In the 1960s, the young novelist was a committed leftist. Toward the end of the decade he began to question dogmatic socialism's intolerance for dissent and individual freedoms. His disenchantment with the hard-line Left started with the Soviet invasion of Czechoslovakia in 1968 and was sealed by the arrest of the writer Heberto Padilla by Cuba's revolutionary government in 1971. For the remainder of the 1970s, Vargas Llosa was something of a centrist, albeit one who appeared more interested in criticizing the communists for their excesses than in endorsing any other political option as a viable alternative. It was not until 1980, while on a fellowship at the Woodrow Wilson Center in Washington, DC, that the novelist read with interest the writings of the economist and Nobel laureate Friedrich von Hayek, one of the intellectual fathers of modern free-market liberalism and a critic of socialism's planned economies. In Hayek he found a set of ideas that he would embrace with greater and more sustained enthusiasm than he had ever exerted in his early support of the revolutionary Left. Reading Hayek led Vargas Llosa to the study of other proponents of open markets and free societies—including Karl Popper, Isaiah Berlin, and Milton Friedman—and in short order the former Marxist was reborn as a freemarketeer. The question that remains, therefore, is not how or when Vargas Llosa changed his world view but when and how that change manifests itself in his fiction.

In an effort to respond to this question, I will focus on one particular aspect of Vargas Llosa's neoliberalism: the unbridled enthusiasm for open markets that has led him to admire not just traditional capitalist entrepreneurs but black-marketeers as well.[1] Indeed, he even conflates the two when, in, "La revolucion silenciosa" ("The Silent Revolution"), his introduction to Hernando de Soto's 1986 treatise *El otro sendero* (*The Other Path*), he praises the informal or underground economy as a form of *capitalismo popular.*" In his nonfiction pieces of the 1980s and 1990s, Vargas Llosa regularly claims that the presence of *informales* or black-marketeers is not a problem governments must solve but the solution to the very problems that governments themselves have created. Informal markets, therefore, should not be viewed as a form of delinquency that impedes economic development but as evidence of workers' creativity and resiliency that actually favors economic development.[2] We find these claims expressed as early as 1986 in the essay "La revolución silenciosa"[3] ("The Silent Revolution") and as late as 1997 in the opinion piece "El desquite de los pobres" ("The Revenge of the Poor") where he writes the following:

> The submerged or informal economy is not the problem; it is the solution to the problem created by the construction of artificial barriers that prevent all citizens in a given society from earning a living decently and legally . . . What is certain is that the existence of an important submerged economy is, on the one hand, a serious challenge to the injustice of hindering or preventing people from finding work; and, on the other hand, it is a demonstration of poor people's creative spirit and will to survive. When faced with the dilemma of either respecting a legality that would condemn them to hunger and ignorance or surviving, they chose the second option. ("El desquite de los pobres")[4]

It was with strong statements such as these that Vargas Llosa repeatedly endorsed the informal economy. Indeed, his support was so unwavering that it almost appears to have been an article of faith with him during the 1980s and 1990s. Evidently the avowed agnostic believed after all—he believed in the invisible hand of the economy and the redemptive power of its caress. This is quite a belief, and one I wish to examine more closely.

In his efficient and fair assessment of Vargas Llosa's novels, which appears in this volume, critic Gene Bell-Villada makes the following statement just before his concluding remarks: "Curiously, even though in his opinion pieces Vargas Llosa routinely extols entrepreneurs for 'creating wealth,' and singles out street hawkers as the carriers of a vibrant future society, in none of his latter-day novels does he venture to include such a figure either as a hero or as a passing if representative cameo-character. Whereas in Vargas Llosa's later world view, business people may have replaced the working class, in his fiction they do not take over let alone usurp the saving role of the left-wing militants in *Conversation in the Cathedral*" (156).[5] This is an interesting assertion for two reasons. If Bell-Villada is right, then we have before us a curious case of disconnect between the author's worldview and his fictional worlds. Such a lack of congruence would be counterintuitive and somewhat disconcerting. After all, we would expect a realistic writer's fiction to reflect to some extent his firmly held and oft-stated beliefs about the desirability of open markets. If this is not the case, then we might conclude that when it comes to his artistic creation—the very basis of Vargas Llosa's substantial professional reputation—the author's economic ideas are inconsequential. Fortunately, we can escape such unsatisfying conclusions by reexamining the initial claim. While Bell-Villada is certainly correct in claiming that Vargas Llosa does not make informal workers the heroes of his novels, it is something of an overstatement to say there are no cameo roles for these characters. If we look carefully, we can find a few. Indeed, as this essay will demonstrate, in four of his novels the Peruvian narrator creates exemplary secondary characters that are all eager to participate in the market. A close reading of their brief appearances will give us the opportunity to appreciate the small but not insignificant role such free marketeers have in his fiction.

The first case I wish to consider is that of Big Pablito, a minor character in *Aunt Julia and the Scriptwriter* (1977). Big Pablito is introduced to us as an amiable "mestizo in his fifties" who first appears in the fifth chapter as an incompetent and rather lazy office employee and who ends up a successful restaurant entrepreneur in the closing pages. The novel itself marks a change in direction for the prolific, young Vargas Llosa. After the decade of the 1960s, during which the leftist sympathizer produced *The Time of the Hero, The Green House*, and *Conversation in the Cathedral*, three tremendously dense and complex works that present disturbing visions of Peru, in the mid-1970s along comes *Aunt Julia and the Scriptwriter*, a delightful comic romance with a happy ending.[6] The novel presents the story of Marito, an adolescent scribbler with great literary expectations. Under the tutelage of two Bolivians—the radio scriptwriter Pedro Camacho and Marito's aunt by marriage Julia Urquidi—the immature adolescent manages to develop into a successful writer and a mature adult but not without many hilarious missteps along the way.

Big Pablito, an amusing secondary character in this comedy, is employed at the same radio station where both Marito and Camacho work. Because the successful new scriptwriter, Camacho, cannot tolerate his amateur efforts at special effects, Big Pablito finds himself reassigned to the news department under the direction of cub reporter Marito, where, presumably, his lack of talent and training will be less of an impediment to production. When presented with his first assignment, the new assistant sputters, "The thing is, sir, I don't know how to read or write" (94). Although clearly unqualified for the job, Big Pablito settles into his new position quite comfortably. His duties, however, are limited to napping at his desk and running errands for another newsroom employee, Pascual. Already in his fifties, Big Pablito appears destined to fritter away his remaining years until retirement in his pointless but secure office job.

The final chapter comes as something of a surprise, therefore, as far as Big Pablito is concerned. Twelve years after the events of his personal and professional formation that were the focus of the earlier chapters, Marito, now a successful novelist, returns to Lima from abroad. He encounters the city utterly transformed by the presence of Andean immigrants who have descended from the highlands to settle in the capital. While walking along Abancay Avenue among the hordes of informal workers—shoeshine boys, ice cream vendors, and sandwich makers—he runs into Big Pablito. His former assistant is physically unchanged but better dressed in a necktie and shiny shoes. Over coffee the two catch up, and Big Pablito tells the story of his success.

When television replaced radio at the station, Big Pablito found himself demoted from reporter to doorman. The change in title was rather meaningless, since his principal activity continued to be running errands for the staff. While fetching food he made the acquaintance of the talented cook at a popular restaurant who took a shine to his uniform and winning personality, and this woman transformed his life. Big Pablito describes her with obvious admiration: "The brunette had energy to spare, was filled with ambition, and had her head chockfull of plans" (363). It was she who came up with the idea that the couple should open their own restaurant with the severance pay Big Pablito would collect on quitting his job at the station. Accustomed to a steady paycheck, the doorman was skeptical of the scheme. Fortunately for him, his partner forced the decision.

The couple could only afford a shabby storefront to start, and they had to borrow left and right to furnish the place. After investing their own sweat equity, the proud owners of El Pavo Real Restaurant were finally ready to open for business. The first year they barely made ends meet, and the work was back-breaking. Big Pablito recalls that they would get up at dawn to get the best ingredients at the best price. Then they would work all day cooking, serving, cleaning, and manning the register. At night they even slept on the floor between the tables. The sacrifice paid off, however, and in the second year the business began to grow. Additional staff were hired—a waiter and an assistant cook—yet, they still found themselves unable to keep up with the demand. The business then relocated to the building next door and tripled in size. The couple eventually bought themselves a house across from the restaurant and finally formalized their common law union through marriage.

Big Pablito's story, which is less than three pages long, reads like a parable about the virtues of entrepreneurship. So long as he works in the inefficient formal sector (the radio station), the individual is unable to unlock his economic potential. It is only when he has the courage to strike out on his own that he finally learns to put in an honest (long) day's work and reaps the profits. In the process he contributes to the local culture and economy by developing an attractive eatery that creates jobs for a number of his compatriots. It is only after the business grows from a small rented storefront to a large owner-occupied building that the entrepreneurs decide to formalize their union, and the traditional happy ending, marriage), follows.

Big Pablito's professional success is all the more dramatic when juxtaposed with the failures of his fellow employees at the station, Pascual and Pedro Camacho, who also appear in the final chapter. Both of Big Pablito's former superiors now eke out a living at the sleazy tabloid *Extra*, which is housed in a dilapidated garage in a run-down section of the city. There the phone service has been cut due to unpaid bills, one of many signs that the business is tanking. Through the editor-in-chief's comments we learn that the history of the failed enterprise is enmeshed in Peruvian politics: "*Extra* had been born in the Odría era, under very favorable auspices: the regime placed ads in it and slipped it money under the table to attack certain individuals and defend others. Moreover, it was one of the few publications that were allowed to appear, and it had sold like hotcakes. But once Odría had been ousted, cutthroat competitors had appeared on the scene and *Extra* had gone broke" (366–67). The current director picked up *Extra* for a song and converted it to a tabloid that libel lawsuits have brought to the brink of collapse. It is in this morass that the narrator finds Pedro Camacho, who, stripped of his former fanaticism, has become a weak, disheveled "a caricature of the caricature he had been twelve years before" (369). Camacho, once a sensational scriptwriter, now runs errands for the tabloid (Big Pablito's former activity at the radio station) and earns less than a servant. The restauranteur refers to him simply as "a guy whose luck has run out" (373). The assessment, by the way, is true enough given that Camacho had the misfortune of marrying a horrible Argentine who is little more than a prostitute rather than an ambitious *limeña* with a head for business.

Although *Aunt Julia and the Scriptwriter* was finished years before Vargas Llosa began thinking seriously and writing about the free market, we can see emerging in the fiction certain notions that would later be cornerstones of his neoliberalism. One such notion is the critique of the way the Peruvian government and certain businesses with connections to the government collude to shut out competition in the marketplace. To wit, as *Extra's* editor-in-chief himself points out, the magazine's early success was due less to its attractive contents than to its protected position in a closed market. Under General Odría's dictatorship, freedom of expression was limited and only publications favorable to the unelected government flourished. When Odría left power in 1956 and democracy returned, *Extra* faced competition for the first time. At that point the publication's fortunes changed and it sank to the level of sensationalist rag, where it remained even after the return of military rule in 1968. When Mario returns to Peru in the mid-1970s, *Extra*, which no longer enjoys the favor of those in power, is on its last legs.

Another aspect of Vargas Llosa's economic worldview found in the novel is the celebration of the self-made businessman. As we have seen, Big Pablito embodies the traditional capitalist entrepreneur. Willing to take risks in the marketplace, he invests his severance pay, which allows him to open his first restaurant. He then reinvests the profits to fund expansion and more growth and profit follow. It is interesting to note that this favorable portrait of an entrepreneur appears in Vargas Llosa's fiction before the author begins to espouse this idea in his nonfiction. Published in 1977, *Aunt Julia and the Scriptwriter* is situated after the author's definitive split with the Left yet substantially before his public embrace of market economics in the 1980s. Thus we may conclude that it is in his fiction that we catch the first glimpse of the change that is to come.

In his next novel set in Peru, *The Real Life of Alejandro Mayta* (1984), Vargas Llosa offers us a very different portrait of a free marketeer, that of an informal worker.[7] Set in an apocalyptic Peru on the verge of an international war between the forces of the Left and Right, the novel records the narrator's attempts to research and write about the life of an obscure Trotskyist who participated in an earlier leftist rebellion. Again, it is in the final chapter of the novel, which functions as a curious coda to the rest of the work that we find the free marketeer. The character in question is, ironically enough, the former leftist revolutionary Alejandro Mayta. The Mayta of the final chapter is not the protagonist of the novel-in-progress that the narrator has been researching and writing; he is the elusive historical figure on whom that fictional character was loosely based. In other words, the Mayta we meet in the final chapter is not the fictionally false Mayta that appears in chapters 1–9 in the fragments of the novel the narrator is writing, but the fictionally real Mayta, the historical figure whom the narrator tracks down in the final pages of the book and convinces to share his story.[8] This second Mayta differs markedly from the first. For starters, he is not now and has never been a homosexual, nor, for that matter, is he a political fanatic, at least not at this point in his life. He appears before the narrator a sad and exhausted man whose only desire is to leave Peru some day. As he relates the tale of woe that is his string of repeated arrests, imprisonments, injustices, and betrayals over the past quarter of a century, he recalls only one truly happy memory: his successful concession stand in the Lurigancho Prison.

When the narrator finally meets the real Mayta, the former prisoner is reticent about his revolutionary past and resentful about his prison years. It is only when he speaks about the concession stand that he is more forthcoming and his tone of voice softens:

> "We created a genuine revolution," he assures me with pride. "We won the respect of the whole place. We boiled the water for making fruit juice, for coffee, for everything. We washed the knives, forks, and spoons, the glasses, and the plates before and after they were used. Hygiene, above all. A revolution, you bet. We organized a system of rebate coupons. You might not believe me, but they only tried to rob us once. I took a gash right here on my leg, but they didn't get a thing. We even set up a kind of bank, because a lot of cons gave us their money for safekeeping. (294)

Mayta's choice of words here is significant. When the former leftist militant calls to mind a "genuine revolution," he thinks not of the leftist rebellion he organized in the highlands but of the successful small business he ran while locked up. In the immeasurable filth and depravity of the prison, he managed to build an oasis of honesty and safety that benefited both clients and proprietor. Mayta recalls with pride that with his earnings he was able to contribute to the support of his wife and children even while incarcerated. Further evidence of the worth of the enterprise is that the business outlasted its founder. When Mayta was released his partner took over, and the concession stand continues to operate back at the prison.

Unfortunately, Mayta is unable to repeat the success of the stand outside the prison walls. Upon leaving Lurigancho he joined the ranks of the underemployed in Peru, a country in which he finds absolutely no prospect of work that pays a living wage. Mayta's testimony in the final chapter serves to personalize Peru's poverty by allowing the reader a glimpse of how grueling life in the informal sector can be, specifically in the areas of transportation and housing. Mayta now works the counter in an ice cream parlor in the well-to-do neighborhood of Miraflores. The job barely pays enough to cover the employee's transportation costs. From work to home the ailing Mayta must take three buses and endure two hours of discomfort. Obviously the commute consumes far too great a portion of the poor man's income and work day, and it takes a toll on his already frail health. Home for Mayta, as for the vast majority of Lima's poor, is a ramshackle dwelling in a *pueblo joven* (essentially a squatters' settlement), which he describes in grim detail:

> My wife was one of the founders of this new town. Eight years ago. Some two hundred families started it. They came at night in small groups, without being seen. They worked till dawn, nailing boards together, hauling rope. The next day, when the guards came, the place already existed. There was no way to get them out. . . . The façade is brick, and the side walls too, but the roof hasn't been finished yet. It's corrugated sheet metal, not even nailed to the house, but held in place by piles of stones set at regular intervals. The door is a board held to the wall with nails and rope. (308–9)

Mayta adds that now that they have secured control of the land, the residents are fighting for water and trash service. Where Mayta's dismal description leaves off, the narrator's picks up, and the novel concludes with his chilling observations about the desperation he sees in Mayta's neighborhood. For the narrator, the mountains of trash are evidence that the population has finally given up; besieged by terror, the country is drowning in its own garbage. Thus concludes an utterly pessimistic portrait of Peru.

According to Vargas Llosa's remarks in the novel's prologue, the portrait of Mayta in the tenth chapter was rewritten after he met the living model for the fictional character.[9] That may well be the case, but the characterization of Mayta in the final chapter also appears to owe much to the representation of the informal sector of Peruvian society that appears in Peruvian economist Hernando de Soto's widely read and highly influential book *The Other Path* (1987). It should not escape our notice that the subtitle of this study echoes Mayta's description of his concession stand as "a genuine revolution," and Mayta's experiences in the informal sector of the Peruvian economy could easily be those of the flesh-and-blood workers whom de Soto describes. Furthermore, *The Other Path* includes a lengthy "Foreword" by Vargas Llosa written in 1986, some two years after *The Real Life of Alejandro Mayta*,[10] in which the novelist uses his literary talents to summarize de Soto's economic argument in a neat narrative.

The informal sector, as de Soto argues in his book and Vargas Llosa summarizes in the "Foreword," is not the problem but the solution to the problem of Peru's economy. In order to support this radical claim, they criticize Peru's formal economy, which they see as open only to elites with powerful financial and political clout and who have no interest in promoting fairness, competitiveness, or creativity in the marketplace, and they strive instead to secure monopolies for themselves, often through corruption.[11] According to de Soto, this traditional economy prevailed until demographic shifts during the second half of the twentieth century began to challenge it. When the poor, driven out by droughts, floods, overpopulation, and declines in agricultural production, migrated from the sierra to the coastal cities in search of greater opportunity, they found the formal economy unable or unwilling to absorb them. In an effort to survive, the masses of marginalized Peruvians turned to the informal sector and sought work outside the protection and limitations of the law.[12] Informality was risky, of course, but the poor had no alternative. In as much as they lacked any capital or technical training, they could not hope to obtain the services and protections of the formal economy such as bank loans, insurance policies, and police or legal protection. What they lacked in resources, however, they made up for with will, imagination, and effort. Thanks to these efforts, in the areas of commerce, industry, housing, and transportation, the informal sector has proven to be far more productive than the state. Finally, since the state has proven incapable of creating wealth, it shifted its attention to redistributing it. This redistribution, however, remains in the hands of powerful elites who assure that what limited wealth there is does not get effectively redistributed. Thus the economist de Soto concludes and the novelist Vargas Llosa concurs that the formal system as it exists in Peru only perpetuates underdevelopment.

Vargas Llosa and de Soto are united in their optimistic view that the informal economy in Peru can actually provide an escape from underdevelopment.[13] As the novelist describes them in his "Foreword," informal workers are in fact microentrepreneurs, and as such, they are national heroes who stoke the economic engine that will power Peru's success:

> [These] men and women who through almost superhuman hard work and without the slightest help from the legal country (in fact, in the face of its declared hostility) have learned how to create more jobs and more wealth in the zones in which they have been able to function than the all-powerful state. They have often shown more daring, effort, imagination,

and dedication to the country than their legal competitors. Thanks to them, our throngs of thieves and unemployed are not larger than they are. Thanks to them, there are not more hungry people wandering our streets. Our social problems are enormous, but without the black-marketeers they would be infinitely worse. (xvii)

Vargas Llosa's praise of the informal workers extends even further. Not only do they suppress the amount of street crime, but also they are true democrats who form the firewall that prevents destructive ideologies from causing social conflagration: "If we listen to what these poor slum dwellers are telling us with their deeds, we hear nothing about what so many Third World revolutionaries are advocating in their name—violent revolution, state control of the economy. All we hear is a desire for genuine democracy and authentic liberty" (xvii).

This notion that Peru's legions of workers in the underground economy are actually popular capitalists who choose to exercise their economic freedom and democratic ideals by circumventing stifling governmental regulation and participating directly in the marketplace is an idea that Vargas Llosa adopts directly from de Soto.[14] As we shall see, he later incorporates this idea into his fictional and political discourse throughout the following decade, during which he makes an unsuccessful bid for the presidency of Peru and publishes two more novels in which small-scale entrepreneurs appear.

In his novel *The Storyteller* (1987), released shortly after he wrote the "Foreword" to *The Other Path*, Vargas Llosa offers us another minor character whose desire is to participate directly in the free market, and in this case the results are tragic. As in *The Real Life of Alejandro Mayta*, *The Storyteller* features a narrator who is a novelist in the process of writing a novel. The novel in question is the story of an anthropology student, Saúl, who 'goes native,' abandoning intellectual life in Lima in order to join a prehistoric tribe in the jungle, the Machiguenga. Alternating between chapters set in urban landscapes and those set in the forest, the novel establishes a fascinating counterpoint between the two cultures that make up Peru: one industrialized and literate, the other premodern and oral. As the novel alternates between these two worlds, it invites the reader to ponder difficult questions about the benefits of assimilation versus isolation of fragile minority cultures.

In chapter four of *The Storyteller* the unnamed narrator recalls that, during his first trip to the jungle in 1958, he visited the Aguaruna settlement of Urakusa, where he had his first encounter with a victim of torture, Jum.[15] Working through an interpreter, the narrator learns that a posse of whites and mestizos, comprising all the civilian authorities of the town Santa María de Nieva and a soldier from one of the bases on the frontier, descended on the indigenous settlement one day. They burned huts, raped women, beat the men who tried to defend themselves, and carried off Jum, the tribal leader. Back in Santa María de Nieva, Jum was publicly tortured, an act the interpreter describes in horrifying detail, "They flogged him, burned his armpits with hot eggs, and finally hoisted him up a tree the way they do paiche, large river fish, to drain them off" (74). After a few hours he was released and allowed to return to his village. The purpose of this brutality was retaliation. Jum had angered his attackers by exercising his economic freedom by organizing a cooperative among the Aguaruna settlements of the Alto Marañón.

Chief Jum was a clever and determined man who was identified as a strong leader by the Summer Institute of Linguistics missionaries working in his settlement. They arranged to have him study in the town of Yarinacocha in order to train to become a bilingual teacher who would be capable of teaching his people to read and write in their own language. Although the program did not realize the lofty goal of bringing literacy to the Amazonian tribes, in Jum's case it did have the effect of putting the chief in contact with "civilization" in Yarinacocha—with unintended consequences. There he discovered that he and his people were being exploited by the white and mestizo middlemen with whom they traded rubber and hides. The middlemen set the prices for the raw materials and then paid the Indian suppliers in goods for which they also determined the value. When the clever *cacique* realized that his people could sell their raw materials in the cities for greater profit and buy their goods at better prices there as well, he informed the middlemen of Santa María de Nieva that he would no longer trade with them. Right after Jum communicated this decision, he was punished. As the posse tortured Jum, they told him repeatedly to forget about the cooperative.

The narrator, while reflecting on Jum's sad story, mulls over a particular articulation of the so-called indigenous question, which has been debated among Peruvian intellectuals for over a century. Given that the Urakusa dwellers live in a state of abject exploitation, what should be done to better their lot? Should they move backward toward the isolation they knew before coming into contact with Western civilization? This might be achieved by herding them into protected reservations where they could continue living according to their ancient traditions. Or should they move forward toward economic integration by establishing their cooperative and gaining the economic security that would allow them to enforce their physical security? It is clear that the narrator, as a young man in his twenties, believes the answer is assimilation, and he suspects that his old friend Saúl would disagree:

> Would he admit that in a case like this it was quite obvious that what was to Urakusa's advantage, to Jum's, was not going backward but forward? That is to say, setting up their own cooperative, trading with the towns, prospering economically and socially so that it would no longer be possible to treat them the way the "civilized" people of Santa María de Nieva had done. Or would Saúl, unrealistically, deny that this was so, insist that the true solution was for the Viracochas to go away and let the inhabitants of Urakusa return to their traditionally way of life? (76)

At the time he is reflecting on Jum's story in the 1950s the narrator obviously equates progress with the advent of socialism. (In this respect, he looks a lot like the young Vargas Llosa on whom he is clearly modeled.) He sees the Urakusas' problem in terms of class conflict that could be resolved through the successful transition to socialism:

> By substituting for the obsession with profit—individual gain—the idea of service to the community as the incentive to work, and reintroducing an attitude of solidarity and humanity into social relations, socialism would make possible that coexistence between modern and primitive Peru that Mascarita thought impossible and undesirable. In the new Peru, infused with the science of Marx and Mariátegui, the Amazonian tribes would, at one and the same time, be able to adopt modern ways and to preserve their essential traditions and customs within the mosaic of cultures that would go to make up the future civilization of Peru. (78)

This socialist solution never pans out for the Urakusa, and we can infer from his comments elsewhere in the novel that the narrator eventually distances himself from that political position. *The Storyteller*, however, does not focus on the efficacy of any particular economic plan but on the inevitability of assimilation. Looking back on the ideas of his youth some three decades later, the narrator understands that it was highly romantic of him to believe that industrial development, whether socialist or capitalist, would preserve rather than annihilate the fragile forest cultures. As he writes in the 1980s, Machiguenga culture is well on the way to extinction, and its only possibility for preservation is in texts such as the one the novelist-narrator is writing.

The appearance of Jum in this novel, therefore, is all the more interesting. The Urakusa chief, as we have seen, is no socialist. (As soon as he saw the market's potential, he was eager to exploit it.) I would argue that his presence in *The Storyteller*, however brief, constitutes a persuasive little plug for a market-oriented economy. This implication was lost on the narrator when he was a young socialist blinded by his utopian ideals but should not be lost on the attentive reader. We do not have to look too hard to see that as a free marketeer Jum embodies the neoliberal notions of his creator, author Vargas Llosa. In addition to being a creative and resourceful human being, the chief is motivated by profit, naturally acquisitive, and capable of understanding money and the market. By representing the Indian in a way that is consistent with his own market-oriented ideology of the mid-1980s, the novelist is actually following a pattern established by earlier works of Andean indigenism. Earlier in the twentieth century non-Indian authors such as the Ecuadorian Jorge Icaza and the Peruvian José María Arguedas wrote novels for their white and mestizo urban readership in which they represent the Indian in his rural environment as a natural communist, a portrait consistent with their own leftist worldviews. Like his literary predecessors, in his depiction of Jum, Vargas Llosa, a non-Indian intellectual writing for a non-Indian urban readership about the Indian in the state of nature, describes the Indian in a way consistent with his own worldview. By making the utterly sympathetic *cacique* of the Urakusa a natural capitalist, Vargas Llosa continues the indigenist tradition, albeit with very different political implications.[16]

Just about the time that *The Storyteller* was going to press, Vargas Llosa's professional life took a sharp turn. He became actively involved in Peruvian politics in response to then-president Alan García's plan to nationalize the banks in 1987, a position the novelist vigorously opposed and successfully thwarted. Vargas Llosa then became involved in Libertad, the political movement that emerged from this successful opposition to position itself against García's populist policies and in support of political reforms that would "create a free society in which everyone would have access to the market and be able to live under the protection of the law" (Vargas Llosa, "A Fish Out of Water" 30). As a consequence of his participation in the Libertad movement, Vargas Llosa later ran as a candidate in the 1990 presidential elections. Backed by the newly formed FREDEMO coalition party and closely allied with the Instituto Libertad y Democracía, a public policy think tank intent on promoting private enterprise and the doctrine of market economics in Peru, Vargas Llosa ran on a platform of neoliberal reforms. His policy initiatives included what Alfonso W. Quiroz calls a "thorough economic restructuring" (358) of Peru: the creation of entrepreneurial incentives through privatization of state monopolies; a promise to permit Peruvians in the informal sector immediate access to legality; and the assurance that there would be no more privileges for the powerful elites once businesses were forced to compete not to gain the favor of the state but rather that of the consumers. Vargas Llosa's neoliberal idealism was evident on the campaign trail, which during his political speeches featured the optimistic slogan "¡Hagamos un país de propiatarios y de empresarios!" [Let's make a country of owners and entrepreneurs!] (Álvaro Vargas Llosa 46).

Ironically, and perhaps predictably, the very informal workers whom Vargas Llosa claimed to support in his campaign promises, failed to support him. Either they rejected his political message outright, or they rejected the well-educated, white politician who delivered the message. Álvaro Vargas Llosa, the candidate's son and campaign manager, writes, "We knew that our ideas were profoundly popular in a country where so many millions of people, guided by need and adversity, were already practicing a primitive form of a free economy. Nevertheless, it was impossible for us to get the poorest Peruvians, those that truly embodied the virtues of freedom, to identify our message with their daily lives like two sides of the same coin" (46).

In a runoff election, the voters chose the opposition candidate Alberto Fujimori, a Peruvian of Japanese descent (i.e., a nonwhite) who stood on a platform of populist issues. In another ironic twist of the election, the populist Fujimori implemented much of Vargas Llosa's economic plan once elected.

After his defeat, Vargas Llosa returned to writing fiction and produced the fourth and final novel we shall consider in this study, *Death in the Andes* (1993). The novel, which was conceived of prior to the campaign but written after Vargas Llosa's defeat,[17] is a detective story set in the Peruvian highlands at the height of the Sendero Luminoso violence. Two important figures from the novel's large cast of characters are pertinent to this study of Vargas Llosa's fictional free marketeers: they are Casimiro Huarcaya and Pedrito Tinoco. Both lose their livelihoods due to terrorist activity and both eventually become victims of human sacrifice in the bizarre rituals practiced by the antagonists. Before they meet their hideous fates, however, each works to build a livelihood in the inhospitable Peruvian economy.

Unlike Jum, whose brief appearance in *The Storyteller* is not really relevant to the development of the plot, Casimiro Huarcaya is essential to *Death in the Andes*, and his character is more memorable than the others we have examined thus far. Casimiro is an exemplary individual who overcomes his physical and material limitations to become a relatively prosperous salesman. Not content with simply being a good businessman, Casimiro struggles to become a good man as well. That his efforts to achieve material and moral success are cut short by the violence in the

Andes illustrates the extent to which Peru's development was paralyzed by this problem in the 1980s.

Born fair skinned, with white hair and light eyes among a uniformly dark Andean population, the albino boy has to fight rejection both at home and school. Despite his circumstances, Casimiro grows up well-adjusted. He is strong, alert, good with his hands, and "loved life" (127). Fed up with the limitations of life in his remote village, Casimiro decides at age fifteen to strike out on his own. He teams up with a traveling sales-man, Don Pericles Chalhuanca, and the two begin to crisscross the prov-ince together in Chalhuanca's old truck. Their business consists of selling products from the city in rural areas and buying agricultural products from these areas to sell back in the city. From his mentor, Casimiro learns a number of lessons including the secrets of the trade, the intricacies of truck repair, and how to seduce women on the road. The young man is thrilled with the freedom of his new life. Although the business is never highly lucrative, it does provide the two with enough to live on. Over the years Casimiro's relationship with his boss evolves from that of apprentice to that of surrogate son and finally to that of full partner in the enter-prise. When the old man is ready to retire, Casimiro buys him out and becomes sole proprietor of the business. Once he takes charge, Casimiro redoubles his efforts. He is the first to open his stall in the market in the mornings and the last to close at night. The extra hours pay off, and eventually he is able to replace the old truck with a larger, newer model.

Casimiro's relationship with Asunta demonstrates that he is not just a good capitalist but one with a conscience as well. When the indigenous girl approaches him with the news that she is pregnant with his child, Casimiro's initial reaction is to heed the advice of his mentor: "Don Peri-cles had advised, in a situation like this, to get behind the wheel and drive away" (130). He insults Asunta and accuses her of trying to trap him. Some hours later, he regrets his reaction and begins to search for the girl. He finds her on the outskirts of town and gives her a ride to her settlement. Along the way he offers her his condolences and money for an abortion. Casimiro's feelings of responsibility do not wither with time. A month later he returns to check up on the girl and learns that she has not aborted. This time Casimiro gives her a pair of shoes and a shawl, which she gratefully accepts. The next time the salesman stops by to check up on her, Asunta is gone, and her family will not reveal her whereabouts. Casi-miro tells himself that he has done all that he can for the girl and that he should stop losing sleep over her. Nevertheless, he continues the search.

Just about the time Asunta disappears, Casimiro's trade is transformed by insurgency in the sierra. His roads are blocked, his bridges are burned, and armed groups of both terrorists and counterinsurgency forces continually stop him along the way and that demand that he hand over a portion of his goods. As if this were not enough, his clientele are disappearing. The abuse of the civilian population by both armed groups has unleashed a mass exodus of families who are abandoning their highland homes for the relative security of the coast. The impact of this violence on his business is devastating. One day Casimiro realizes that he is actually losing money and that the only thing that motivates him to keep traveling is the challenge and obsession of finding the mother of his child. For three years he continues his circuit, and everywhere he goes he asks for the girl. As he is beginning to give up hope entirely, Asunta reappears. The encounter occurs in a small town in the southern part of Ayacucho where one night the salesman finds himself surrounded by a group of superstitious drunks who see in his light complexion the face of a *pishtaco*, or devil. Just when the mob is about to lynch him, shots ring out overhead and a band of insurgents led by a cold, commanding young woman appears—it's Asunta. She dispels the crowd's fears by explaining that Casimiro is not the devil but an evil man who raped and impregnated her and then gave her money to abort. Turning a deaf ear to his claims that he has tried for years to right that wrong, the woman warrior sentences Casimiro to death on the spot and raises her pistol. Asunta, however, is a *senderista* (member of the guerrilla group Sendero Luminoso, or Shining Path) with a conscience; she aims high, thus sparing Casimiro's life. Devastated by the shock, the salesman never recovers, and he spends the remainder of his days in a senseless, alcohol-induced stupor.

This section of just over eight pages works effectively as a self-contained short story within the novel. The story efficiently and sympathetically covers a young terrorist's personal motivation for taking up arms (Asunta's initial abandonment) and explores the socioeconomic impact of Sendero Luminoso on the sierra (Casimiro's business goes bust). Thus the characters personalize what was a tragedy of epic proportions. Through Casimiro and Asunta's plights we come to appreciate the tremendous human toll of the violence. If not for the bloodthirsty insurgency and the ruthless counterinsurgency, this young couple might well have formed a financially and emotionally secure future together in Ayacucho.

Although *Death in the Andes* is not one of Vargas Llosa's strongest or more satisfying works, it has moments of brilliance. The portrait of Pedrito Tinoco is one such moment. Like Casimiro, Pedrito is a Peruvian who pursues his livelihood quite contentedly until the violence of the 1980s puts an end to it. Unlike Casimiro, Pedrito embodies the very poorest of the poor. In this poignant characterization Vargas Llosa captures a human being's struggle for spiritual and physical survival in utter depravation. Born mentally retarded and abandoned as a baby on the steps of a church, Pedrito ekes out a living on the streets of Abancay, where he takes what work he finds: "He was a porter, a bootblack, a sweeper, a helper, and a stand-in for watchmen, mailmen, and garbagemen, a caretaker of stalls at the market, an usher at the movies and the circuses that came to town for the Patriotic Festival" (37). Indeed, during his youth Pedrito appears to embody the informal workforce in all its variety and all its discomforts. Here Vargas Llosa certainly does not romanticize poverty. Pedrito's childhood is spent shoeless, unwashed, and dressed in rags. He sleeps on the streets and eats thanks to the charity of the others. Despite mental limitations that render him almost speechless, he eventually finds work on a government-sponsored vicuña preserve. The pay is not much, but it is certainly much more than Pedrito has ever had before, and it allows him to live frugally but contentedly. As promised by the authorities, money and provisions are delivered regularly—until the day these suddenly stop coming. Though this portion of the narrative is focalized through the shepherd's limited faculties, we can clearly grasp the reason for the cutoff. We may infer, however, that the bloodthirsty insurgency has frightened off the government workers who thence abandon the vulnerable shepherd and his flock.

It is when Pedrito is alone with the animals that we truly see his humanity in his profound solitude and selflessness: "He had established a more intimate relationship with these delicate creatures than he ever had with anyone of his own species" (39). He plays with, cures, pets, and even talks to the animals in their language, but he cannot protect them. When a band of *senderistas* comes across the preserve, they promptly slaughter the herd. Using revolutionary rhetoric, the insurgents try to justify to the stricken shepherd the destruction of the herd because the herd was the invention of the imperialist enemy. Confounded by what he has witnessed, Pedrito does not flee as the revolutionaries order him to do. Our final image of him is of the shepherd sitting silently in the center of the slaughter as the birds of prey circle.

Again the portrait of Pedrito Tinoco works as a finely crafted short story inserted into the larger novel. For the purposes of this study, we should observe that in this story Pedrito is neither an owner nor an entrepreneur since his mental limitations do not allow him to participate in the market in this way—he is just a lowly laborer. With his enthusiasm for work and his befuddlement before the terrorists, Pedrito illustrates a basic tenet of Vargas Llosa's conception of the nature of poor Peruvians: given the choice between revolution and work, they choose work.

Unfortunately, Pedrito is not given this choice. Because the government abandons its obligations to the highlands, Sendero Luminoso is able to go on a rampage in the area. In his opinion pieces on the uprising Vargas Llosa has maintained that the real blame for the bloodshed rests with the Peruvian government that turned its back on the highlands and thus allowed the absurd insurgency to spread like wildfire when it otherwise would have been a short-lived, local phenomenon.[18] Thus, the portrayal of the poor laborer as victim of the government's economic mistakes, as seen in the case of Pedrito in *Death in the Andes*, is consistent with Vargas Llosa's political and economic views of the 1980s through the presidential campaign of 1990.

Although entrepreneurs and informal worker characters disappear from his novels after *Death in the Andes*, Vargas Llosa continues to champion the informal economy in his nonfiction writing for some time after 1993. He concludes his book-length study of the narrative of José María Arguedas. *La utopía arcaica (The Archaic Utopia)*, with a chapter titled "La utopía arcaica y el Perú informal." In this chapter he claims that Arguedas's indigenism (which portrayed two separate Perus, one white and western, the other Indian and traditional) has been challenged by the onset of the informal economy. He argues that the traditional Andean society of which Arguedas wrote was dismantled by the mass exodus from the highlands to the coast, where the Indians shed their traditional ways and acculturated to form *la cultura chicha*—the hybrid culture that rose up in the shanty-towns among these migrants.[19] For Vargas Llosa, *chicha* culture appears to be another term for the burgeoning informal sector in which he finds so much to admire. After praising the energy, vitality, and willpower of the *informales*, he continues: "Thanks to those ex-Indians, *cholos*, blacks, *zambos*, and Asians, there has emerged for the first time a popular capitalism and a free market in Peru" (332).[20]

The author continues to sing the praises of informality in his essay "El desquite de los pobres" (1997), in which he simply recycles those ideas from the mid-1980s that first appeared in his "Foreword" to de Soto's *The Other Path*. To demonstrate that he has in no way shied away from these views, he even goes as far as to assert that the informal economy is good not only for Peru and other developing countries but also for advanced European countries like Spain. Such assertions, which would have seemed radical and provocative in 1986, before the neoliberal economic strategies had been implemented in Peru and other parts of Latin America, sound tired and dated in 1997. However, just as we might feel inclined to write off Vargas Llosa's socioeconomic ideas as stale and repetitive, the writer shifts gears again.

For readers accustomed to associating Vargas Llosa with his embrace of informal workers and the underground economy, his more recent opinion pieces come as something of a surprise. Of late, the author is sounding more optimistic about Peru's official economy and his reasons for optimism are more in line with mainstream capitalism. In his opinion piece titled "¿Otro país?" ("Another Country?") he marvels at the accomplishments of the formal sector, which over the past twenty years has managed to develop the agro-export economy of Ica, Peru, to the point that it now purrs along at full employment. The author is impressed not only by the variety and quantity of the produce being harvested from the Peruvian desert but also by the cleanliness, safety, and order of the enterprise. His only criticism is that increased income alone cannot end underdevelopment if official corruption prevents that income from being equitably distributed. Now that Peru's formal economy has demonstrated itself capable of producing wealth, he calls on the government to do a better job of redistribution. This is quite a shift from his earlier claim that only the informal sector was capable of producing in Peru and that the government was incapable of redistributing wealth. Indeed, all that remains of his former position is his consistent admiration for the entrepreneurial spirit.

Although he has diverted his attention from informal workers, Vargas Llosa remains an admirer of entrepreneurs. In another column titled "Los Añaños" ("The Añaños") he offers his readers an inspirational account of a family from Ayacucho that managed to build a soft drink empire among the ruins of the economy of the highlands of Peru. In the late 1980s, at the height of the Sendero violence, the Añaños family founded Kola Real, a remarkably successful company that now is sipping up market share once dominated by the soft drink giants Coke and Pepsi. Vargas Llosa uses the case study as a parable to teach us what Latin American entrepreneurs are capable of in the free market. We don't have to look too hard to see that the Añaños of 2003 are the nonfictional counterparts of the fictional Big Pablito from 1977. Their narratives bookend a quarter of a century during which Vargas Llosa thought and wrote about free markets frequently, and they testify to the fact that the author cannot resist an entrepreneurial success story. For that matter, who can?

So what have we learned by studying Vargas Llosa's fictional free marketeers in the context of his neoliberal period? We have seen just five secondary characters in a total of four novels. That's not many when compared to other types that Vargas Llosa has examined. Idealistic young leftists are sprinkled among the early novels. Overbearing fathers show up regularly as secondary characters throughout these early works as well.

Novelists function as highly visible and dynamic narrators in three novels from the middle of his career. And perhaps most importantly, ideological fanatics of every stripe appear as the protagonists of a number of his novels from *The War of the End of the World* (1981) on through *The Way to Paradise* (2004). Clearly, when it comes to picking a protagonist, the fanatic wins out every time over the free marketeer, and that raises the question of why Vargas Llosa does not present us with more of these economic success stories during the years when he believes wholeheartedly that the unfettered free market is the answer to Peru's problems. Perhaps it has to do with the author's belief that the purpose of literature is not to propose solutions but to present problems.[21] Furthermore, Vargas Llosa's lasting obsession with ideological fanatics in his fiction might actually account for the lack of concentration on small business owners and entrepreneurs. The thing about these folks is they are so physically exhausted from their work that they don't have time left over to dedicate to ideological flights of fancy. For fictional purposes, fanatics are a lot more fun. Also, in Vargas Llosa's hands, it is the frustration of the desires of these fanatics that make the novel a vehicle for social criticism.

The few entrepreneurs and informal workers we do find scattered among the novels are therefore all the more interesting for their rarity and their subtle significance. All five are clearly positive figures, and this implies that the open market with which they are associated is also desirable. With the exception of Big Pablito, all are ultimately frustrated in their efforts to earn their livelihoods in the asphyxiating Peruvian economy. Nevertheless, despite the failures of the other four, all of Vargas Llosa's entrepreneurs and informal workers give us cause for hope. By their very existence they testify to that energy and creativity that the country could harness from its human capital. Thus even when the writer is most pessimistic about Peru's potential—as he is in *The Real Life of Alejandro Mayta* and *Death in the Andes*—he sows what he believes are the seeds for its salvation.

NOTES

1. Support for open markets is, to be sure, only one component of a wider neoliberal worldview. A more comprehensive analysis of Vargas Llosa's neoliberalism is beyond the scope of this essay.
2. Vargas Llosa undoubtedly owes this perspective on informality to the Peruvian economist Hernando de Soto, who in the mid-1980s studied the informal sector of the Peruvian economy as an example of primitive capitalism. More will be said about this important influence on Vargas Llosa's economic thinking later in this essay.

3. The essay "La revolución silenciosa" "The Silent Revolution" was first published as the "Foreword" to Hernando de Soto's socioeconomic study of the informal economy in Peru, *The Other Path*.
4. This translation is my own.
5. This quotation comes from Gene H. Bell-Villada's essay "Sex, Politics, and High Art: Vargas Llosa's Long Road to the *Feast of the Goat*" included in this volume (137–158).
6. It should be noted that *Aunt Julia and the Scriptwriter* is actually Vargas Llosa's second comic novel, although the first with a happy ending in which the hero is able to realize his aspirations. In the hilarious satire of the Peruvian military, *Captain Pantoja and the Special Service* (1973), there is no happy ending. The young officer's efforts to fulfill his duty and open brothels for the soldiers in the jungle ultimately result in the complete frustration of his professional aspirations.
7. Following the release of *La Aunt Julia and the Scriptwriter* in 1977 Vargas Llosa published his weighty and profound portrayal of the effects of fanaticism in the Brazilian backlands, *The War of the End of the World* (1981). Because this is a historical novel set outside Peru, it is not surprising that we do not find informal workers here. In his fiction, these figures appear only in novels set in contemporary Peru.
8. Of course, the relative "reality" of the two Maytas is just an illusion sustained by the conventions of fiction. Technically speaking, the Mayta of Chapters 1–9 is made of words on paper just as the Mayta of Chapter 10.
9. This prologue appears in the Punto de Lectura edition of *Historia de Mayta* from 2008.
10. Curiously, Hernando de Soto chose to cut Vargas Llosa's "Foreword" from the most recent edition of his book. Given that the "Foreword" is so favorable and readable, it appears that the reason for this omission is a personal animosity that developed between the two former friends.
11. We have already seen this criticism of the corrupt formal system presented as the explanation for *Extra*'s early success under the Odría dictatorship in the final chapter of *La Aunt Julia and the Scriptwriter*.
12. We catch a fictional glimpse of this urban transformation in the final pages of *Aunt Julia and the Scriptwriter* when mature Mario returns to Lima in the 1970s and finds the streets teeming with hawkers of every stripe.
13. Efraín Kristal makes the interesting observation that in their social diagnoses, neoliberals such as de Soto and Vargas Llosa echo some of the socialist claims of their youthful sympathies to leftist doctrines by speaking in the name of the poor and blaming the state for the poverty that persists in Peru. Like communist intellectuals they equate their own economic solutions for the country's most pressing problems with the wishes of the oppressed masses. They distinguish themselves from the communists, however, by proposing the unfettered free market and not the socialist state as the solution (*Temptation of the Word* 110–11).

14. Of course, the underground economy is not unique to Latin America, nor do Vargas Llosa and de Soto present the only possible perspective on what should be the public policy implications of the phenomenon. More recent commentators, who have studied cases of informality elsewhere in the world, do not find the evidence makes a clear case for market-oriented reforms. See, for example, Robert Neuwirth's *Shadow Cities: A Billion Squatters, A New Urban World* and Sudhir Aladi Venkatesh's *Off the Books: The Underground Economy of the Urban Poor.*

15. The attentive Vargas Llosa reader may notice that both of these characters have appeared in the author's fiction before. The novelist-narrator figure shows up in *Aunt Julia and the Scriptwriter* and *Historia de Mayta*, and his biography closely resembles that of the real author. For a more extensive analysis of this character, see my book *The Story of the Storyteller: La tía Julia y el escribidor, Historia de Mayta, and The Storyteller.* And Jum, the indigenous chief, tried to form a cooperative once before in the second chapter of *The Green House* (1965) where he also makes a brief appearance.

16. For a thorough study of the early history of Andean indigenism and the political implications of the genre, see Kristal's *The Andes Viewed from the City.*

17. In an essay on the campaign, Vargas Llosa mentions that he was planning to write a novel about human sacrifices and political crimes in a village in the Andes when he was tapped to run for president ("A Fish Out of Water" 17).

18. For the author's perspective on Sendero Luminoso see, for example, his "Piedra de toque" column entitled "El Perú en llamas" ("Peru on Fire").

19. *Chicha*, originally a fermented drink made from corn, has become the name used to describe the musical hybrid between traditional Andean and Caribbean musical styles created by Andean migrants in the coastal cities of Peru and, by extension, the culture that they developed.

20. This high praise is tempered, however, by Vargas Llosa's observation that this same *chicha* culture was responsible for electing President Alberto Fujimori to power in Peru, and thus ushering in an authoritarian regime (La utopía arcaica [*Archaic Utopia*] 335).

21. He reiterates this idea in the "Foreword": "Unlike good literature, which teaches us indirectly, *The Other Path* preaches an explicit lesson about contemporary and future Third World reality" (xi).

Part II

The Writings of the 1980s and 1990s

Chapter 4

Appropriation in the Backlands

Is Mario Vargas Llosa at War with Euclides da Cunha?

Nicholas Birns

As the Mario Vargas Llosa papers in the Princeton University's Firestone Library show, Vargas Llosa began *The War of the End of the World* in Lima in 1979 and continued to draft it during his stay at the Woodrow Wilson Center in Washington in early 1980. This was just after the Soviet invasion of Afghanistan, when sentiment in the United States was alarmed about Soviet aggression, and the menace of left-wing radicals in third world countries seemed very real. In the Latin American sphere of Vargas Llosa's primary interest, the Sandinistas had come to power in Nicaragua in July 1979 and were already showing signs of hewing more closely to the Moscow/Havana line than their foreign celebrants had promised. Furthermore, the remnants of the Velasco regime, with its Left-nationalist rhetoric, were still present in Peru, although the August 1980 inauguration of Fernando Belaunde Terry for the latter of his far-separated terms as president of Peru, signaled democratization. Yet Vargas Llosa's then-ideological soulmate Hernando de Soto first conceived the agenda, in 1979, that led to the founding of the Instituto Libertad y Democracia two years later, this promotion of free-market, libertarian attitudes seemed to fly in the face of a hegemonic socialist consensus among Latin American intellectuals. What Efraín Kristal in *Temptation of the Word* (110) calls Vargas Llosa's "antiauthoritaran" ideas were not, in their incipience, comfortably "establishment" in torque. Vargas Llosa had been an avowed 'liberal' anticommunist since at least the brouhaha over Fidel Castro's treatment of the political prisoner and writer Heberto Padilla in 1971. But for much of the next ten years, Vargas Llosa looked as if he was standing athwart the currents of history.

This appearance changed during *The War of the End of the World*'s publication and translation. By the time the novel was published in Spanish in 1981, Ronald Reagan had been elected and the rise of Solidarity in Poland had given a clear signal of discontent in the Soviet bloc. Although discrete leftist revolutionary movements would still make noise in the 1980s (such as, obviously, Sendero Luminoso in Peru) Vargas Llosa's novel came into a reading context very different in terms of political ambience from the context of its authorial production.

When the novel appeared in English translation in 1984, it was "morning in America," to cite Reagan's successful reelection slogan. The review of *The War* by the respected novelist Robert Stone in the August 12, 1984, issue of the *New York Times Book Review*, despite some nominal criticism of the Reagan administration, read the novel as a valuable critique of leftist utopianism. Stone observed that "as a 'third world' writer in an age of upheaval . . . Vargas Llosa has the temerity to question the uniqueness of the revolutionary mythos. Implicitly, by assigning revolution its place among the ritual dramas of history, he questions its salvific function" ("Revolution as Ritual"). Stone no doubt thought of Vargas Llosa as a liberal skeptical of both political extremes. But also influencing his perspective was the belief, which lingered even into the writer's 1990 presidential run, that Vargas Llosa could not be a supporter of Reagan or Margaret Thatcher; that, as a Latin American writer, a Boom novelist, he was apodictically left-wing. He was associated with the general leftism of the Boom. Since Vargas Llosa was mentioned in the same breath as canonical leftist icons like Gabriel García Márquez, in terms of representing the new flourishing of Latin American literature, he could by definition not be of the right.

What remained unanswered by Stone's reception of *The War*, though, is the question of whether this skeptical awakening ends up endorsing liberalism or a revived belief in the free market, and if this participates in another sort of received revolutionary mythos, of what Jeffrey Nealon calls the "almost complete triumph" of the free market (81). Though many would stipulate that Vargas Llosa eventually emerged as a fervent defender of free-market capitalism, it is again crucial to note that the text of *The War* was originally conceived and composed amid conditions seemingly far less propitious for such an ideology. A utopian-capitalist reading of its critique of leftist utopianism is an effect of context and readership, across a textual and temporal fold from the circumstances of its production.

It could be argued, though, that the textual history of the novel begins even earlier, well before the novelist conceived the work, well before the novelist was even born. The events in Vargas Llosa's novel concern the late nineteenth-century utopian visionary Antonio Conselheiro. Conselheiro brings disaster to the rural backlands people of Canudos in northeastern Brazil with his millenarian visions. But is Conselheiro meant to be a figure for leftist utopianism or for utopianism *tout court*? Is there such a thing as a utopianism of the Right? And can a sage skepticism about utopianism of the Left eventually bend to an opposite utopianism?

That this is not just an ideological but a formal question can be examined in the light of the novel's relation to its predecessor text, Euclides da Cunha's *Rebellion in the Backlands* (1902).[1] Da Cunha's work, an experimental piece of nonfiction, had received international exposure by the time Vargas Llosa published his novel. In 1944, Samuel Putnam's translation was, like Vargas Llosa's novel forty years later, featured on the front page of the *New York Times* Book Review, and was for a time in the 1960s the favorite book of the then-first couple of American letters, Robert Lowell and Elizabeth Hardwick. (Presumably their friend Elizabeth Bishop, long resident in Brazil, also knew of it, or perhaps introduced it to them.) But the Peruvian writer's rendition of the Canudos story reached a far wider and more popular audience. Was Vargas Llosa retelling da Cunha's story for his own imaginative purposes? Was he giving it worthy exposure through embedding it in the more immediately appealing narrative mode? Or was Vargas Llosa, writing in a more widely spoken language and in a more popular genre than the Brazilian journalist, appropriating da Cunha? I will suggest that the implied contest between Vargas Llosa and da Cunha over the imaginative 'territory' of Canudos is a question parallel to that of any rightist counterutopianism.

In this sense, *The War of the End of the World*'s chief antagonist may not be the Conselheiro *but da Cunha himself*. Da Cunha is a scientist, a positivist, a believer in modern progress, and whether consciously or not, an experimental writer—all aspects potentially held at bay by the (to adapt Jerome C. Christensen's phrase) "corporate populism" of Vargas Llosa's narrative.[2] Moreover, the very idea of 'novelizing' da Cunha's text is ipso facto postmodern, thus refuting Raymond L. Williams's contention that Vargas is a modern, not postmodern, writer (*Mario Vargas Llosa* 173). Does a revived novel genre, touting a reinvigorated realism with the fillip of self-reflexive technique, provide complement to a revived conservatism?

As early as 1970, in "The Latin American Novel Today," Vargas Llosa declares that the novel is inherently "subversive" and that pre-Boom writing tends toward an "aggressive provincialism" (denouncing his own countrywoman Clorinda Matto de Turner) and was "primitive" (7, 8). In a 1997 interview, the novelist speaks of "the ambition of all fiction to impose itself on the reader as the truth" ("Demons and Lies" 17). Vargas Llosa's strong belief in the autonomy of literature, combined with his denigration of pre-Boom Latin American writing, offers a literary as well as a compositional basis for the tacit self-positioning of his own work on a higher aesthetic level than da Cunha's. Inevitably, though, Vargas Llosa's declaration that, effectively, Latin American writing worthy of world notice begins with the Boom generation is a form of self-advertisement and generational boosterism.

The antagonist of the novel is not, inside the text, the messianic Conselheiro, or, outside the text, any *sandinista*, *senderista*, or Soviet-inspired agitator, but da Cunha himself. Da Cunha's beliefs (his racialism, scientism, positivism) and his identity as a nonfiction writer are generally opposed by Vargas Llosa's text. Some aspects of this balance sheet weigh heavily in Vargas Llosa's favor; the Peruvian writer utterly eschews the racial superiority and determinism of da Cunha, which is the Brazilian writer's least admirable aspect. But it cannot be denied that the implied conflict between Vargas Llosa and da Cunha is at least as energetic as that between Moreira César and Conselheiro.

Vargas Llosa was aware of da Cunha's text after 1972, when, as Efraín Kristal points out, he thought of collaborating with the Brazilian filmmaker Rui Guerra on a cinematic adaptation of da Cunha's work (*Temptation of the Word* 125). That the novel does not assert that it is an adaptation of an anterior work (da Cunha is mentioned in the front apparatus of the novel as a dedicatee, and a figure based on him functions as a partial narrator in the novel, but there is no statement of the novel's indebtedness to da Cunha's narrative within the text) when the process that produced it was generated by such an attempt at adaptation, illustrates a certain concealment of the text's relationship to its source. Vargas Llosa was clearly intrigued by da Cunha's work; Kristal notes that the influence is discernible as early as *Captain Pantoja and the Special Service* (1973). As an added element of this influence, the very name Pantoja is found in da Cunha (where a Colonel Pantoja is mentioned as leading a battalion engaged in a pitched battle) (326). Presumably, this passage is Vargas Llosa's source for the name.

Thus, by the time he came to write *The War*, Vargas Llosa was already well enmeshed with da Cunha's work. Yet a Brazilian brought the work to Vargas Llosa's notice. It was not part of his cradle literary inheritance. It would be absurdly puritanical to fault Vargas Llosa for encountering inspiration in this way. The claim of the novel's prerogative to reframe reality is a motif running through the literary self-justification of romanticism and modernity. Yet Vargas Llosa's interaction with da Cunha exists in a network of context and affiliation. It cannot simply be seen as the outcome of a pure, uninflected act of reading.

Vargas Llosa's book should have served as a kind of advertisement for da Cunha; this has happened many times with postmodern rewrites or re-presentations of classics. But da Cunha's text was not given this push by the great success of a novel based on it; it has continued be read by Brazilianists, studied by comparative literature scholars, and valued by those in the know—but such was the case before 1981, and it could even be argued that its exposure has *lessened* since the publication of *The War*. For instance, Putnam's 1944 English translation is widely criticized. Yet despite the publicity afforded the text by Vargas Llosa's novel, a new translation did not appear in the quarter-century following the English-language publication of *The War of the End of the World*, a lack only remedied in 2010 with the appearance of Elizabeth Lowe's Penguin translation.

Does Vargas Llosa foreground his dependence on da Cunha's text in the novel? Vargas Llosa does dedicate the novel to da Cunha, along with the Brazilian novelist Nélida Piñon, who guided the novelist through the sertaõs of Bahia. But he characterizes da Cunha as being in the other world, a way of course of saying he is not alive; but one that echoes the old woman's assertion of that "archangels took him up to heaven" (Vargas Llosa, *The War of the End of the World* 568), as well as asserting a transcendence for a scientific positivist who did not believe in such. Vargas Llosa may grant da Cunha literary immortality. But there is a latent assertion that da Cunha's positivism is a form of transcendental belief, therefore debunking its empirical self-assertion.

In effect, Vargas Llosa's text *replaces* da Cunha; substituting fiction for nonfiction, a Spanish-speaker's viewpoint over a Portuguese-speaker's; a nonnative of the country depicted over a native; the perspective of a *litterateur* over that of a scientist; a skeptical liberalism over a bewildered positivist optimism.[3] One sees this when comparing the works at a crucial juncture in the underlying *histoire*: the point when the Brazilian army comes to a reluctant admiration for the rebels. Da Cunha says,

> Something then happened that was extraordinary and rather unexpected. The battered enemy now appeared all of a sudden to have a new lease on life and began displaying an incredible degree of vigor. Even the troops that that had faced him from the start of the conflict had not really come to know him or, rather, they knew him only from the glimpses they had had of him, as an astute foe, slipping away from the maze of dugouts and luring them on, indomitably repelling the most valiant of charges, and without

an equal when it came to eluding the most unforeseen of attacks. He was
beginning to loom as a hero in their eyes. (435)

This is one of the places where da Cunha is at his most narrative and
most character-centered, yet the vantage point is abstract, unindividu-
ated—the 'him' is not Conselheiro but the *jagunço as a combatant and,
even more, as a sociological phenomenon*. Vargas Llosa's presentation is very
different. The nearsighted da Cunha stand-in, speaking to the Baron de
Canabrava, says that the dissolute Father Joaquim was transformed by
Conselheiro into "something of a hero" (*The War* 418) and then goes on
to say that "culture, intelligence, books have nothing to do with the story
of the Counselor. . . . but that's the least of it. The surprising thing is not
that Father Joaquim became a jagunço. It is that the Counselor made a
brave man of him, when before he had been a coward. That's the most
difficult, the most miraculous conversion of all" (418).

Like da Cunha, Vargas Llosa is both repelled by and admires the rebels of
Canudos, but the dry, analytic detachment is gone. Vargas Llosa is passionately involved in the lives of these individuals and can appreciate change
and growth even in the service of a misguided and tragic way of life. Vargas
Llosa sees these characters as flesh-and-blood, three-dimensional individuals and, whatever his animadversions about the ideology by which they
lived, is willing to commit to telling their stories. Whatever his critiques
of the futility of Conselheiro's ideology. Vargas Llosa is unswerving in
registering its transformative effects on the lives of its adherents, who
become different and better people, undergo change and growth, are not
static types or emblems. Vargas Llosa's narrative intricacy and psychological depth may actually be less experimental than da Cunha's use of expository prose to delicately register the contradictions of a complex nations
coming to terms with the different and often self-fissuring strands in its
fabric. But Vargas Llosa's capacity to acknowledge the individuality and
moral freedom of the rebels of Canudos—their capacity to grow—may
signal that da Cunha's assessment of them is bound by a racialism and
Eurocentrism that the postmodern Vargas Llosa, who is generally both
multicultural *and* neoliberal, lacks.

Recent work on da Cunha has foregrounded the racialist and Darwin-
ian side of his positivism, what Adriana Johnson has called his "hegemonic articulation" of a national project that would usurp the testimonial
ability of the unlettered and impose the "intelligibility" of a "lettered
elite" (356). In this way, da Cunha's viewpoint solidly adhered to the
intellectual consensus of the *paulistas* (people from Saõ Paulo) who dominated the early Brazilian republican government and the general mentality of "Ordem e Progresso" highlighted on the Brazilian flag and mirrored

by other Latin American analogues such as the Porfirio Díaz regime in
Mexico from 1876 to 1910. Yet this needed reappraisal should not blind
us to the eminently modernist aspects of what Thomas Beebee calls da
Cunha's "dense, hypotactic, paradoxical style" (Beebee 195) characterized
by, as Walnice Nogueira Galvão puts it in her introduction to the Biblioteca Ayacucho's Spanish-language edition of da Cunha's text, "the inces-
sant repetition of contradictory statements" (Galvão xxiii). Nor should it
occlude the way in which da Cunha's scientific training gave him a sense
of idiosyncratic witness that might prove more fructifying than the narrative mechanisms of the novel.

One could aver that *Rebellion in the Backlands* is "not a novel" (Wasserman 471); thus his novel cannot be accused of being an imitation. One
would agree with Vargas Llosa that the novelists should not have to refrain
from borrowing from other sources, even great writers such as da Cunha.
Certainly what it at issue here is not plagiarism or even derivativeness.
The two writers agree on the specificity of the Latin American landscape;
its insusceptibility to European models; the need for urban Brazilians to
look inland and not be pale imitations of Europeans; the fatuity of Conselheiro's rebellion and the tragedy of Moreira César's bloody suppression
of it. But the difference between the two writers that is the most crucial
is just the one Vargas Llosa makes the greatest effort to foreground in his
self-defense: that da Cunha was a scientist who believed in notions of scientific progress and Vargas Llosa is a creative writer who claims preroga-
tives for the novel that are fundamentally beyond reason. In this respect,
and given the pejorative characterization of all those who associate themselves with science or progress in the novel, Vargas Llosa's stance toward
da Cunha is not just that of a Spanish to a Portuguese speaker, novelist
to extraordinarily gifted expository writer, but a late twentieth-century
reanimator of tradition who trusts in the powers of the novel form over
the inferentially discredited truisms of scientific order and progress.

Perhaps it was Vargas Llosa's anti-leftist politics, or the fact that a
Spanish-speaking writer has dared to appropriate a great classic of the
Portuguese language, not any outrage on the alleged plundering of da
Cunha, that made this a contested issue. This is fair; that this is a con-
tested issue is indeed probably due to Vargas Llosa's politics. Yet it could
also be argued that the particular characterization and displacement of
Euclides da Cunha within Vargas Llosa's text also, from the start, has
political implications.

There is an inevitable atmosphere of churlish sour grapes, of being a
kind of dour spoilsport about making these complaints, and the general
reader who just wants to enjoy the book may find them frustrating. But

it is the critic's obligation to at least attend to them and to avoid either *ad hominem* castigation or literary carte blanche. Moreover, Vargas Llosa defends his right as a Peruvian to write on Brazilian material, aptly pointing out that the book, in Spanish translation, was in Angel Rama's Biblioteca Ayacucho series. This is perhaps the strongest point in his rebuttal to his critics, asserting that *Rebellion in the Backlands* was part of his immediate heritage—his birthright, as it were, as an American—and that his relation to it therefore cannot be one of imperialism or straightforward appropriation. Furthermore, there is a history Spanish-language reception of da Cunha going back at least to the pioneering work of the Argentine *littérateur* Braulio Sánchez-Sáez in the 1930s.

Yet Vargas Llosa takes da Cunha's textuality in a decidedly different direction. One need look, in this respect, no further than the fundamental tripartite division of *Rebellion in the Backlands* into geography, anthropology, and event. The story of Conselheiro and the Canudos revolt only comes at the end. Even Adriana Johnson, who does not give undue credence to the 'creative' aspects of da Cunha's work, discerns that "*Rebellion in the Backlands* is full of aporias, moments in which the Republican, positivist and scientific codes of Da Cunha find their epistemological limits." (359)

Da Cunha even parades some of those himself, such as his overt references to "the Hegelian scheme" (*Rebellion in the Backlands* 41) of development, far more speculative than the Comtean ones to which he officially subscribed—though one that da Cunha positions the Brazilian landscape as evading. Da Cunha's text also deploys botanical and local-gazetteering aspects in which Vargas Llosa is not outstandingly interested. The elements of local history that for da Cunha are the crucial referents in his account are only indices of a global meaning for Vargas Llosa, who in any event concentrates on ideology, character, and language; landscape for him is setting, not, as it very nearly is for da Cunha, the de facto "protagonist" or perhaps more fittingly "antihero." Da Cunha devotes four paragraphs to the umbú tree; Vargas Llosa exfoliates the story out into areas of sex and religion, neither of which da Cunha shows much avidity for, but that, to generalize, provide a more reader-friendly narrative approach.

Furthermore, da Cunha's stance of scientific scrutiny is exemplified textually in the segmented, almost encyclopedic subsections that accumulate to an overall effect, like tesserae in a mosaic, but do not accumulate any narrative force from one section to the next. Vargas Llosa's novel is in four parts, and after a very short second section, the third and fourth are the longest and parts of the book and display the most narrative force; even their subsections are much longer than da Cunha's, and the discursive flow is far less interrupted by the advent of a new segment. With respect to its predecessor text, Vargas Llosa's novel manifests a declared affirmation of narrative. In its defense, it also can be said to carnivalize, in a Bakhtinian way, the historical standpoints reveals by *Rebellion in the Backlands*, as everybody—republican, anarchist, *sertanejo*—becomes characters is a cavalcade that sometimes threatens to envelop them all. Peter Elmore points out that, with regard to the internal thoughts of the key characters, Vargas Llosa imposes "a cloak of silence" ("Los duelos de la historia"). What we do have access to is the novelist's own discourse, superimposed over the various ideological standpoints expressed in the novel as characters. Indeed, the most significant genre-based strategy Vargas Llosa can deploy to his benefit is the novel's capacity to subject every referent within it to a universal parody and anarchy, far more fissiparous than the version of anarchy espoused by Galileo Gall, the Scottish anarchist in the novel. The novel has the capacity not to take itself wholly seriously and indeed totally negate any determinate position of seriousness, which da Cunha's nonfiction narrative, however experimental and self-conscious it may be, does not.

Yet paradoxically, it is in the novel's overall registering of da Cunha's presence within it that its force seems least anarchic, most premeditated.[4] It is important to note that Galileo Gall and Epaminondas Gonçalves, two invented characters, not only represent stock ideological viewpoints but also have aspects of da Cunha's belief systems in them, even if they are far more sympathetic to the *jagunços* than Euclides. As a Scottish anarchist, Galileo Gall is a send-up of foolish Enlightenment aspirations, of making something like the measurement of heads into a science—phrenology—that is inherently unclassifiable. As a Scotsman (revised, according to Kristal, from an originally Irish character; in his current-work-in progress, on Roger Casement's journeys to the Belgian Congo, Vargas Llosa is finally concentrating on an Irishman) he is a symptom of Enlightenment gone overboard and also perhaps of a strain of sober Scottish industriousness—a trait that had yielded many entrepreneurs no doubt admired by Vargas Llosa, not to mention Adam Smith himself—loosened and driven mad by ideological fervor. In both the cases of Galileo Gall and of Epaminondas Gonçalves, scientific, positivistic optimism—the sort with which da Cunha is customarily associated—is subject to mockery, jest, derision. Da Cunha virtually ends his book by saying, "let science have the last word" (476). Vargas Llosa would hardly concur.

Vargas Llosa has been critical of the strands of postmodernism that would privilege identity categories such as race, class, and gender or would reduce reality to a series of simulacra or a net of textuality. Nonetheless, Vargas Llosa, in his reusing of anterior forms (whether popular genres in

Aunt Julia and the Scriptwriter, or an anterior text like da Cunha's in *The War,* or the historical record of the Trujillo dictatorship in *The Feast of the Goat),* participates in the style of pastiche, borrowing, and appropriation commonly associated with postmodernism, particularly in architecture but also in the visual arts and in writers who reuse previous canonical narratives, such as the many practitioners of what Linda Hutcheon has termed "historiographic metafiction," (105) a postulated genre that, in its emphasis on both fictionality and a reflexive look back at concrete history, has powerful applicability to *The War.* Leopoldo Bernucci, as cited by Efraín Kristal, speaks of Vargas Llosa's book as a "rewriting" (*Temptation of the Word* 127) of *Rebellion in the Backlands,* This act of rewriting may at once give new life to da Cunha's story yet excessively annex it to what Vargas Llosa elsewhere called the "sovereignty" (*Wellsprings* 30) of the novel, which Vargas Llosa has persistently linked with the sovereignty of the individual and individual freedom. And the reemergence of the traditional, realist novel—with the bells and whistles of self-reflexive technique attached to it in a nondeterminative way—may be a structural parallel to the reemergence of nineteenth-century economic liberalism, laced by the awareness of coming "after" a Marxism that had positioned itself in critique of the original liberalism.

Angel Rama, in his treatment of the relation of *The War* to *Rebellion in the Backlands,* likened it to the relation of Joyce's *Ulysses* to Homer's *Odyssey.* This comparison certainly implies that Vargas Llosa is not out to *replace* or *oppose* da Cunha's text, an assertion fortified by the detailed study Leopoldo Bernucci has made of the relationship between Vargas Llosa's novel and da Cunha's work. Certainly, in both the detail of the relationship and the ingenuity with which the novelist meticulously hews to the source yet devises a new creation, the conjecture of this notable critic is resonant. Yet one would respectfully contend that there are differences here, not so much in novelistic practice as in canonicity. Homer's epic had been around for millennia and is a staple of modern Western culture since the Renaissance. Da Cunha died just a generation before Vargas Llosa was born, Homer's epic was a widely known classic, familiar to millions that had not read it, and Joyce's relation to it was not only textual but also cultural, relating not to the *Odyssey* as such but to what people *knew* about the *Odyssey.* Moreover, Joyce's relation to Homer is parodic, ironic, and ludic; Vargas Llosa's may be so in execution (from a novelist of his ingenuity, one would not expect anything else), but it cannot really come across like this in conception simply because of the relative obscurity of the source; discovering Vargas Llosa's game-playing with his antecedent is a matter for textual scholars, not general readers.

Os Sertões is a great book known largely to Brazilians, Brazilianists, and a very thin layer of connoisseurs of world literature. It is not my impression that it is generally known, for instance, among lay readers in Spanish-speaking countries in the Americas, which would have to be the case for Rama's parallel to be sufficient rather than strikingly suggestive. Vargas Llosa is a more famous writer and was so when he published the novel, than da Cunha ever has been outside Brazil, whereas Joyce still now has not matched the fame of Homer. Rama's parallel, in other words, only fully works within Brazil. The great Uruguayan critic admires the novel as a work of art but despairs of its hostility toward revolutionary action. But perhaps the most salient manifestation of this is the belief that a novelist who was *not there* can *replace* the account of an experimental nonfiction writer who *was* there in taking stock of the events at Canudos.

Vargas Llosa has stated that da Cunha was only one of many sources he used in composing the novel. This is no doubt true—there had been previous "heterolingual" (to use Roberto Ignacio Díaz's term) novels on Canudos by the British writer Cunninghame Graham and the French writer Lucien Marchal—and da Cunha does not have an imaginative stranglehold over Canudos, however outstanding his writing, any more than Vargas Llosa or anyone else does. But this move also evokes what Harold Bloom termed "the anxiety of influence"—rhetorically broadening the field of alternatives so as to outflank one particularly prominent opponent. This is a time-honored psychological, political, and even military tactic (maybe even Moreira César would have recognized it) and operates to discursively tug da Cunha into being an *opponent* of Vargas Llosa. In addition, this "widening of the field" begs the question of why Canudos is of interest in world literature. A writer writing a novel about whaling in the Pacific may use many other sources than the fiction of Herman Melville and some sources that have assets Melville may not. But Melville is why the subject has a *literary* importance.

Renata R. Mautner Wasserman also provides a bracing examination of the relation of the two texts, seeing Vargas Llosa as introducing a fundamental epistemological skepticism into da Cunha's more observational and empirical angle on Canudos. But is the greater skepticism is necessarily more "progressive"? As Bruno Latour has pointed out, the former George W. Bush administration in the United States tended to use a rhetoric of relativism and perspectives that relied on a constructionist view of reality, leaving the Left with the less glamorous, in postmodern terms, terrain of hard facts. This rhetoric has, though, led to a revelation of the empirical on the Left and a lessening of its fixation on cultural relativism. Greg Grandin has asserted that the a precursor of the second Bush administration's desire to ideologically transform the Middle East was the Reagan administration's desire to have the same effect on Latin America. So there is some sort of connection between antileftism in 1980s Latin America and a utopianism of the postmodern unbound.

This potential slippage is fortified by the wide range of utopianisms in the novel. First of all, it must be remembered that, throughout the novel, Conselheiro and his followers are portrayed as nothing but Christian religious fanatics; they are not Marxists, not rationalists, not believers in immanent social progress; indeed, they desire regress. Free-floating anarchists like Galileo Gall want to affix themselves to their cause, and opportunistic outside agitators like Epaminondas Gonçalves want to employ them as tools in a broader ideological game. But these men are followers, not originators of the utopian impulse. In Conselherio's enunciation of it, this impulse is thoroughly Christian. The Euclides stand-in stuns the Baron de Canabrava in his insistence that priests are involved in the Conselheiro movement, not just "phrenologists" or "Scottish anarchists" (417).

Moreover, over a dozen references in the book to Sebastianism—the belief that the Portuguese king Sebastian, who died in crusade in North Africa in 1578, thus guaranteeing the end of the Avis dynasty and Portugal's temporary absorption under the Spanish crown—indicates that Vargas Llosa knows that Conselheiro's millenarianism has deep roots in Portuguese and Brazilian culture. Thus it is not directly traceable to a secular totalizing belief systems comparable to the Soviets, the *sandinistas*, and the *senderistas*. Inevitably, Vargas Llosa is relying on an allegorical equation between the two kinds of fanaticism. He also presumes the reader is aware, directly or indirectly, of the hypothesis of scholars such as Karl Löwith and Norman Cohn that modern socialist utopianisms are but a displacement of Christian messianism. This link between utopianism and messianism was overwhelmingly made as a way to denigrate utopianism, and a familiar critique made by many on the Right and even among anticommunists of the Left from the late 1940s onward. Indeed, without these sort of clues, the untutored reader is likely to conclude that *The War of the End of the World* is a novel pointing, as such, to the dangers of Christian messianism and of millenarianism of the straight, not the displaced, variety.

But Vargas Llosa's tacit propagation of the Cohn/Lowith thesis presumes that Christian messianism was *not totally good in the first place*. This is why Vargas Llosa is more of a neoliberal than a conservative. He does not assign religious belief a sustaining role in the renormativization of Western society in the wake of Marxism. Indeed, normative Christianity in Latin America is associated with a statism and a lack of initiative.

Much of *The War* is skeptical not only of messianism but also of what might be called Christian knightliness: the peers of France in the legends of Charlemagne and Roland are pointedly mentioned several times in the novel, with the *jagunços* being compared to them in a mocking way almost Cervantine in its deflation of chivalric pretensions.

Both Vargas Llosa's and da Cunha's books are great ones, and whatever structural or ideological antagonism there is between them should not force us to choose one or the other. What it does demonstrate, though, is that the historical record—whether ideological, annalistic, or intertextual—is rich and full of ramifications and that neither the sovereignty of the novel nor the suspicion of cultural critique can totally determine it. To see Mario Vargas Llosa's fiction against the full background of its cultural, political, and discursive placement is to reaffirm the scale and significance of its achievement.

What Vargas Llosa opposes in his 1981 novel was worth opposing and perhaps was particularly so in Vargas Llosa's immediate Peruvian context. Moreover, to advocate liberalism and market economics in Latin America in this era had differing implications than to have done so in the rich North. To simply denounce Vargas Llosa for not adhering to the leftist politics many worldwide still expect of Latin American writers is as simplistic as the response of Robert Stone, which took the novel's presentation totally at face value. The formal and political effect of *The War* should be scrutinized in the light of recognition that Vargas Llosa, as one of the most accomplished, most public, and most protean of contemporary novelists, is a key figure in the life of his times. To tell the story of the world's recent past without coming to terms with Vargas Llosa's writing is impossible. Yet the most resonant figure in *The War* is someone only tenuously named there, yet insistently disclosed by the novel's enmeshment in history—Euclides da Cunha.

NOTES

1. Da Cunha's book has a complicated set of defining terms. Its Portuguese title, *Os Sertões*, refers to the geographical terrain around the town of Canudos, in Bahia. The *sertanejos* are the inhabitants of the *sertão* in general; the *jagunços* are those inhabitants constituted into bands in armed rebellion supporting the utopian visions of Conselheiro. The word *sertão* is translated in English as 'backlands'; the normal English equivalent would be 'backcountry' but the sole Anglophone translator so far, Samuel Putnam, did not use this, no doubt because it suggests forested terrain, and a *sertão* is a dry, dusty plain quite unlike that. 'Prairie,' more geographically apt, would give a very misleading connotation. Da Cunha does not have 'Rebellion' in the title, but Putnam added it, to

tell the reader what was going on but also to narrativize it, taking the first step in a process Vargas Llosa will gradually accelerate.

2. Jerome C. Christensen, "Rhetoric and Corporate Populism: A Romantic Critique of the Academy in an Age of High Gossip."

3. Vargas Llosa's interest in Brazil itself, though, is genuine and long-term; in a June 16, 2007 article in the Spanish newspaper *El País*, he applauds the Lula government as a palatable alternative to Hugo Chávez's' twenty-first century socialism' ("Socialismo del siglo XXI").

4. Da Cunha's description of Moreira César is a masterpiece of the freewheeling, unhinged, yet scrupulously observant sarcasm Bakhtin famously found so delightful and destabilizing in Dickens's *Little Dorrit*.

CHAPTER 5

MARIO VARGAS LLOSA, THE FABULIST OF QUEER CLEANSING

PAUL ALLATSON

IN 2005 MARIO VARGAS LLOSA DELIVERED HIS LECTURE "CONFESSIONS of a Liberal" for the Washington-based American Enterprise Institute for Public Policy Research. A summation of Vargas Llosa's intellectual evolution since the 1960s, the lecture confirmed his claim to the mantle of Latin American liberal *par excellence*. Plotted in opposition to ideology as "an open, evolving doctrine that yields to reality instead of trying to force reality to do the yielding," Vargas Llosa's liberalism rests on a number of familiar precepts: political democracy; private property; the free market; and the rule of law in productive tension with "the defense of individual interests over those of the state" ("Confessions of a Liberal"). For Vargas Llosa, moreover, liberalism also signifies "tolerance and respect for others, and especially for those who think differently from ourselves, who practice other customs and worship another god or who are non-believers," hence his support for the "separation between church and state" and "the decriminalization of abortion and gay marriage" ("Confessions of a Liberal"). Given Vargas Llosa's shift from the Left to the Right of the political spectrum and his well-publicized impatience with political agendas opposed to his own, the argumentation here was somewhat disingenuous. Equally disingenuous was Vargas Llosa's celebration of a liberal "natural lack of trust in power, in all powers" ("Confessions of a Liberal"). For there is one power that he does, in fact, trust: his

This chapter revisits and reworks my article "*Historia de Mayta*: A Fable of Queer Cleansing" (*Revista de Estudios Hispánicos* 32.3, 1998: 511–35). I am grateful to Steven Gregory and Diana Palaversich for their contributions to the earlier article, and Jeffrey Browitt for his inputs into this chapter.

own as a writer and as an "author-function," to use Foucault's term for an author's appearance and function in discourse.

Faith in that power has a long provenance in Vargas Llosa's *oeuvre*, but it appeared with a new confidence in his 1984 novel *Historia de Mayta*, translated as *The Real Life of Alejandro Mayta* (1986).[1] *Historia de Mayta*, in fact, is a formative publication in Vargas Llosa's literary and political development alike. It confirmed the author's antipathy for leftist political agendas (ideological lies, destructive fictions), and it announced that such displeasure would henceforth color his authorial concerns (literary truths, productive fictions). Vargas Llosa noted as much in his essay "Transforming a Lie into Truth: *The Real Life of Alejandro Mayta* as a Metaphor for the Writer's Task":

> Ideological fiction is what Mayta and his comrades live. . . . On the other hand *Historia de Mayta* is a description of the other kind of fiction, a fiction that the narrator/writer is trying to write. The reader sees in the novel how this other fiction, which is also an imaginary construction that has some roots in reality, as in the case of this ideological fiction built by Mayta, does not have these negative or even catastrophic results but has positive ones because at least in this world, which is going to pieces, which is practically disappearing in an orgy of violence, this man who is writing finds a reason to resist, to live. (*A Writer's Reality* 153)

Historia de Mayta, moreover, serves Vargas Llosa as a key literary template for his post-1984 career: "The story of Mayta, then, is my own story of a writer writing his fiction. What the narrator does with Mayta is what I do each time I write a novel" (155).

But what does the narrator and the novel's author-function—its textual stand-in for the real-world writer—do with Mayta? Toward the end of *Historia*, after the narrator has travelled across Peru in search of his subject, he finally meets the "real" Mayta. After telling this Mayta of his research for the book he is writing, he says, "The character in my novel is queer" (301). Mayta's incredulous "Why?" elicits the following reply: "To accentuate his marginality, his being a man full of contradictions. Also to show the prejudices that exist with regard to this subject among those who supposedly want to liberate society from its defects. Well, I don't really know exactly why he is" (301). The "real" Mayta's response to this explanation creates a breach between the Mayta or Maytas learned about up to that point and the person finally tracked down and allowed to speak. And when that Mayta says, "They say Mao shot all the queers in China" (301), he has the final word on the novel's queer presence.

Why then, and with what implications, is Mayta, or one version of him, queer? In the critical literature about Vargas Llosa's fictionalization of a specific moment in Peruvian history, the novel's complex figuration of homosexuality has not attracted sustained attention.[2] My interest, aroused in part by that critical oversight, lies in plotting the gradual revelation of one historically situated body signed queer in relation to the novel's figurations of a Peru conceived of as an ailing body politic, within a third body, the text itself. For it is in the structure of a fictionalized history held together by the investigations and inventions of the elusive narrator that the other two bodies are displayed. Somewhere in the convergence of these three bodies lies the answer to the "real" Mayta's, and my own, question: why? In responding to those questions, my analysis regards *Historia* as a doubly important textual moment in Vargas Llosa's post-1984 liberal and writerly career. First, the novel begins to indicate the extent to which Vargas Llosa's political and philosophical embrace of liberalism is haunted by the figuration of queerness. Second, *Historia* confirms that the limits of Vargas Llosa's liberalism are reached in that figuration.

DIAGNOSING PERU

Historia de Mayta opens and closes with images of Lima, but the pleasant ambience through which the narrator runs in the first paragraph will not reappear in the novel "because everything man-made there is ugly" (3). If that brief sentence serves as an initial diagnosis, the following paragraph describes the city's symptoms. Beset by urban decay Lima is ugly, fearful and suffocating. Poverty and misery have spread and are all-encompassing, touching even wealthy and privileged districts. Lima is now a garbage dump, and dogs and people swarm across it like maggots on carrion. At the novel's end, the narrator again passes through the evocative wasteland, thinking of epidemics, wounds, and premature deaths. The narrative thus ends with a return to the diseased present, in which invading garbage, people and epidemics imply that there is no hope of recovery for the patient: "And I'll remember that a year ago I began to concoct this story the same way I'm ending it, by speaking about the garbage that's invading every neighbourhood in the capital of Peru" (310). The patient in this novel is Peru, as the Warden in the last chapter iterates: "The whole country's the problem" (283).

The Peru through which the narrator moves as he gathers testimonies belongs to a present that is also an unspecified, fictionalized future of a Peru outside the text. The present/future Peru contrasts with the reconstruction of events from Peru in 1958. Although the narrator's research is being written twenty-five years later, the futuristic aspect of the present is reinforced by the description of a country at war, invaded by Cuban and Bolivian troops and against which are arraigned the governing junta's armed forces and supporting U.S. troops. Temporally, the novel charts an inexorable decline in the health of Peru from the late 1950s to the moribundity of the narrator's present/future. In chapter three, for instance, the narrator describes his Dantean impression of crossing the circles of hell as he drives from Lima's centre to the outlying slums. The trip evokes the decline of the city from the unremarkable poverty of the past to a present dominated by overwhelming poverty *and* violence. The fearful psychic and physical effects of the environment are quite palpable as the narrator waves his arms at flies, as if the filth of the slums and the apparent lethargy and expressionless of their inhabitants were infectious.

Such images of a terminally ill Peru by no means represent a novel Vargas Llosian invention in *Historia*. They also figure in Vargas Llosa's other fictions, an infamous example being "'En qué momento se había jodido el Perú?" (I, 13) ("At what moment did Peru become fucked?") on the first page of *Conversación en La Catedral* (1969). Moreover, the trope has appeared with startling regularity in Peruvian letters since those of Manuel González Prada, whose writings, from the 1880s on, are rich in exemplary aphorisms: "Peru's is like those patients the doctors claim are beyond recovery" (qtd. in Mariátegui 196); "In the political organism, no disease produces more degeneration than progressive opportunism" (210); and "Peru is a sick organism: when one applies a finger out oozes pus" (204). If these aphorisms foretell Vargas Llosa's diagnoses of the Peruvian malaise, González Prada's aims and the context in which he wrote were very different. According to Higgins, González Prada's targets were specific Spanish colonial and neocolonial state apparatuses: "Spain had bequeathed a sorry legacy of venality, corruption and intellectual obscurantism which had turned Peru into a sick organism, he argued, and the nation would never be made healthy till the oligarchy, the Church, the military and all the other institutions of the past were destroyed, till Lima's stranglehold on the country was broken, and till the mestizo proletariat and the Indian peasantry were freed from their servitude and their servility" (72–73).

Higgins also notes how images of the sick Peruvian body were common in writings from the 1950s and 1960s, including Eduardo Congrains Martín's deromanticizing novel, *No una, sino muchas muertes* (1957), and Sebastián Salazar Bondy's *Lima la horrible* (1964) (192–93). Moreover, the idea of the ailing nation, indeed, of the infirm continent, has a long provenance among Latin American intellectuals, from the Argentinian Sarmiento and the Bolivian Alcides Arguedas to the Puerto Rican Pedreira, all of whom linked national pathologies to racial ones (Franco 55–61; Flores 19, 33). *Historia* thus has a discursive relation to long-standing yet unresolved Peruvian, regional and continental debates concerning what José Carlos Mariátegui called the "Indian problem," although writers such as Mariátegui and José María Arguedas sought to disprove the equation that indigenous Peru equaled diseased Peru.[3]

In *Historia* that equation persists, nonetheless, to underwrite the depictions of Lima and, by extension, of the country. Visiting Vallejos's sister Juanita, a nun working in the Liman slums, the narrator reports Juanita's views on her order's early attempts at combating poverty, by tending to the education of the rich (the head) who, in turn, will care for and improve the status of the poor (the body). Such attempts failed to change the world, as Juanita admits. The implication is that the nation is subject to an entrenched disease, hence the vast array of opportunistic infections from which it is suffering.[4] Lima is host to numerous physiological ills. In its leprous street corners, sordid convents and squalid cantinas swarm the human parallels to the city's inanimate pollution, Indian migrants from the Andean provinces comprising the greatest number. These are, as the narrator puts it, the "cancerous growth" on Lima's buses (119, 105); the beggars who "constitute a sort of grotesque royal court of tatters, grime, and scabs" (109); and the slum-dwellers living in fetid garbage dumps. The narrator's impression of not being in Lima, but rather in an Andean village, makes synonyms of Indians and *basuras* (garbage). These connections support Guzmán's view that "poverty . . . is important in this book mainly by its incidence in the condition of bodies" (138). But while the Peru in *Historia de Mayta* is figured as diseased corporeality, it is also pointedly a racialized, indigenous corporeality.[5]

In *Historia*'s descriptions of Lima, then, two temporal Perus (past and present) and two class-defined Perus (rich and poor) are explicitly related to two disparate Spanish and Quechua Perus. The divide between Spanish and Indian Perus, moreover, is linked to yet more Perus, the capital and the Andean provinces.[6] In this respect, it is significant that the narrator's investigations enable him to extend his national diagnosis by tracing the moribund effects of the capital on all of Peru's parts, including the Andean terrains of Indian Peru. This diagnosis is exemplified by the narrator's responses to Jauja, the former capital and site of Mayta's planned revolution, described in terms of past greatness and a decline attributed to the energy-sapping power of Lima. Jauja was also once the destination for people with tuberculosis, its reputation as a sanatorium, according to the narrator, mythologized in literary texts and by romantic sadomasochists. But now it only signifies "perforated lungs, fits of coughing, bloody sputum, hemorrhage, death from consumption" (117). The city's past reputation, then, is as prone to new pathologized significations as Lima.

And lest this example fail to remind the reader that the provinces have not been immune to the contagions afflicting Lima, the narrator later reinforces his impressions of "dirt as disorder" (Douglas 2) with the following imagined conversation: "Yes, Mayta, millions of Peruvians lived in this same grime, in this same abandonment, amid their own grime and excrement, without light or water, living the same vegetable life, the same animal routine [as . . .] this woman . . . with whom . . . he hadn't been able to exchange more than a few words, because she barely knew any Spanish" (254). Peru has been subject to an inexorable contamination of which there are few differences, except in degree, between the conditions that Mayta is reported to be witnessing and those the narrator encounters twenty-five years later.

The incipient nature of this national indisposition, directly linked here to the racial, linguistic and economic gulf between "civilized," non-Indian Spanish speaker and "primitive," non-Spanish-speaking Indian, suggests that the national syndrome not only targets high-risk and marginalized groups but also originates with and is spread by them. In the novel, then, the viral metaphor used to apportion blame reveals a peculiarly Peruvian crisis in signification of epidemic proportions, to rework Treichler's description of AIDS discourses (32) in an era defined by an illness, coincidentally enough, whose spread into bodies and international consciousness is coterminous with both the present/future in the novel and Vargas Llosa's writing of it.

In keeping with the pathogenic tropes deployed to describe the infirm national body and its inhabitants, the narrator utilizes similar metaphors in his investigation into the ideological sources of infection, which have long historical roots in Peru: "Violence of all kinds: moral, physical, fanatical, intransigent, ideological, corrupt, stupid—all of which have gone hand in hand with power here. And that other violence—dirty, low, vengeful, vested and selfish—which lives off the other kinds" (109). With such pronouncements, the narrator insinuates himself into the novel as somehow beyond, and therefore uninfected by, his pathologized surroundings. Yet the specific political targets of his investigations suggest an undeclared ideological position on his part. In fact, the narrator's ideological interestedness is implied in his claims that a leftist parasite, genetically programmed for self-interest, feeds on the nation for its own ends. This diagnostics is reinforced by the play of a host of conflict-ridden binaries that are embedded in the many Perus displayed in the novel: first/third world, capital/provinces, rich/poor, bourgeois/peasant, European/Indian, Spanish/Quechua, civilized/primitive, Right/Left, internal/external, normal/abnormal, fact/fiction, private/public, clean/contaminated and, of course, health/sickness. One effect of such ordering principles is that leftist ideologies in the novel are defined as at once impotent cures and powerful contaminants.

For the narrator and the Vargas Llosian author-function alike, the moribundity of Peru, its figuration as an epidemical disaster zone with no immune system, has an identifiable and blameworthy source of dystopian contamination. Speaking of *Historia*, Vargas Llosa is explicit about Peru's particular pathogenesis: "These sometimes elaborate and complex ideological constructions in which one society was described and then another ideal society was also described as a goal to be reached through revolution, as well as a methodology of the way this revolution could be achieved, were, in fact, a mechanism that was destroying our societies and creating major obstacles to real progress and the battle against the things the revolution opposes—social injustice, economic inequalities, lack of integration of the different cultures" (*A Writer's Reality* 150). Indeed, because transmission of the viral ideology afflicting Peru is traced in the novel to a faction-ridden, insurgent Left, the link between violence and infection has serious implications. As Sontag argues, the war metaphor often used to describe disease "implements the way particularly dreaded diseases are envisaged as an alien 'other,' as enemies are in modern war; and the move from the demonization of the illness to the attribution of fault to the patient is an inevitable one, no matter if patients are thought of as victims" (97).

THE PATHOLOGIZING OF MAYTA'S BODY

The pathologized metaphors used to describe Peru provide the discursive territories in which Mayta's body and the conflicting *historias* concerning what he does with his body are revealed. Those territories and *historias* confirm a particularly Peruvian version of a phenomenon that Sander Gilman has described with regard to western cultures: "[There is a] relationship between ideas of national space and ideas of race, between representations of the body and concepts of difference. These concepts are, of course, 'Western' and make use of the basic paradigms of 'race,' of 'difference,' of the 'normal' and the 'pathological' which are to be found in other 'Western' (read: Christian and/or scientific) cultures (not all of them in Europe and North America)" (176). However, Peruvian manifestations of this relationship between, on the one hand, national and racial ideals and, on the other, bodily representations, have been downplayed in the critical responses to the novel that concentrate on the depiction of Mayta as a revolutionary Trotskyite within Peruvian national space.

Dunkerley, for example, has astutely observed that Mayta's "essential character is established by the only constant feature of the text: the understanding that the being of the Left is singularly self-determined and, even more importantly, that the catastrophe that is contemporary Peru is centrally attributable to the agency of this left" (140). Yet Dunkerley's allusion to Mayta's "sympathetically" rendered private life glosses over the intimate convergence in the novel between the diseased national body and the body of Mayta, failed revolutionary and queer subject. For Souza, Mayta's homosexuality can be read as a parody of the concept that socialism represents the feminization of society, a claim that accepts as synonymous homosexuality and (ef)femenization.

Neither Souza nor Dunkerley interrogates the extensive deployment in *Historia* of discourses that simultaneously target the homosexual and the political Left, not to mention the Indian. Mayta can only satisfy the synecdochic tag if his sexuality is regarded as abject and pathological by the narrator and by the novel's readers. He must be seen to bear an identifiable and ultimately incurable, internal sickness that, in turn, parallels and further discredits the leftist and indigenous ills besetting Peru. That link has been made, albeit in passing, by Zapata, for whom, from the novel's opening, Mayta's inevitable failure is indicated by descriptions of Mayta's ugliness, grotesqueness, incapacity for self-reflection and homosexuality (193–94). Clearly, considering the novel's tropology of Peru's ill health and its overt identification of the ideological source of transmission, the convergence of Mayta's political and sexual lives suggests that his symbolic role cannot be explained simply as either an ideological or a national synecdoche. Mayta's textual function will be understood only partially if his negativized sexualization is not acknowledged and confronted.[7]

From his first appearance, everything about Mayta points to the truth of the later description of him as a complete orphan. At the beginning of *Historia* Mayta is an empty signifier, a nonbeing, a corporeal space that requires fleshing out and a history. The narrator is determined to fulfill that requirement, however contradictory the results of his investigation-cum-reconstruction. He thus poses a series of unanswerable but rhetorically telling questions about his subject: "Because his case was the first in a series that would typify the period? Because he was the most absurd? Because he was the most tragic? Because his person and his story hold something ineffably moving, something that, over and beyond its political and moral implications, is like an X-ray of Peruvian misfortune?" (15).

As the last question intimates, the political and moral essences of Mayta's persona signify a two-sided identity requiring both exposure and diagnosis. To this split identity adhere descriptions of a sorry physical appearance and other indicators of his marginality. The first description of Mayta—a fat child with flat feet, gaps between his teeth, and an ungainly manner of walking—reveals his physical ludicrousness. Further-more, Mayta is the only school child with an Indian name, a Quechua word that signifies to roam aimlessly or without knowing one's direction (Souza 173). Most significantly, the name indicates a cultural and racial positioning that unambiguously links Mayta, despite his ignorance of Indian cultures, to the novel's traffic in images of Indian squalor.

Up to the fourth chapter, the gathering of information about Mayta is framed by juxtapositions between sensualization and political rigor, by pointed questions, and by words and phrases (rumors, insinuations, gos-sip, secrets) chosen for their undermining suggestiveness and capacities to indicate Mayta's repressed ontological condition. The narrator's inves-tigation thus focuses on the oppositions between public and private and between secrecy and disclosure that hover around the emerging Mayta. While it is clear that much of Mayta's secrecy can be attributed to an underground Trotskyite party that demands discretion of its members, the continual contrasts between political and moral secrecy also prepare the narratorial ground for the revelation of Mayta's homosexuality in the fourth chapter. The signs of Mayta's particular sexual interests, however, have always been present. They are hinted at in the first chapter with the narrator's questions about whether the friendship between Vallejos and Mayta was based on a political alliance, or, like love, signaled a deeper affinity formed at first sight. The insinuations continue with Vallejos's confession that he has been teaching Marxism to a group of boys in the mountains and Mayta's response that such "bad" matters should not be spoken about. Most suggestive of all, Mayta's "trembling" desires, kindled by his excitement at impending revolutionary action, begin to exceed the boundaries of political fraternity when he imagines the women who must have tasted the *alférez's* (second lieutenant's) well-defined lips and enjoyed his hard body.

Mayta is closeted, present but hidden, an open secret. The use of clos-etedness here is not intended as an anachronistic imposition of a post-1960s liberal concept of gay identity onto the novel's late-1950s frame. Rather it is to suggest that the western closet trope, by which homosexu-als are conventionally revealed, concealed, and potentially "liberated" as sexual identities is at work in the narrative and in the narrator's investiga-tion of his subject. As Miller argues, the logic of the discourse of sexual-ity signposted by the closet and its correlate coming out highlights the policed production of identities in "the private and domestic sphere on which the very identity of the liberal subject depends" (ix). The open secret of Mayta requires reader familiarity with the closet trope in *Historia* as Mayta's sexual essence is at once concealed and exposed to diagnostic scrutiny. Mayta, then, is doubly closeted: anxiety-laden secrecy applies to his political allegiances and his homoerotic desires alike. Both can be interpreted in terms of a stigmatizing behavioral passivity unfitting for a *machista*—or better yet, a *machista* leftist—and of a concealed but essential sexual identity core as understood in post-1960s gay liberation terms. Mayta's open secret thus impels "journalistic scrutiny and exposure" and makes him into a doubly troubling sign "of inauthenticity and of a difference all the more subversive because [it is] simultaneously threatening . . . and potentially unidentifiable" (Edelman 152).[8]

The fourth chapter confirms the implied links between Mayta's political and sexual inclinations made up to that point. As the narrator records the testimony of Senator Anatolio Campos, he also constructs a revolutionary and sexual relationship between Mayta and the youthful Anatolio. These personal revelations occur in a chapter in which the futuristic parameters of the narrator's fictionalized present are also detailed. Apocalyptic war and the invasion of foreign troops meet political treachery, duplicity, factional conflicts and guilt among the Left of an earlier era, these narrative threads intertwining with the first description of a sexual act between Mayta and Anatolio. The threads infect each other in a dense play of contrasting significations. For example, a description of a smiling Mayta, his body tense with anticipation, is followed by the narrator's loaded commentary: "The self-sacrificing Mayta transformed into a two-faced monster, weaving a really risky plot just to trap his comrades?" (89). Introduced in the same insinuating language used to describe his political activities, Mayta's subsequent request to Anatolio—"'Let me jerk you off,' he whispered in an agonizing voice, feeling that his whole body was burning" (95)—adds weight to the implied link between political and homosexual recruitment.

In this respect, the ensuing conversation between the senator and the narrator about the deceptions practiced by so-called inverts is particularly telling. In that conversation, the senator defines the typical homosexual, and hence Mayta, as an incomplete feminized being prone to treachery and a discredit to the fixed and true sex allocated at birth. The definition reflects the conflation of a leftist dismissal of homosexuality as bourgeois decadence with the conventional *machista* view of sexuality as conforming to an active/passive matrix, one in which the full weight of hypermale opprobrium is directed at the passive and hence inferior partner in sexual acts.[9] For the narrator, Anatolio has reasons of his own to emphasize the distinction between sexual passivity and activity. Mayta belongs to the former category. The demonization of a passive, feminized Mayta signifies the senator's desire to preserve untarnished his own macho reputation:

he has always been on top, his masculinity unquestionable. At the same time, the narrator wants to discredit the senator's testimony by interlacing it with his own reconstructions of a presenatorial dalliance with Mayta, thereby indicating the senator's hypocrisy.

Neither the senator's demonization nor the narrator's construction of Mayta as queer, however, can be isolated from the narrative strands in which Mayta is accused of being a political traitor. Furthermore, sexual and political accusations are connected, because of proximity on the page, to the powerfully rendered descriptions of a national apocalypse. It thus becomes impossible to extract a nonabject Mayta from the narrative. In the narrator's account, Mayta emerges from his encounter with an accusatory Anatolio as a sad picture of internalized self-hatred, admitting to shame and imagining himself purged of his contaminating desires. Mayta's supposed self image and the senator's self-preserving image of him is, as would perhaps be expected of the 1950s, cast as a pathological condition, one reinforced by the narrator's third person description of Mayta's weakened physical state, just before Anatolio permits Mayta to give him a handjob. The incident, followed by the fusing of the narrator's and the imagined Mayta's reactions to a posited national preoccupation with violence in the Museum of the Inquisition, confirm Mayta as a paranoic space in and on which are conjoined "the form of knowledge that represents at the same time 'knowledge itself' and a diagnostic pathology of cognition, or the cognition of a diagnosable pathology" (Sedgwick 97). Secrecy, disguise, dissembling, intrigue, treachery, invasion, entrapment, seduction, confession, shame, filth, anxiety, alienation, infection, and disease all converge in this chapter to characterize the entrance of Mayta's homosexualized body in the text.

THE MARICÓN IN GOTHIC PERU

After the fourth and pivotal chapter, the interplay between Mayta's erotic life and his revolutionary ambitions continues to overdetermine his novelistic existence as a pathologized being in a pathologized environment. In this respect, it is significant that in chapter five, Jauja is the setting for Mayta to be immobilized by altitude sickness that makes him resemble one of the city's former tubercular patients. Under the influence of that sickness, Mayta is reported as wondering what sort of country Peru is, given that the mere movement from one region to another changes him into "a gringo, a Martian" (126). Already othered as a *maricón*(fag), the *marciano* Mayta becomes a native-born alien within, the alarming patient zero who presages the foreign soldiers and other woes that later overrun the body politic.

Chapter five also details the expulsion of Mayta from his party for treachery, an accusation that encompasses both sexual and political perversion. The link is emphasized by the reported thoughts of Mayta himself at the imminent prospects of revolution as he recalls his night with Anatolio: "He had had in his arms the boy he had desired for so many years. He had made him experience pleasure and he had experienced pleasure himself. He had heard him whimper under his caresses" (142). For Comrade Joaquín in chapter six, however, the problem presented by Mayta is clear: how can an invert be a revolutionary? The narrator's commentary, interlaced with Mayta's purported thoughts, supposedly emphasizes the petty and confused prejudices that motivate the expulsion of Mayta from the party, not for lack of discipline, error, or treachery but "for having slid his tongue, like a stiletto, between Anatolio's teeth" (177).

Yet in a chapter also concerned with the unforseen consequences of accidents, rumors, and new knowledge, the narrator's asides betray a more insidious ulteriority behind the chapter's homosexual characterization. At one point during his conversation with Blacquer, the narrator isolates what he finds likeable about one Mayta—the older revolutionary who rediscovers his youthful vigor and throws himself into the cause—who has emerged in his research. He then follows this with an analysis of what was wrong with his subject: "If he had been able to control his sentiments and instincts, he wouldn't have led the double life he led, he wouldn't have had to deal with the intrinsic split between being, by day, a clandestine militant totally given over to the task of changing the world, and, by night, a pervert on the prowl for faggots" (166).

In the Spanish original, pervert is *apestado*, a word here highly charged (212). Mayta's pestilential, twilight sexuality is causally linked to both his revolutionary failure and the epidemics of violence, terror, poverty and indigenous backwardness that the narrator blames for the destruction of Peru. In short, Mayta's homosexuality becomes a pathogenic signifier. Mayta's shadowy and health-threatening activities situate him in and as—to use Williamson's formulation—a "morass of unthinkability" in "a Gothic territory where fears are flung out into a sort of mental wasteland beyond the castle walls of the [narrator's/author's?] ego" (70). An indisputably Gothic territory, in the form of a narrative strand detailing the massacres perpetuated by the invading Chilean army in 1881, shadows the descriptions of the narrator's meeting with Mayta's former wife in the seventh chapter. Adelaida is perhaps the novel's only true synecdoche of a Peru conceived as victim. She could also be read as a synecdoche of the novel itself, the literal screen—"*pantalla*," in the original Spanish (241)—on which Mayta dissimulated his political and sexual li(v)es.

Adelaida's account of her discovery of Mayta's homosexuality, one that made her retch, is caught in the narrative between images of contemporary apocalyptic progress and the epidemiological consequences of the Chilean invasion, as infections spread from the many unburied dead. Yet Mayta's revolutionary aim to cure the diseased body politic is deflated by his wife's suggestion that he, not Peru, requires medical treatment. At the same time, descriptions of violent social change, of smoking ruins and pestilence, undercut Mayta's utopian dreams for a revolution so that Peru will no longer be a rotten society, a revolution that will also be for the country's queers.

Mayta's self definition in this chapter as a *maricón*, his avowals that he does not want to stop being one, and his utopian dream of a revolution for homosexuals suggest an epistemological understanding of sexual identity unlike the passive betrayer of masculine behavioral conventions already noted. Mayta's dream suggests, again, an internationalist concept of gay identity and liberation, an unlikely intrusion of a post-1960s liberal sexual utopia into the novel's late 1950s frame that serves to fix Mayta within a "morass of unthinkability" (Williamson 70). The conflicting models beg the following question: how many homosexuals can Mayta signify? The answer is legion, for in chapter eight, Mayta the revolutionary is also insinuated into a deviant position as corruptor of minors. The at-risk group represented by the Josefinos is taken in by the erotic charge emanating from Mayta's game of revolution. As one school boy describes it, the experience was like losing his virginity. Mayta in this chapter is also impugned as the sensualist who lacks control and discretion and as the aging revolutionary who regresses to a teenage realm when he rubs his gun against his fly. The image of Mayta as a homo-sensualized revolutionary thus undermines his pretensions to collective selflessness and self-discipline. The following chapter, which details the failure of the revolution continues to link Mayta's lack of control or vigor, both leftist and sexual, with images of expelled body waste, Indian squalor, and disabling altitude sickness. Mayta's body now metaphorizes the narrator's insinuations of the Left's inability to comprehend Andean conditions. Physical weakness, political ineptness, sexual inaptness, disease, filth, poverty, Indian abjectness, the sinister landscape, and more apocalyptic rumors frame the penultimate chapter's characterization of Mayta: sad, defeated, and imagining Anatolio's head on his chest. Then, the chapter ends with the narrator's sudden, destabilizing aside that the story told so far has been a lie, akin to fiction.

EXCISING THE *MARICÓN*

Lies and fiction, truth and reality, past and present, history and invention: as these binaries play through the text, producing competing knowledges about Mayta, the reader turns to the final chapter nonetheless assuming that this participant in a failed, if not farcical, revolution is also queer. His politicized and sexualized identities alike have been implicated in the processes that have destroyed the health of the nation. Mayta enters the novel's final pages as the symbolic and literal agent responsible for Peru's decline. But the narrator's encounter with the real Mayta enacts a breach in the knowledge of Mayta accrued by the reader up to this point in the novel. The queer Mayta is a narratorial invention. As it turns out, the only signifi-cant revolutionary achievements of the real Mayta—the one speaking to the narrator in the final chapter—have been to establish a coupon system and to lobby for better standards of hygiene in prison. As for being queer, the idea is rejected by this Mayta, now figured as a homophobic paradigm of Latin American leftism: "I was never prejudiced about anything . . . But, about fags, I think I am prejudiced. After seeing them. . . . Tweez-ing their eyebrows, curling their eyelashes with burned matches, using lipstick, wearing skirts, creating hairdos, letting themselves be exploited the same way prostitutes are exploited by pimps. How can you not be sick to your stomach?" (301)

The real Mayta is a good family man, *machista*, and leftist. This Mayta has the final word, uttered between gritted teeth, on the homosexual pres-ence in the novel: "They say Mao shot all the queers in China" (301).

According to Huston, in the interplay between truth and lies, Mayta becomes the text's only "autonomous and compelling lie," an achieve-ment that "creates the book, and which brings the real Mayta to judge-ment, convicts him of the sin of resignation" (116). The success of the novel for Huston, then, lies in its "revolutionary storytelling," by which "Vargas Llosa discovers not the real life of Alejandro Mayta, but his truer and more necessary fictional life" (117). Yet whether or not the final chapter's Mayta can be read as the real one, in his final appearance this Mayta has been given an unambiguous role: he becomes the mouthpiece by which the queer subject is excised from the narrative. That excision is not simply explicable as a laying bare of the lie of either leftist ideology, or the deceptive devices employed in historical or fictional narration alike. In the novel, such devices and lies have made great use of the homosexual as an abject device. Indeed, that abjection is reiterated in the novel's final chapter in a brief passage before the moment of fabulous surgery. Here, the narrator details the layout and appearance of Lurigancho prison.[10] The prison, like the national body politic, is a congested, garbage-swamped, chaotic space populated by the mad and the violent, with a special section reserved for *los maricas* (fags) to prevent fights and rapes. Moving in that space, the narrator recalls asking a prison doctor about the effects of rape among the inmates. He receives this response: "'The most common problem is infections of the rectum, complicated by gangrene or cancer.' I ask Carrillo if there are still as many rapes. He laughs: 'It's inevitable, with people who have nothing else, don't you think? They have to let go somehow'" (285).

In a text congested with pathologized bodies, but only one queer body, that body cannot dodge the taint of, to cite the original Spanish, "*el recto supurando, gangrenado, cancerizado*" (355) ["the rectum, complicated by gangrene or cancer" (285)][11]. This sodomitically charged image, casually placed in the novel's end pages, evokes what Edelman has called "the scene of the voiding of waste" as it "gets entangled in the national imaginary with a fantasy of cultural and historical vastation" (168). For Edelman, that fantasy "bespeaks a narcissistic anxiety about the definition of (sexual) identity that can only be stabilized and protected by a process of elimination or casting out" (169). Extrapolating that insight to *Historia*, and therefore to a Peruvian national imaginary, the final chapter confirms what the entire novel has insinuated: the novel's most vital excrescence is the queer, signified throughout the text as a pathogen responsible for transmitting a deadly ideological epidemic. The only hope for the health of the body politic and for the health of Peru's contaminated history is a swift excision to remove the offending Mayta, site of Bersani's provocatively defined rectal grave. Mayta and the abject sexuality he signposts represents "a disposable constituency" (Bersani 204).

THE QUEER LIMITS OF VARGAS LLOSIAN LIBERALISM

Speaking of Vargas Llosa's 1993 autobiography, *A Fish in the Water*, Ellis notes that a key to understanding the literary evolution of Vargas Llosa lies in his comparison between the (implicitly male) writer of fiction and the (assumed female) stripper. That is, "whereas the stripper . . . exposes herself to an objectifying gaze, the male writer shields himself from scrutiny in order to avoid objectification altogether" (*They Dream not of Angels* 79). Vargas Llosa plays this shielding game by "cloak[ing] the autobiographical persona in what might be called the gender and racial drag of masculinity and whiteness," that in *A Fish in the Water*, at least, means that the author's identity core of white hetero-masculinity is counterpointed by and made meaningful in opposition to "homosexual femininity" (80).

A similar process is at work in *Historia de Mayta*. By making the real Mayta responsible for disposing of the queer Mayta, the shadowy narrator appears to survive the novel untainted. Indeed, he alone of all the novel's characters is implied to be the only uncontaminated body in Peru. This construction is achieved because in his fictionalizing the narrator so insistently casts everything—nation, populace, history—beyond himself into an abject zone. Yet as Kristeva has argued, such relations to the abject are fraught, tenuous, and always self-defeating. Thus, while it might seem that the narrator is "opposed" to the abject, "the jettisoned [abject] object" nonetheless "draws" the narratorial I "toward the place where meaning collapses" (1–2). In that place, rendered in *Historia* as moribund Peru, "the abject does not cease challenging its master" (2). In Vargas Llosa's novel, various indigenous, leftist, and sexual abjections fill the spaces created by the narrator's silences regarding his own ideological interests and identifications against multiple Others. However, in the end the clamoring of these "jettisoned objects" demands critical attention. The abundant representations of the abject ensure that neither the narrator, nor the Vargas Llosa author-function, nor the author can guarantee that their fictional immunity from ideological self-interest will be recognized, endorsed, or applauded by the novel's readers.

Indeed, by allowing what was once an empty signifier to signify so much and to characterize the queer Mayta as the pathogenic source and symptom of Peru's moribundity and by removing that offending signifier at the tail end of the novel, Vargas Llosa resorts to an unambiguous rearguard action in his fictive game of truth, lies, and lives. He posits a quick cure for infection and degeneracy. Despite the novel's identification of multiple abjections, Vargas Llosa's cure nonetheless overtly targets the queer. Thus, as with the discourses of AIDS that began to circulate in the world outside Vargas Llosa's novel during its writing, *Historia de Mayta* demands to be read, as I do here, as a fictional attempt to represent "male homosexuality as a stage doomed to extinction . . . on the enormous scale of whole populations" (Sedgwick 128–29). Yet while the queer Mayta may be cleansed from the narrative, the consequences of his narratorial presence are not so easily discounted. As a trope of subjective negativity, impossibility, and disposability, the queer Mayta in *Historia* is not alone in Vargas Llosa's novels. Many other characters have served the same function in works such as *Conversation in the Cathedral*, *The Time of the Hero*, *The War of the End of the World*, *In Praise of the Stepmother*, and *The Notebooks of Don Rigoberto*. However, as a template of Vargas Llosa's author-function since the early 1980s, *Historia de Mayta* stands out from this competition. The novel does not merely grate against a liberal celebration of "tolerance and respect for others." By making the "*recto supurando, gangrenado, cancerizado*" of all who may share in Mayta's desires its central target, *Historia de Mayta* also lays bare the Vargas Llosa author-function's broader operations as a fabulist of queer cleansing.

NOTES

1. Page references in this chapter come from *The Real Life of Alejandro Mayta*.
2. Most attention has been paid to two areas: Vargas Llosa's problematizing of history, his contamination of notions of truth, objectivity and fact by constructing history with the same inescapable lies as are employed in fiction; and his (mis) treatment of the Peruvian Left. See, for example, Newman, Reisz de Rivarola, Chrzanowski, de Grandis, and Muñoz.
3. Latin America's post-1945 right-wing dictatorships also conceived the ideological enemy-within as a cancer to be excised if national health was to be saved. My thanks to Diana Palaversich for reminding me of this connection.
4. The passage also allows the narrator to allude to and dismiss liberation theology as a potential force of change in the Perus constructed in the novel.
5. It is worth noting that Vargas Llosa's pitting of Spanish/European against Indian does not provide space for mestizo Peru to emerge in the Peruvian realities dealt with in the novel. This suggests a view of the "Indian problem" that is conceptually and ethically antithetical to the work of Arguedas, for example in his *Formación de una cultura nacional indoamericana*. See Spitta for a nuanced discussion of Arguedas's ideas, and Rowe for an astute argument that Vargas Llosa has consistently misread Arguedas's intellectual position.
6. Vargas Llosa also elaborated on this host of antagonistic Perus in "Discovering a Method for Writing" (*A Writer's Reality* 41–42).
7. Caro and Booker are among the few critics to note the negative treatment of homosexuality in *Historia*. This critical neglect is surprising, given that what Ellis calls "talk of homosexuals" forms a narrative thread throughout Vargas Llosa's writing. Ellis regards such talk as "a concerted effort to publicly affirm a heterosexual identity" (*They Dream not of Angels* 78) on the part of the author. Browitt notes that Vargas Llosa's "portrayal of homosexuality and the working out of Oedipal complexes . . . are worthy of a book-length study in themselves," for they imply "a deeper attachment to heterosexual male machismo on the writer's part than perhaps Vargas Llosa realises or would care to admit" (132).
8. A key depiction of another closeted homosexual occurs in Vargas Llosa's *Conversación en La Catedral*; the revelation of Don Fermín's hidden homosexual condition (II, 245-53) functions as a destabilizing literary device that, like Mayta, reveals and confirms the unhealthy truth of the ailing nation. Don Fermín's homosexuality is inextricably linked to the notion of a fucked Peru cited on the novel's first page (Pope 215–16).

9. For elaborations of this bodily economy, see Allatson.
10. Vargas Llosa's own 1981 account of this prison is contained in "Una visita a Lurigancho."
11. A literal translation of the Spanish original of this phrase is "the rectum, festering, gangrened, with cancer."

CHAPTER 6

GOING NATIVE

ANTI-INDIGENISM IN VARGAS LLOSA'S *THE STORYTELLER* AND *DEATH IN THE ANDES*

IGNACIO LÓPEZ-CALVO

IN 2005, PERUVIAN WRITER MARIO VARGAS LLOSA RECEIVED FROM the American Enterprise Institute, one of the premier right-wing think tanks, the Irving Kristol Award. He opened his reception speech by thanking his hosts for seeing him as a "unified being," in contrast with many of his Hispanic critics who tend to separate his literary work from his political views. In light of the author's statement, in this essay I shall contextualize the representation of indigeneity and indigenism in his fiction with the evolution of his political thought. As Efraín Kristal reminds us, according to Vargas Llosa's "doctrine of the demons of artistic creation, a writer is not responsible for his literary themes, and his personal convictions may contradict the contents and messages of his literary works" (*Temptation of the Word* 197). Nevertheless, as we shall see, there is an ideological common ground between the novels considered in this essay and the author's political thought at the time he published them even if, as can be expected of the novelistic genre, in the fictional discourse we can often find polyphonic contradictions and ethical ambivalence.

The Chinese-Peruvian author Siu Kam Wen, in his autobiographical novel *Viaje a Ítaca* (Voyage to Ithaca, 2004), comments on how Vargas Llosa's political image during his 1989 campaign for the following year's presidential elections was widely seen as white-oriented and elitist. Among other political mistakes, he argues, the famed author and inexperienced politician "formed alliances with worn-out parties and discredited politicians when it would have been more sensible to run by himself; he recruited his running mates and technical advisers from among the white elite, thus alienating the indigenous and mestizo majority of the population" (19). This last sentence brings us back to Vargas Llosa's request that critics see him as "a unified being." How do his perceived political stance and his statements as an intellectual translate into the novelistic representation of indigeneity and indigenism? In a recent article, Vargas Llosa expresses his concern for the oppression of indigenous people and shows, as he has always done, his compassion for their plight. Concomitantly, in direct contrast with the tenets of various versions of Peruvian indigenist discourse, he endorses *mestizaje* (mixing of races) as the solution to Latin America's social ills, regardless of the danger it poses to their cultural specificity: "Fortunately, the mixing of races (*el mestizaje*) is very extensive. It builds bridges between these two worlds, drawing them closer and slowly merging them . . . In the long run it will win out, giving Latin America a distinctive profile as a mestizo continent. Let's hope it doesn't homogenize it completely and deprive it of its nuances, though this seems neither possible nor desirable in the century of globalization and interdependence among nations" ("Latin America" 34).

In this same article, he goes on to explain that whereas, for indigenists, the genuine reality of Latin America resides in pre-Hispanic civilizations and indigenous people, he believes that, culturally, Latin America is an intrinsic part of the Western world and that, after five centuries of inhabitation, nonindigenous Latin Americans are as native to the continent as indigenous people: "The fact is that Latin America is Spanish, Portuguese, Indian, African all at once, and a few other things as well . . . Five centuries after the Europeans set foot on the continent's beaches, mountain chains and jungles, Latin Americans of Spanish, Portuguese, Italian, German, Chinese, and Japanese origin are as native to the continent as those whose ancestors were the ancient Aztecs, Toltecs, Mayas, Quechuas, Aymaras and Caribs" ("Latin America" 35–36).

From this perspective, how is Vargas Llosa's political opposition to indigenism reflected in his fiction? As we shall see, some of his novels offer a rather ambiguous and ambivalent rendering of indigeneity. Paradoxically, in his book of essays *A Writer's Reality* (1991) he criticizes the writings of Jorge Luis Borges (an author who, incidentally, he admires deeply) for their cultural ethnocentricity: "The black, the Indian, the primitive often appear in his stories as inferiors, wallowing in a state of barbarism apparently unconnected either to the accidents of history or to society, but inherent in the race or status. They represent a lower humanity, shut off from what Borges considers the greatest of all human qualities, intellect and literary refinement" (18). Vargas Llosa believes that the Argentine writer's discrimination toward so-called third world cultures was uncon-scious: "Those other cultures that form part of Latin America," he insists, "the native Indian and the African, feature in Borges's world more as a contrast than as different varieties of mankind" (18). After reading these statements, one cannot help but wonder: does not Vargas Llosa's fiction suffer from a similar ethnocentric tendency to associate Andean and Ama-zonian indigenous beliefs with barbarism? To answer this question, I shall concentrate on two novels published after he had rejected socialism and turned his political convictions toward neoliberal free-market economics: *The Storyteller* (1987), and *Death in the Andes* (1993).

In *La utopía arcaica* (The Archaic Utopia, 1996), a study of the birth of the indigenist movement through the life and works of José María Arguedas, Vargas Llosa expresses his admiration for this Peruvian writer who, as a professional anthropologist and a person who grew up sur-rounded by indigenous culture, enjoyed the benefits of being an expert in the two main realities of Peru, the Indian and the white-mestizo: "Privi-leged because in a country split in two worlds, two languages, two cul-tures, two historical traditions, he knew both realities intimately, in their misery and greatness, and, therefore, had a much wider perspective of our country than mine and most Peruvian writers" (9). In spite of this modest acknowledgment of his own limitations (which he also confesses in the first chapter of *A Writer's Reality*), Vargas Llosa, in the two nov-els mentioned previously, faces the challenge of following in Arguedas's footsteps and exploring Peru's violent race relations in this clash between "modern" Western on one hand and "traditional," indigenous cultures on the other. Before he published *The Storyteller*, however, there were occa-sional glimpses of this interest (which would eventually become one of his literary "demons") in two previous novels: *Aunt Julia and the Scriptwriter* (1977) and *The Real Life of Alejandro Mayta* (1984). Referring to *Aunt Julia*, Peruvian critic Antonio Cornejo Polar notices how the autobio-graphical narrator is so surprised by the changes brought about by rural migration to Lima in the ten years he has been absent that he feels like a tourist in his own city:

> On leaving the Biblioteca Nacional around noon I would walk down the Avenida Abancay, which was beginning to turn into an enormous market of itinerant peddlers. On the sidewalks a dense crowd of men and women, many of them dressed in ponchos and peasant skirts, sold the most heterogeneous collection of wares imaginable . . . This Avenida Abancay was one of the thoroughfares in Lima that had changed the most. Jam-packed now and possessed and possessed of a distinct Andean

flavor, a street on which it was not rare to hear Quechua spoken amid the strong odor of fried food and pungent seasonings. (361)

Cornejo Polar underscores the contrast evident in this passage between the quiet library where written Spanish language predominates, a symbol of the lettered city (Angel Rama's *ciudad letrada*), and the noisy indigenous market that surrounds it, where written Spanish has been replaced by oral Quechua. At the same time, there is another implicit opposition: order versus the "indomitable plebeian disorder of the streets, which is seen explicitly and repeatedly as Andean" (837). In more simple terms, the protagonist finds himself surrounded by the ethnic Other in his own city.

A similar passage will surface seven years later in *The Real Life of Alejandro Mayta*, in which the unnamed and semiautobiographical first-person narrator (who is gathering information about a former revolutionary pioneer named Alejandro Mayta in order to write a novel about the first socialist insurrection in Peru) wonders, "From time to time I have the impression that I'm not in Lima or even on the coast but in some village in the Andes: sandals, Indian skirts, ponchos, vests with llamas embroidered on them, dialogues in Quechua. Do they really live better in this stink and scum than in the mountain villages they have abandoned to come to Lima? Sociologists, economists, and anthropologists assure us that, as amazing as it may seem, this is the case" (53). This passage seems ambivalent at best. Its first sentence gives the impression that the narrator is not only surprised but also disturbed by the omnipresence of indigenous people in "his" city; it is implied that this people do not belong in Lima but in their ancestral homeland in the Andes. In the next two sentences, however, he somewhat redeems himself by expressing his sympathy for their trials.

And the imagery reappears again in *The Storyteller* when the semiautobiographical narrator sees an Andean boy cleaning the filthy floor of a café: "A zombie? A caricature? Would it have been better for him to have stayed in his Andean village, wearing a wool cap with earflaps, leather sandals, and a poncho, never learning Spanish? I didn't know, and I still don't. But Mascarita knew" (27). These scenes in the three novels are reminiscent of the "informal Peru" or "Chicha culture" that Vargas Llosa describes in *La utopía arcaica* in derogatory terms that emphasize the confusion and lack of harmony of the hybridization. In the last chapter of this study, he mentions the unexpected results of the deindianization and forced cohabitation produced by Andean migration to the capital: "A strange hybrid in which the rudimentary Spanish or Creolized jargon that people use to communicate reflects a taste, a sensitivity, an idiosyncrasy, and even aesthetic values that are virtually new: a Chicha culture" (331–32)

These two ethnic realities are inseparably linked to Peruvian geo-graphical locations. In *La utopía arcaica* Vargas Llosa includes a quotation from an indigenist academic essay titled *Ruta cultural del Perú* (Cultural Route of Peru), by the historian Luis E. Valcárcel, which the novelist considers an example of the "Andeanist" perception of Lima: "In the long run, the coast, because of its geographic location and its social composi-tion, came to represent the Anti-Peru" (169). This passage is also repre-sentative of the archaic utopia initiated by El Inca Garcilaso de la Vega, who claimed that Quechua culture would be metaphysically preserved throughout the centuries, waiting for the appropriate moment to restore, in modern times, the Incas' egalitarian society. This indigenist "historical-political fiction" (in Vargas Llosa's terms; *Utopía* 168) is echoed in the fictional discourse of a character in *Mayta*, a twenty-two-year-old second lieutenant jailer named Vallejos who leaves Lima outside the essence of Peruvianness: "Mayta then heard him launch, with no preamble, into the discourse about Indian life. The real Peru was in the mountains and not along the coast, among the Indians and condors and the peaks of the Andes, not here in Lima, a foreign, lazy, anti-Peruvian city, because from the time the Spaniards had founded it, it had looked toward Europe and the United States and turned its back on Peru" (19). Vallejos will expand his argumentation in chapter 5: "Then, when Lima snatched the scepter from it, Jauja, like all the cities and cultures of the Andes, went into an irreversible decline and servitude, subordinate to that new center of national life set in the most unhealthy corner of the coast, from which it would go on ceaselessly expropriating all the energies of the country for its own use" (116). These statements by the leftist lieutenant, together with the revolutionaries' efforts to "save" indigenous Peruvians and bring them back to a position of national leadership, are later satirically refuted and mocked through the passive reaction of Jauja's inhabitants to the parade of the minuscule group of adolescent insurgents: "When people did turn to look at them, it was with indifference. A group of Indians with ponchos and packs, sitting on a bench, just followed them with their eyes. There weren't people for a demonstration yet. It was ridiculous to be marching" (232). A few pages later, the same indifferent reaction to the presence of their "saviors" further ridicules the insurgents' sacrifice: "In the plaza, the Indians went on buying and selling, uninterested in them" (254).

Therefore, even though, to Vargas Llosa's dismay, most critics have interpreted *Mayta* as a fictionalized political treatise against socialist revo-lutions and political utopias, there is also a subtle lucubration against indigenist discourses (by which I do not mean that the novel or Vargas Llosa are anti-indigenous) that will be later developed in more depth in

The Storyteller and *Death in the Andes*. In the same way that *La utopía arcaica* criticizes José Carlos Mariátegui's appropriation of the Indian plight to justify the Marxist theorist's own political objectives (without his knowing much about their culture) *Mayta* condemns, in an implicit way, the revolutionaries' flagrant attempt to use indigenous people in order to materialize their own political utopias, even as they pusillanimously hide out in their garage when the opportunity to take the arms arises. Although their attitude changes following the triumph of the Cuban Revolution at first Mayta's fellow Trotskyist militants choose to continue with their byzantine discussions instead of joining the uprising (which they had ostensibly been planning for years) alongside the indigenous people in the Andes. Yet all of them are convinced that indigenous people hold the key for the success of a socialist revolution: "When the Indians rise up, Peru will be a volcano" (12), Mayta promises. Only Vallejos and a somewhat reluctant Mayta eventually join the armed struggle, even though the latter avowedly knows nothing about Indians or their way of life. In a sort of poetic justice (which, according to *A Writer's Reality*, faithfully echoes the life of the historical Vicente Mayta Mercado), the last chapter shows him living a miserable life in a slum and laboring in an ice cream parlor.

Moving on to the novels specifically dedicated to the clash and lack of communication between the two main Peruvian cultures, in *The Storyteller* we have one of these indigenists: an idealistic, half-Jewish student from Lima's San Marcos University named Saúl "Mascarita" Zuratas who, after doing anthropological fieldwork in the Amazonian jungle, decides to join "the men who walk"—that is, the nomadic Machiguenga tribe. That *The Storyteller* is sympathetic toward the Amazonian Indians is suggested by the novel being dedicated to them. Yet it takes for granted (since both Mascarita and the narrator agree) that the assimilation of Andean Peruvians to Western culture is inevitable and even advisable. Thus Mascarita states, "I know very well that there's no turning back for the descendants of the Incas. The only course left them is integration. The sooner they can be Westernized, the better: it's a process that's bogged down halfway and should be speeded up. For them, it's the lesser evil now. So you see I'm not being utopian. But in Amazonia it's different. The great trauma that turned the Incas into a people of sleepwalkers and vassals hasn't occurred there" (100).

By contrast, in the case of the Amazonian tribes the dilemma is presented, in line with postmodern skepticism, from two contrasting perspectives, neither of which is clearly defended within the novel. This is reflected in the fact that the conundrum remains somewhat unresolved in the book. In a first reading, it seems that Vargas Llosa lets the reader decide on her own which of the two arguments seems more appropriate for Peru: Mascarita's indigenist return to a pre-Colombian way of life, which, as Gene Bell-Villada points out, is "portrayed as something of an eccentric, utopian impulse" (150), or the Westernizing approach of his unnamed novelist-narrator, who no longer believes in socialist indigenism.[1] However, a second reading reveals that this would-be dialogical and polyphonic *tour de force* that takes place in 1958 between the neoindigenist Mascarita and the ostensibly anti-indigenist first-person narrator is stacked. Inevitably, the fact that the narrator has autobiographical traits gives more weight to the second option. In O'Bryan-Knight's words, "As the narrator's voice breaks away from and begins to overpower that of the *hablador*, stylization gives way to critical parody. The voice of ethnography is ultimately subverted when it becomes clear that it is not a Machiguenga storyteller who is speaking out but, rather, the narrator speaking through Mascarita's mouth. Indeed, Mascarita emerges as a parody of an anthropologist" (90). Furthermore, the three odd-numbered chapters narrated in a style that imitates indigenous orality expose negative aspects of this culture.[2] The credibility of this criticism is enhanced by the fact that it comes from an anthropology student who obviously empathizes with the Machiguenga and now sees their culture from within.

Yet the impossibility of completely abandoning Western ways is proven by the fact that Mascarita resorts to adapted versions of written texts, such as the plight of the biblical Jews and his favorite story, Franz Kafka's "The Metamorphosis" (1916). Mascarita's adoption of the Machiguenga worldview has not completely erased the written culture he learned in Lima. As Raymond L. Williams puts it, "Rather than an authentic storyteller, he is the perfect imitator of the storyteller" (262). In any case, Mascarita has found his destiny living as an *hablador* (storyteller) in the Amazonian jungle and trying to convince the Machiguenga, from this privileged vantage point, about the dangers of changing their ancestral customs. In the last chapter, for example, he warns them against abandoning their traditional nomadic life and trading with the *Viracochas* (non-Indians) through the story of a Machiguenga man who has joined up with the mercantile economy that, in his view, is so detrimental for the Amazonian tribes. Soon, this Machiguenga man becomes unhappy and begins to suspect that the whites with whom he has been trading products are devils. Tormented and suffering from insomnia, he regrets having committed the mistake of deviating from Machiguenga rules and moves with his family elsewhere, leaving all those "impure" objects behind.

Another element of Vargas Llosa's criticism of indigenism is his accusation against the movement of being openly male chauvinistic. In *La utopía arcaica* Vargas Llosa provides examples of stereotypical representations of masculinity and femininity, including Valcárcel's foretelling, in *Tempestad en los Andes* (Tempest in the Andes, 1927), of the eventual hegemony of the "virile sierra" over the "feminine coast" (68). In *The Storyteller*, this machismo is transplanted to the Machiguenga themselves. Misha Kokotovic has argued that "for Vargas Llosa, the Machiguenga are just a vehicle for a story about the importance of stories, and of storytelling" (182). Yet they also serve perhaps more important function: they illustrate the backward gender discrimination that, according to Vargas Llosa, permeates Amazonian indigenous cultures. Thus the Machiguenga man who had been trading with the Viracocha loses his temper and strikes one of his wives after accusing her of being a liar when she is obviously telling the truth. The deplorable situation of women in the Amazonia is also emphasized in the following passage: "'What I gave them is worth more than she is,' he assured me. 'Isn't that so?' he asked the Yaminahua woman in front of me, and she agreed" (110). The girl, who was purchased from a Yaminahua family in exchange for some food, has not yet had her first menstruation. These passages can be interpreted in the context of feminist political philosopher Susan Moller Okin's criticism of multiculturalism in the sense that "culture" and the concern for preserving cultural diversity should never be an excuse for allowing the oppression of women and ignoring gender discrimination in minority cultures:

> In the case of a more patriarchal minority culture in the context of a less patriarchal majority culture, no argument can be made on the basis of self-respect or freedom that the female members of the culture have a clear interest in its preservation. Indeed, they *might* be much better off if the culture into which they were born were either to become extinct (so that its members would become integrated into the less sexist surrounding culture) or, preferably, to be encouraged to alter itself so as to reinforce the equality of women—at least to the degree to which this value is upheld in the majority culture. (Okin 22–23)

In any case, this is another controversial argument. While the scene may describe the situation of women among the Machiguenga, this type of discrimination cannot be generalized to all indigenous Peruvian cultures. The status of women in pre-Columbian societies, for instance, varied greatly according to the ethnic group, as revealed by the archaeological discovery in 1991 of several tombs of high-level Mochica priestesses in San José de Moro, in the department of La Libertad on the northern coast of Peru. Likewise, the discovery in 2005 of a mummified Moche woman with complex tattoos in her arms, baptized the Lady of Cao, at the Huaca Cao Viejo, part of the El Brujo archeological site on the out-skirts of Trujillo, has also raised many questions about the role of women in the ancient civilizations of Peru, as it contained precious ornamental and military artifacts, including war clubs and spear throwers.

The novel, therefore, suggests that Peru should never try to return to what Vargas Llosa seems to consider the archaic and backward indigenous ways. The semiautobiographical narrator himself makes this assumption explicit when he lightheartedly accuses his classmate Mascarita: "'You're an Indigenist to the nth degree, Mascarita,' I teased him. 'Just like the ones in the thirties. Like Dr. Luis Valcárcel when he was young, wanting all the colonial churches and convents demolished because they represented Anti-Peru. Or should we bring back the Tahuantisuyo? Human sacrifice, quipus, trepanation with stone knives?'" (99). In this regard, it is worth noting that he presents trepanation as backward when, considering the century when it was practiced, most anthropologists consider it proof of the scientific sophistication of Inca and pre-Inca societies. For instance, in a recent sur-vey of pre-Colombian technology and science, Rómulo Lins and Marcos Teixeira argue that "the medical and botanical knowledge of the Inca was substantial and, in some cases, quite sophisticated for the time," singling out trepanation as an example of such medical sophistication (627).

The narrator provides many other reasons to consider these tribes' culture inferior, including their polygamy, animism, head shrinking, and witch doctoring with tobacco: "The fact, for instance, that the Aguarunas and the Huambisas of the Alto Marañón tear out their daughters' hymen at her menarche and eat it, that slavery exists in many tribes, and in some communities they let the old people die at the first signs of weakness, on the pretexts that their souls have been called away and their destiny fulfilled . . . That babies born with physical defects, lame, maimed, blind, with more or fewer fingers than usual, or a harelip, were killed by their own mothers, who threw them in the river or buried them alive" (25). This last part is particularly relevant if one takes into account that had Mascarita been born a Machiguenga, his own mother would have killed him after seeing the birthmark that covers half of his face. Underscoring the paradox, Mascarita himself admits that this is in fact what would have happened to him and actually criticizes this barbaric custom. For this reason, he saves a parrot that its mother was trying to kill because it had been born with physical handicaps. Among several other anti-indigenist arguments used by the narrator to support indirectly the colonization of the Amazonian jungle is the small number of indigenous people that live there. In accord with Vargas Llosa's well-known epigraph that opens this essay, the narrator argues,

That in order not to change the way of life and the beliefs of a handful of tribes still living, many of them, in the Stone Age, the rest of Peru abstain from developing the Amazon region? Should sixteen million Peruvians renounce the natural resources of three-quarters of their national territory so that seventy or eighty thousand Indians could quietly go on shooting at each other with bows and arrows, shrinking heads and worshipping boa constrictors? . . . If the price to be paid for development and industrialization for the sixteen million Peruvians meant that those few thousand naked Indians would have to cut their hair, wash off their tattoos, and become mestizos—or, to use the ethnologists' most detested word, become acculturated—well, there was no way around it. (21–22).

In the narrator's opinion, instead of worrying so much about the future of the few thousand Indians that belong to these small and primitive Amazonian tribes, Mascarita should concentrate on the predicament of the millions of Andean Indians.

At any rate, the narrator argues that Mascarita's indigenism (and indigenism in general, for that matter) is an archaic, romantic, unrealistic, and antihistorical utopia. At one point, he actually maintains that assimilation to Western ways would also be desirable for Amazonian tribes: "Was going on living the way they were, the way purist anthropologists of Saúl's sort wanted them to do, to the tribes' advantage? Their primitive state made them, rather, victims of the worst exploitation and cruelty" (73–74).

Other scenes in the novel corroborate his intuition that assimilation is the only solution to the exploitation of indigenous tribes. In one of them, Jum, the *cacique* (local authority) of Urakusa, realizes (after his contacts with Western civilization while taking a course to become a bilingual teacher) that the men with whom they trade rubber and animal skins are exploiting his tribe. When the white or Amazonian mestizos with whom he trades find out that he has set up a cooperative between the indigenous villages, they brutally torture him. Upon seeing these abuses, the narrator recalls his debates about the colonization of the Amazonia with Mascarita and wonders, "Would he admit that in a case like this it was quite obvious that what was to Urakusa's advantage, to Jum's, was not going backward but forward? That is to say, getting up their own cooperative, trading with the towns, prospering economically and socially so that it would no longer be possible to treat them the way the 'civilized' people of Santa María de Nieva had done" (76). In line with the polyphonic approach of the novel, however, an alternative interpretation is subsequently offered:

Matos Mar thought that Jum's misfortune would provide Mascarita with further arguments to support his theory. Didn't the entire episode prove that coexistence was impossible, that it led inevitably to the Viracochas' domination of the Indians, to the gradual and systematic destruction of the weaker culture? Those savage drunkards from Santa María de Nieva would never, under any circumstances, lead the inhabitants of Urakusa on the path of modernization, but only to their extinction; their "culture" had no more right to hegemony than that of the Aguarunas, who, however primitive they might be, had at least developed sufficient knowledge and skill to coexist with Amazonia. (77)

Regarding this argumentation presented by Vargas Llosa in both his novels and his political discourse, Kokotovic has questioned the author's thesis that preservation is the only alternative to modernization: "The very terms in which the dilemma is posed predetermine its resolution. Vargas Llosa sets up a false dichotomy by opposing Western modernization to the straw man of 'cultural preservation,' by which he means literally freezing 'primitive' indigenous cultures in time. Having thus limited the options he skips 'from choices the Indians face to choosing for them,' to use Doris Sommer's felicitous phrase" (177). As Kokotovic contends, indigeneity is not incompatible with modernity and, therefore, does not have to be necessarily replaced and sacrificed by the hegemonic Western culture; instead, a transculturation process can bring about Arguedas's ideal of a modern but not acculturated or Westernized Quechua culture.

In spite of his obsession with the figure of the Machiguenga storyteller, the narrator, who admittedly struggles to accept that these primitive cultures are part of his country, continues to find reasons for the modernization of the Amazonia. Unlike his friend Mascarita, he initially applauds the work that the Schneils, a couple of religious North American linguists, are doing with the Machiguengas. Because of this external influence, half of the five thousand Machiguengas now live in a village, have become Christian, and even have a *cacique*. As a result, their moral disintegration and helplessness, which made them refuse to take care of themselves once they fell ill, has now disappeared. A few lines later, however, the polyphonic counterpoint returns and he begins to have some doubts: "Was all this a good thing? Had it brought them real advantages as individuals, as people, as the Schneils so emphatically maintained? Or were they, rather, from the free and sovereign 'savages' they had been, beginning to turn into 'zombies,' caricatures of Westerners, as Mascarita had put it?" (163).

In the book he is writing, the novelist-narrator imagines that Mascarita, the born-again storyteller, has internalized the Machiguengas' superstitious and magico-religious interpretation of the reality. His opinions, therefore, now come from within the indigenous culture. But even before he becomes a Machiguenga, he contests the narrator's observations by providing his own arguments against the colonization of the Amazonia. One of them is based on his disparagement of Lima's Andean Indians. Looking at them, Mascarita insists that Amazonian tribes should never follow in the footsteps of their Andean brethren in the capital city: "Or do you believe in 'civilizing the savages,' pal? How? By making soldiers of them? By putting them to work on the farms as slaves to Creoles like Fidel Pereira? By forcing them to change their language, their religion, and their customs, the way the missionaries are trying to do? What's to be gained by that? Being able to exploit them more easily, that's all. Making them zombies and caricatures of men, like those semiacculturated Indians you see in Lima" (26). In Mascarita's view, even though we may find some Amazonian customs cruel and offensive, aboriginal cultures should be respected. And the only way to do that, he argues, is to avoid contact with them. For centuries, he explains, their beliefs and traditions have helped them to survive in the jungle, to repel numerous colonization attempts (by Incas, then colonial missionaries, *criollos* [Euro-Peruvians] and, more recently, by anthropologists), and most importantly, to live in harmony with nature.

In spite of their discrepancies, the narrator and Mascarita are equally patriotic; both of them want the best for their homeland and, at one point or another, show sincere concern for the autochthonous tribes' adversity. Yet whereas Mascarita proposes to save the Machiguenga and their culture by isolating them, the narrator has more of an ethnological interest in them. His literary interests account for his fascination with their *habladores*: "'They're a tangible proof that storytelling can be something more than entertainment,' it occurred to me to say to him. 'Something primordial, something that the very existence of a people may depend on. Maybe that's what impressed me so'" (94). This passage is crucial to understand the common background behind the works considered in this essay. What the narrator has actually discovered here is that fictions are something that humans cannot live without. This need for fiction may account for oral storytelling and novels, or it may have a darker side: racists and fanatics of all kinds, including religious fundamentalists and members of terrorist groups such as Sendero Luminoso (Shining Path), may very well end up believing the bizarre fictions (ideological utopias) they have fabricated to justify their crimes. And in the author's mind, indigenists, behind their ostensibly good intentions, may also create their own dangerous ideological fictions. Vargas Llosa has formulated these views in *A Writer's Reality*: "One day I reached this conclusion: that ideology in Latin America was fulfilling this task for many people; that ideology was the way they incorporated fiction into their lives, as other people incorporated the fictitious experience through fiction, through novels, or through religious ideas" (149). Even though in this passage, the author is referring mostly to political ideology in *Mayta*, one can easily conclude that he considers indigenist discourse just another fiction, another imagined world, another fantasy fabricated by Peruvian academics.

In *The Storyteller* we find the opinions of a character that has been partially invented by another, twenty-five years after the events took place. This invention contributes to the creation of a set of ambiguities that, in postmodernist fashion, eliminates the need for an epistemological center. Likewise, the additional interpretations provided by other characters (interviewees in *Mayta*'s case), some of whom may be lying or may suffer lapses of memory, create a perspectivism with differing and at times contrasting views of the same facts. To complicate things even further, in both works the novelist-narrator is not as interested in unearthing the historical truth as he is in creating a fictional story and a protagonist with verisimilitude; if those events could have happened, that is all that matters. Thus, in *The Storyteller*, after the narrator speculates about possible reasons for his classmate's obsession with safeguarding aboriginal culture, he realizes that he will never find out what they are and chooses instead to invent them and make them part of a novel. Kristal has analyzed this ventriloquistic narrative device: "The narrator chooses to identify the individual in the photograph as Mascarita . . . but because he only does so in the last pages of the novel the resolution of the mystery coincides with the reader's retrospective realization that the novelist's recollections are intertwined with his fictional inventions. The novel is a Borgesian game of Chinese boxes: the story of Mascarita's integration into the world of the Machiguenga is a fiction of the unnamed novelist whose obsession with Mascarita is a fiction of Vargas Llosa's" (*Temptation of the Word* 159). The reason Vargas Llosa used this narrative device is revealed in *A Writer's Reality* when he is actually explaining the creative process of his novel *The Green House* (1966): "I wanted to have an Indian character, a primitive man from a small tribe in the Amazon region, as the central figure in the novel. I tried hard to invent this character from within in order to show the reader his subjectivity, how he had assimilated some kind of experiences with the white world. But I could not do it . . . I felt I was making a caricature of this character and finally decided to describe him through intermediaries, through characters whom I was able to divine and to perceive" (19).

All these factors suggest, in a very postmodern way, the difficulty of reconstructing historical facts and of taking sides on delicate issues such as indigenism or revolutionary activities without falling into simplistic conclusions. It is not too difficult, however, to read between the lines and infer the negative views about socialism and indigenism that permeate *Mayta* and *The Storyteller*. Both discourses are discredited not only as anachronistic and naïve fictions but also as dangerous ideologies. In other words, they try to uncover the naïve and perhaps innocent ideological background that gave birth in the late 1960s to the Maoist guerrilla organization Sendero Luminoso. Could racist indigenism or a meeting of a handful of utopian leftist militants have ever developed into the embryo of a bloodthirsty terrorist group that will hold the country hostage for several decades? According to these works, that is the way *senderismo* began in Peru.

As to the relation between dogmatic socialism and radical indigenism, it is widely believed that, following Mariátegui's notion that the Inca Empire or Tahuantisuyu (or Tawantisuyu) constituted a sort of primitive communist society, *senderistas* and their leader, the former philosophy professor at Ayacucho's Universidad Nacional de San Cristóbal de Huamanga, hoped to create a new Peru that would be a combination of pre-Columbian Inca society and the Maoist revolutionary regime. Vargas Llosa, however, rejects this idea that Sendero Luminoso was trying to preserve indigenous cultures and bring back the Inca Empire in all its glory: "In contrast with the image that some irredeemable enthusiast of local color would like to fabricate, Sendero Luminoso was not an indigenist movement, of Quechua ethnic vindication, anti-Western, contemporary expression of the old Andean messianism" (*Utopía* 330). Instead, argues the author, what they really wanted was quite the opposite: erasing every trace of the cultural past as Mao Zedong tried to do with during the Cultural Revolution. The interconnection between indigenism and revolutionary thought proposed by Mariátegui is also discussed when a professor named Matos Mar describes socialism as the only solution for the dilemma of the integration of indigenous communities. Ultimately, even if going in different directions, Mayta and Mascarita share a common fanaticism guided by what the implicit author considers naïve fictions. Likewise, whereas in *Mayta* the narrator uses the widespread homophobia among leftist militants as a way of unveiling their hypocrisy, in *The Storyteller* it is gender discrimination and the killing of "imperfect" newborn babies that serves the same purpose.

While Jean O'Bryan-Knight and other critics have discussed the technical, structural, and thematic similarities that can be found among *Aunt Julia*, *Mayta*, and *The Storyteller* (all three novels share the presence of a protagonist who is also the narrator and a semiautobiographical writer), the latter resembles *Death in the Andes* in a different aspect. It portrays the existence of two parallel Perus that are oblivious to each other: on the one hand, the Andean (Quechua and Aymara) and Amazonian indigenous and on the other, the coastal indigenous that has become mestizo. Still within the anti-indigenist discouse underscored previously, in *Death in the Andes* we have a different response to indigenists such as Valcárcel, Manuel González Prada, and Mariátegui who conceived Indians as the true Peruvians: what if modern Latin American citizens went back to pre-Columbian ways? Vargas Llosa's answer is this novel in which two outsiders, a tavern keeper named Dionisio and his wife, Doña Adriana, convince the inhabitants of a fictional Andean town called Naccos to practice human sacrifice and cannibalism in order to placate evil mountain spirits. When three men, Pedrito Tinoco, Don Mellardo Llantac and Casimiro Huarcaya, suddenly disappear, two civil guards, Corporal Lituma (a recurring character in Vargas Llosa's fiction) and his adjutant, Tomás Carreño, are put in charge of the investigation. Although at first they suspect that the Sendero Luminoso guerrillas are responsible for the disappearances, Lituma eventually realizes, thanks to the remarks of a Danish archaeology professor named Paul Stirmsson who is doing field-work in Peru, that the resurgence of pre-Incan ritual human sacrifices may be the answer to the mystery.

In fact, the novel suggests in several passages that Sendero Lumino-so's massacres are nothing but a continuation or modern version of pre-Columbian human sacrifice. For instance, a minor character, "the blond engineer," wonders "if what's going on in Peru isn't a resurrection of all that buried violence. As if it had been hidden somewhere, and suddenly, for some reason, it all surfaced again" (153). In the opening of the novel Lituma had already suggested that there were more than political objectives to Sendero Luminoso's assassinations: "Weren't the terrucos [Sendero Luminoso] killing people left and right and saying it was for the revolution? They got a kick out of blood, too" (19). Beyond the practice of human sacrifice, in the denouement of the novel we learn that the locals have also been practicing ritual cannibalism, to which they refer, in Catholic terms, as "communion." This unexpected development had been prefigured when one of the locals mentioned that Dionisio's Quechua last name meant "Eater of Raw Meat" (165). Later, it is also foreshadowed in a conversation about the Sendero Luminoso's so-called people's trials between Lituma and Dionisio:

> 'The lucky ones were whipped, the rest had their heads bashed in.'
> 'All we need now is for them to suck people's blood and eat them raw.'
> 'It'll come to that?' The cantinero replied. (81)

And once again, the gruesome finding is linked to Stirmsson's explanations about pre-Inca cannibalism:

> As far as horrible things are concerned, he could give a few lessons to the ter-rucos, mere novices who only knew how to kill people with bullets or knives, or by crushing their skulls, which was child's play compared to the techniques employed by the ancient Peruvians, who had achieved the heights of refinement. Even more than the ancient Mexicans, despite an international conspiracy of historians to conceal the Peruvian contribution to the art of human sacrifice . . . how many people had heard about the religious passion of the Chancas and Huancas for human viscera, about the delicate surgery in which they removed their victims' livers and brains and kidneys and ate them in their ceremonies, washing it all down with good corn chicha? (146)

Three years after the publication of *Death in the Andes*, Vargas Llosa coincides with the arguments of his character, Stirmsson, when he develops, in *La utopía arcaica*, his interpretation of the birth of Peruvian indigenist discourse. In this essay, he analyzes the writings of Valcárcel, in which the latter idyllically conceives of pre-Columbian Peru as a lost paradise that epitomized socialism's collectivist utopia. Among the Incas, maintains Valcárcel (coinciding with the character of Matos Mar in *Death in the Andes*), work was not oriented by a mercantile spirit but by an altruistic will to serve the community. By the same token, the benevolent government took care of its subjects' needs and respected the idiosyncrasies and the autonomy of the peoples incorporated to the Empire. In turn, Vargas Llosa denounces these texts as romanticized fictions inspired by European mythification: "This description of that lost paradise is not historical, even if the one who wrote it was a historian: it is ideological and mythical. To make it possible, it was necessary to perform a surgery that eliminated from that perfect society everything that could make it ugly or attack its perfection" (171). Then he mentions human sacrifice, a widespread practice in Peru during and before the Inca Empire, with a special emphasis on the *capacocha*, a ceremony in which a great number of children brought from all over the Tahuantisuyo were immolated. Also coinciding with his character, Stirmsson, Vargas Llosa explains that the reason the Huancas and Chancas helped the Spanish conquistadors was that they were subjugated nations in the Inca Empire. He also mentions the *mitimaes*, or massive deportations by which the Incas uprooted entire peoples from their homelands in order to control them more easily. Finally, the author points out that when Francisco Pizarro arrived in Peru, the Inca Empire was not the ahistorical Arcadia described by indigenists but a land torn by a bloody civil war due to the disputes with respect to the dynastic succession. All these passages in his novels and essays are Vargas Llosa's moralistic (and arguably essentialist) response to those Peruvian academics who rhetorically longed for a return to pre-Columbian ways. However, he fails to point out, for example, that at the time the European Inquisition was burning hundreds of people alive at the stake.

This historical research had previously found its place in *Death in Los Andes.* Thus, according to his character Stirmsson, in the ancient, central Andean cultures of the Huancas and the Chancas it was common to sacrifice humans when they were going to build a new road, divert a river, or build a temple or fortress. In this way, they showed respect for the *apus*, or spirits of the mountains whom they were otherwise going to disturb, and thus prevented avalanches, floods, and lightning from killing their people. The professor, however, does not present these facts as criticism of these cultures but as proof of their religious devotion. He also reminds his interlocutors that one has to think about these rituals and conquests from a historical perspective: "Of course they were animals. Can any ancient people pass the test? Which of them was not cruel and intolerant when judged from a contemporary perspective?" (153). In fact, perhaps going against the grain of contemporary Peruvian academic discourse, he sees the Huancas and the Chancas as the victims of Inca imperialism: "They had helped the Conquistadors in the belief that they, in turn, would help the Huancas gain their freedom from those who had enslaved them" (151).

Stirmsson also contends that we should not make the mistake of trying to understand Sendero Luminoso's killings with our minds because they have "no rational explanation" (153). In fact, not only the terrorists' killings, which are supposedly motivated by political ideology, but also the religious rituals of human sacrifice and cannibalism are depicted in the novel as irrational behavior that the reader should not try to approach with a Western rationalistic mindset. The very name of one of the two persons responsible for convincing locals about the benefits of human sacrifice, Dionisio, suggests precisely the Dionysian nature of this underworld: he is proud of having taught local men to enjoy life. Like Dionysus, he represents the instinctual and irrational side of human nature. Without this Peruvian Dionysus, local men agree, there would be no festivities. In his cantina, he organizes orgiastic parties in which, instead of wine like Dionysus and Bacchus, he uses pisco to make his customers uninhibited and to manipulate them into a frenzy. It would be worth mentioning here that the indirect references to Greek mythology (Dionysus, the labyrinth of Theseus, etc.) could be one more proof of the author's Eurocentric mentality.

On the other side of the temperamental spectrum, we have Lituma's critical rationalism that mocks what he considers ignorant and anachronistic superstitions: "'You're all very gullible, very naïve,' replied Lituma. 'You believe anything, like stories about pishtacos and mukis. In civilized places, nobody believes things like that anymore'" (86). Toward the end of the novel, however, he gives in to the imposing landscape of the Andes and begins to accept and unconsciously internalize the intuitive values of the locals. Thus, after miraculously surviving a *huayco* (an Andean avalanche of snow, mud, and rocks), Lituma surrenders to their worldview, while using a seriocomic tone that hints at his cultural transformation, "as if he had passed a test, he thought, as if these damn mountains, this damn sierra, had finally accepted him. Before starting out, he pressed his mouth against the rock that had sheltered him, and whispered, like a serrucho: 'Thank you for saving my life, mamay, apu, pachamama, or whoever the fuck you are'" (180). It seems, therefore, that the orgiastic Greek religion that celebrated the power and fertility of nature and its counterpoint in the Peruvian Andes have found a new follower. How is it possible that westernized laborers with at least a grade school education and who live in the modern world have ended up believing in human sacrifice? And how is it possible that Lituma himself is reluctantly accepting a worldview that he had been criticizing so harshly? Again, we find an explanation in the irrational instincts that all human beings possess, whether or not censored by a social or parental superego. Congruent with Vargas Llosa's interest in irrationality, in *Death in the Andes* the spokesmen of Sendero Luminoso justify their killings with absurd conspiracy theories about secret strategies devised by imperialist and capitalist states. Beyond this, their revolutionary trials in which they force locals to kill "antisocial types" with their own hands or with stones and sticks and then prevent them from burying the bodies are depicted in the context of a pre-Columbian irrational, magico-religious mentality.

In contrast with Stirmsson, Lituma is much less tolerant of contemporary Andean mentality. As in other novels of Vargas Llosa where he appears, we are told that Lituma is a mestizo who grew up in the coastal town of Piura, in northern Peru, and does not feel at home in the Andes; in fact, in *Death in the Andes* he repeatedly expresses his dislike of Andean people. From the opening paragraph, he expresses his rejection of the indigenous worldview and behavior and even of the Quechua language, which makes him feel uneasy because it resembles "savage music" (3). Even though his adjutant and close friend, Carreño, is also Andean and speaks Quechua, Lituma rejects a world that seems impenetrable to him. He feels particularly frustrated by what he perceives as Indian indolence and by his inability to engage the locals in productive communication. This invisible barrier created by cultural differences had previously been

pointed out by the French tourists killed by Sendero Luminoso opera-
tives in the first chapters: "He had made several attempts, in his poor
Spanish, to engage his neighbors in conversation, with absolutely no success. 'It isn't race that separates us, it's an entire culture,' *la petite* Michèle
reminded him" (11). In the denouement of the novel, once Lituma realizes that the human sacrifices respond to the ancient tradition of appeas-
ing the *apus* before disturbing the land, he vents his rage against the locals:
"'You motherfuckers!' he bellowed then at the top of his lungs. 'Fucking
serruchos' [mountain people] Goddamn Indians, you superstitious pagan
sons of bitches!'" (174).

In *Death in the Andes*, therefore, Vargas Llosa tries to prove that, no
matter how well-intentioned and inspirational indigenism may be for
indigenous peoples that have been oppressed, neglected and marginalized for centuries, one should not romanticize pre-Columbian history
or create false fantasies about a world that, from today's ethical perspective, was far from peaceful and idyllic. By creating contemporary fictional characters who adopt Amazonian (in *The Storyteller*) and pre-Inca
(in *Death in the Andes*) cultural ways, he also warns about the dangers
of a neoindigenist philosophy that, in his view, shows its ugliest face in
the massacres committed by the Maoist guerrillas of Sendero Luminoso.
Evidently, in Vargas Llosa's literary discourse human sacrifice and cannibalism represent the archaic and irrational ways of pre-Columbian
civilizations. Indeed, as Elizabeth P. Benson's book *Ritual Sacrifice in
Ancient Peru* (2001) contends, ancient Peruvians (especially the Inca
and the Moche) practiced human sacrifice to maintain a proper recip-
rocal relationship with the supernatural world. To focus exclusively on
these rituals in order to discredit their culture, however, seems somewhat simplistic and reductionist, particularly if we consider that these
were two of the most recurring arguments (along with paganism and
homosexuality) used by the conquistadors to justify the conquest of the
Americas and the subjugation of its people. Therefore, perhaps making
the same mistake of which he accuses the indigenist movement, Vargas
Llosa ends up creating an alternative "fantasy" or "fiction" of the pre-
Columbian world.

In *Death in the Andes*, these primitive beliefs have weathered the Spanish
Christianization of Peru. Yet could we affirm that the actions of Dionisio
and his wife Adriana also respond to irrational instincts? The fact is that the
couple shows no guilt or remorse for the assassinations they have instigated.
This proves that, rather than acting like inebriated, irrational beings as do
some of the locals in Naccos, they sincerely approach the ritual sacrifices
from a religious (rather than cruel or evil) perspective. Whereas Sendero

Luminoso's massacres respond to a fanatical, ideological take on Peruvian reality, Dionisio and Adriana go beyond this more common violence by actually eating their victims, not as a result of an irrational reaction but for premeditated, religious reasons.

At any rate, in Vargas Llosa's worldview both types of violence are intimately related not only by the leitmotif of the irrational side of human nature (beyond political ideology and religion) but also by the characters' fanatical, utopian, and indigenist desire to return (either rhetorically or in praxis) to pre-Columbian ways.[3] In his view, they also respond to humans' need to create fictions. In this sense, Kristal maintains that while Vargas Llosa has demonstrated his concern for the suffering of the Andean population, in *Death in the Andes* "he is also weary of the violent tendencies of the local populations. In Vargas Llosa's analysis all of the parties involved [Sendero Luminoso, the government, and Peruvian peasants] are prone to violence and all have committed crimes. A feeling of mistrust of the military, the guerrilla movement, and the indigenous population also pervades *Death in the Andes*" (188). The character of the mute Pedrito Tinoco, who is first attacked by Sendero Luminoso, then tortured by Lituma's superior and then singled out by locals for their ritual human sacrifice, symbolizes the way in which Andean villages were exposed to all types of blind fanaticism and were also caught in the middle of a bloody war between terrorists and governmental forces.

Perhaps anticipating criticism about the verisimilitude of these plots, in *Death in the Andes* Vargas Llosa contextualizes the human sacrifices and cannibalism in Naccos with the fact that, as his character Lituma explains, in Ayacucho people are scared about a *pishtaco* invasion and in Lima there is widespread paranoia about foreign eye thieves. Later, referring to human sacrifice, Lituma insists, "Around here they kill anybody for anything. They're always finding graves, like that one outside Huanta with the ten Protestant missionaries. Why shouldn't there be human sacrifices too?" (173). In the end, however, the Corporal never arrests the murderers because he is convinced that the facts are too outlandish to be taken seriously by his superiors in Lima. By the same token, in *The Storyteller* the strange adventures of Mascarita in the Amazonian jungle are revealed as a fantasy of the novelist-narrator who, in his imagination, is trying to make sense of the mysterious disappearance of his friend. The narrator's fictional reconstruction of the Amazonian indigenous world is even more questionable if we consider that rather than conducting research on site (or interviewing the protagonist and the people who knew him, as the narrator does in *Mayta*), he writes about his friend's Indian adventures from faraway Florence, Italy.

As regards the novelistic portrayal of indigenism as just another Latin American fiction, Kristal maintains that "Vargas Llosa has not resolved his own dilemmas about the preservation or eventual modernization of indigenous cultures" (*Temptation of the Word* 157). Indeed, in direct contrast with his interviews, lectures and essays, in his novels Vargas Llosa wrestles with arguments for and against the assimilation of Andean and Amazonian Peruvians into the Westernized national life and explores, through the different opinions of his characters, the best possible options. In the end, however, he brings closure to all this speculation, despite admitting that there are both advantages and disadvantages to this process, when he labels the indigenist movements in Ecuador, Peru, and Bolivia as "collectivism," a term he has associated with the socialism, Nazism, and fascism of the past, as well as with today's nationalism and religious (Christian and Islamic) integrism. As one can notice in the following passage from *Making Waves* (1997), as well as in the public declarations previously quoted, Vargas Llosa leaves little doubt as to where he stands on this issue: "Perhaps there is no realistic way of integrating our societies other than by asking the Indians to pay this high price. Perhaps the ideal, that is, the preservation of America's primitive peoples, is a utopia incompatible with a more urgent goal: the establishment of modern societies where social and economic differences are reduced to reasonable proportions and all can attain, at the very least, a free and decent life" (377).

All things considered, is there truly a divide between Vargas Llosa's fiction and his public persona, as his Hispanic critics seem to suggest? Or can we rather see him as a "unified being," as the author requested in the reception speech for the Irving Kristol Award? While it is obvious that his fiction changed dramatically from an ideological standpoint after he affiliated himself to liberalism (in the European sense) or neoliberalism, the truth is that it never ceased to reflect the author's ethical and moral commitments; he is still a politically engaged writer, albeit of a different sign. However, as expected from the novelistic genre, in his fiction he uses a dialogical, polyphonic, and heteroglossic approaches that, in his lectures and essays, could seem otherwise unnecessary. In the case of indigenism, Vargas Llosa acknowledges a positive side in its revalorization of indigenous cultures but condemns the extremism that, when used as an instrument of power, can lead it closer to antidemocratic intolerance and racism. In his ultimate view, indigenism is merely a product of ahistorical idealizations and mystifications.

NOTES

1. This quotation comes from Gene H. Bell-Villada's essay "Sex, Politics, and High Art: Vargas Llosa's Long Road to *The Feast of the Goat*" included in this volume (137–158).
2. Actually, the novel presents the inventions of a fictional novelist-narrator who is trying to imagine Mascarita's imitation of a Machiguenga storyteller.
3. As several critics have pointed out, this novel was influenced by the author's participation in a 1983 committee that investigated the ritual massacre of eight journalists in the Andean village of Uchuraccay, near Ayacucho.

CHAPTER 7

THE RECOVERED CHILDHOOD

UTOPIAN LIBERALISM AND MERCANTILISM OF THE SKIN IN *A FISH IN THE WATER*

SERGIO R. FRANCO

BECAUSE OF ITS BUILT-IN HETEROGENEITY AND MULTIPLICITY OF intentions and its proximity to the time of its writing, Mario Vargas Llosa's *A Fish in the Water* (1993) occupies a unique position in the growing corpus of Latin American autobiographical writing. In effect, only three years before its publication, Vargas Llosa had been a candidate for the Peruvian presidency. He was the candidate for Frente Democrático, or Democratic Front (FREDEMO), a coalition that included traditional parties, like Acción Popular and Partido Popular Cristiano, and the new Movimiento Libertad, led by the writer. Vargas Llosa was defeated by Alberto Fujimori, a then-unknown Peruvian engineer of Japanese descent, after two electoral rounds (April and June, 1990). This defeat not only ended an intense political campaign but also constituted a major surprise for those involved. The unexpected turn of events of the last two weeks of those presidential elections two decades ago was also a surprise to average citizens like myself. Without a doubt, those are the events that explain the immediate reception of *A Fish in the Water* as a chronicle of the political campaign. This is an impoverishing interpretation of a text that exceeds such a characterization. However, it is also true without this defeat the memoirs would not exist.[1] It is the magnitude of the endeavor that undeniably marks a key moment in the life of the protagonist. There is no other way of understanding his attempt at looking at his life from that viewpoint in order to explain the reasons for his defeat, offer eyewitness testimony, and undeniably, polemicize with his antagonists.

A Fish in the Water consists of two narrative lines that alternate in the discourse of the text. The first begins in 1946, with recollections about the novelist's childhood and his family background, and concludes when the beginning writer, thanks to a Javier Prado fellowship, leaves with his wife for Madrid. The second begins in late July 1987 when Vargas Llosa is apprised of President Alan García's proposal for the nationalization of Peru's private banks, financial institutions, and insurance companies and concludes with his postelectoral voluntary exile to Europe, in June 1990. As is obvious, this conscious desire for symmetry—which implies in itself a desire to organize the story of his life—establishes a counterpoint between two possible conceptions, that of the politician and that of the writer, as well as two distinct "educations." And a subliminal educational imperative is undeniably what leads to the Max Weber epigraph with which the text opens: "Primitive Christians also knew very explicitly that the world is ruled by demons and that anyone who becomes involved in politics, that is to say, anyone who agrees to use power and violence as a means, has sealed a pact with the devil, so that it is no longer true that in his activity the good produces only good and the bad, but that the contrary frequently happens. Anyone who does not see this is a child, politically speaking" (unnumbered page after title page).

This quotation comes from *Politik als Beruf* (*Politics as a Vocation*, 1919), where Weber presents an interpretation of politics that eschews ethics while delineating the constitutive traits of a political personality, with its extremes of voluntarism and vanity. The quote also anticipates the general meaning of the text, thus reinforcing the idea that politics is the *raison d'être* of *A Fish in the Water*. Nevertheless, the relationship between epigraph and text is more complex than it would seem at first and deserves to be explored. This is especially so, given that the epigraph anticipates the simple and efficient binarism that organizes the text, with its two plot lines, as well as ideas that reappear in Vargas Llosa's discourse. First, there is the idea of politics as a worldly activity marked by violence and power; second, the mention of demons who govern the world cannot but provoke a precise resonance in any one who is familiar with the weight ascribed to the irrational as the origin of the act of writing in Vargas Llosa's poetics. It is true that in Weber "demons" have an ethical connotation foreign to Vargas Llosa's reflections. But in both cases, one finds the idea of hidden forces capable of leading down unpredictable paths. On the other hand, the clear opposition between good and evil points in the direction of a Manichaeism intuited by means of belief rather than reflection, a fact that appears underlined by the reference to a *primitive* Christianity. But perhaps the most significant aspect of the quote from Weber consists in the idea of a "child" regarding politics. The child introjects us to the field of the private, of the intimate. Moreover, childhood connotes ideas not only of purity, naiveté, inexperience but also of immaturity, lack of development, and potentiality, since childhood is by definition a state of transition toward adulthood. Every child is a savage and its evolution toward maturity mimics the development of humanity. Thus the likeness to the child possesses a peculiar ambiguity that must be scrutinized, since it will reappear with different connotations throughout the text.[2]

Weber's figurative child precedes the literal child under whose image the author decides to present himself at the start of *A Fish in the Water*. Mario Vargas Llosa, a child of ten, walks hand in hand with his mother to meet the man who is his father: Ernesto J. Vargas. The latter had been a problematic husband from the start. Aggressive and temperamental, he controlled his wife, forcing her to live as if in a prison during the five and a half months that their life together lasted. He then abandoned her despite her pregnancy, exposing her to shame and gossip. During the time the separation lasted, she was received by the Llosa family, with whom she created the lie she told the child: that the father was dead. Little Mario's life seemed destined to take place in an Eden of pampering, whether in Bolivia or Peru. But Ernesto J. Vargas reappeared in Mario's life after renewing through letters his relationship with his wife, who despite the separation from and mistreatment by her husband, continued to be in love with him: "My mama took me by the arm and led me out into the street by the service entrance of the prefecture . . . It was the final days of 1946 or the first days of 1947 . . . I had finished the fifth grade and summer in Piura, with its white light and asphyxiating heat, had already come. 'You already know it, of course,' my mama said, without her voice trembling. 'Isn't that so?' 'Know what?' 'That your papa isn't dead. Isn't that so?' 'Of course. Of course' (3).

It is obviously possible that the events did not exactly happen as told. All autobiographical texts imply a specular double movement by means of which authors write and read their life simultaneously. That is why the autobiographical text, as a form of writing, is mainly a form of reading. This disassociation manifests itself in the gap between the "I" that narrates the events and the "I" that experienced them. This gap widens in the case of childhood narratives, which, by definition, are never written during the period being described. In fact, childhood is the one stage of life in which, when narrated, the artificial character of autobiographical discourse becomes clear. This is because regardless of the author's scrupulousness, childhood evocations, which are generally discontinuous, contradictory, full of holes, become, when narrated from a later perspective, coherent, directed, and clear. The fact that generally in autobiographical discourse the author, the narrator, and the character end up fused, tends to fictionalize this discourse. Narrating one's childhood implies an analogous reinvention to that of nations imagining their origins.[3]

A Fish in the Water does not subscribe to the standard modality of childhood autobiography, but does provide us with one of the most intense and painful childhoods in Spanish American literature. It is a "tight" though not closed narrative. For instance, it's "overture" is curious and far from realism: a child of ten years answering "Of course. Of course" when informed that the father he believed dead is actually alive. I find this difficult to believe. In any case, the "overture" establishes a situation that will be recurrent throughout *A Fish in the Water*. I am referring to the fact that the protagonist discovers truths that ultimately lead to disappointment: the overall theme is of disappointment. Ernesto J. Vargas does not resemble the father in the photograph nor the one of family legend (23). And when he attempts to recover his "place" within the family structure he not only puts his overwhelming presence between mother and son, destabilizing their previous harmony and distancing the young protagonist from the close-knit Llosa clan, but also inflicts torments on his son not in the least inferior to those experienced by David Copperfield: humiliation, corporal punishment, and fear. There was also the father's inferred "betrayal" of the mother, whose love for her husband "had that excessive and transgressive nature of great love-passions that do not hesitate to defy heaven and even pay the price of going to hell in order to prevail" (51). We understand then, that one of the functions that the strategy of Vargas Llosa's self-representation as a child is to present himself as a victim and to interpellate the reader from that position, which is easy to do. How not to feel sympathy for that child whom Ernesto J. Vargas beats and frightens? How not to feel compassion when he cries and trembles in fear? How not to feel anger before the brutal process— one cannot avoid thinking of "compulsory heterosexuality"—by which the father attempts to "straighten" him, to make him a "little man" instead of the "sissy the Llosas had raised" (50).

Therefore, the child Vargas Llosa (like the mother) is a victim of the father, but at the same time, the father's violence externalizes a rigid self-control that makes Ernesto J. Vargas also a victim. A victim, in this case, of a rigorous regime of self-mortification: he does not drink alcohol, he has no relations with other women, nor does he indulge in hijinks, remaining a thrall to labor. Of his parents' sex life, the delights and enjoyments of conjugal life, Vargas Llosa says nothing and it would seem it was virtually nonexistent. Nevertheless, his father's malaise has deeper and more complex causes:

But the real reason for the failure of their marriage was not my father's jealousy or his bad disposition, but the national disease that gets called by other names, the one that infests every stratum and every family in the country and leaves them all with a bad aftertaste of hatred, poisoning the lives of Peruvians in the form of resentment and social complexes. Because Ernesto J. Vargas, despite his white skin, his light blue eyes and his handsome appearance, belonged—or always felt that he belonged, which amounts to the same thing—to a family socially inferior to his wife's. The adventures, misadventures, and deviltry of my paternal grandfather, Marcelino, had gradually impoverished and brought the Vargas family down in the world till they reached the ambiguous margin where those who are middle-class begin to be taken for what those of a higher status call "the people," and in a position where Peruvians who believe that they are *blancos* (whites) begin to feel that they are *cholos*, that is to say mestizos, half breeds of mixed Spanish and Indian blood, that is to say poor and despised. (5)

This structure of feeling not only explains the rancor and anger of the father but also illuminates the "impulses," "passions," and "political, professional, cultural, and personal rivalries" (6) that are experienced in Peru. These had already been revealed to the young writer during his teenage years at the military school Leoncio Prado, the setting of his first novel: *The Time of the Hero*. It is of interest that this passage, which attempts to understand his father's animosity toward his mother's family, concludes naturally with a reflection on the explosive social inequality of Peru and the colonial attribution of value to individuals according to race. The concept of race has served in Peru to legitimate the relations of domination that resulted from the conquest.[4] By presupposing the inferiority of the indigenous population—whose humanity was not always recognized and who, in the best-case scenario, were viewed as children—the social hierarchy of the colonial order was naturalized, providing an ethical justification for the need to control indigenous Peruvians. In this worldview, whiteness obliterated the social conditions of its own emergence in order to present itself as the highest level of society's social pyramid, as well as serving as the distinctive trait, or symbolic capital, of the dominant group.[5]

The crusade Vargas Llosa began in 1987 against García's attempt to nationalize banking and other related industries, which culminated in his campaign for the presidency of Peru, is based on more than a simple discrepancy with the economic model. It implies a rejection both of the manner in which the social is organized and certainly of that mercantilism of the skin that informs Peruvian society as a whole and that, in a complicated manner, has victimized him since childhood. In a first stage of his intellectual development, Vargas Llosa thought he had found in the Christian democracy a solution to the ailments that troubled (and still trouble) Peruvian society (297–300). In a second, he thought he had found it in socialism. After a lukewarm approximation to social democratic ideals—a fact not mentioned in *A Fish in the Water*—by the mid-1970s, the Peruvian novelist had found a solution in the liberal and anticommunist ideas of Raymond Aron, Milton Friedman, Friedrich von Hayek, Karl Popper, and Robert Nozick (88).[6] Since then, Vargas Llosa has endeavored to promote liberal ideas, especially in newspaper articles. Thus, against the intervention of the state in economic planning and as granter of privileges in detriment of private initiative and economic and political freedom, he defends the notion of citizenship, the abolition of privileges, protectionism, and monopolies. He favors the creation of an open society in which all have access to markets and enjoy protection under the law (152). (Given these ideas, for Vargas Llosa, socialism and mercantilism are equivalent [154–55].) Or to put it in more concise terms, Vargas Llosa believes in access "to what Hayek calls the inseparable trinity of civilization: legality, freedom, and property" (527).

However, the political program promoted by Vargas Llosa faced, as one might expect, resistance. First, the Movimiento Libertad, its central promoter, reproduced all the endemic vices of Peruvian political life: "bossism, cliques, factionalism" (157). Also, the entrepreneurial sector, which had supported Vargas Llosa's struggle against García's nationalizations, expressed fear and ended up rejecting the free market. Victims of mercantilist practices, entrepreneurs had become used to being passive, were psychologically insecure, feared competing in the global economy, and lacked the enterprising spirit of a true captain of industry (260). On their part, his ideological adversaries—Apristas (followers of the originally populist-leftists APRA party founded in 1924 by Victor Raúl Haya de la Torre), leftists—misrepresented Vargas Llosa's proposals. An example of this distortion of his ideas is the false claim that, if elected, he would have begun his administration by firing half a million state employees. In fact, he was proposing the gradual relocation of surplus workers, who would be given bonuses in order to make it appealing for them to retire or quit (351). One must point out that in this case Vargas Llosa genuinely believed in the virtues of the market to solve the problem through economic growth (354). But large sectors of the population were not convinced by these proposals. And here the notion of childishness reappears as an explanation for this rejection. In fact, Vargas Llosa considers that if he cannot communicate through speeches at large meetings, it is because his rational expository style, proven in multiple intellectual and academic forums, is not appealing to citizens used to the glib or superficially seductive rhetoric of the political orator who "goes up onto the platform to charm, to seduce, to *lull*, to bill and coo" (169; italics are mine). Moreover, the public possesses a fragile attention span and an elementary psychology. Vargas Llosa notes "the ease with which it can be made to pass from laughter to anger, be moved, be driven into a frenzy, be reduced to tears, in unison with the speaker" (169). As should be evident, the author uses the social infantilization of citizens as an explanation for what, otherwise, could be construed as an example of a poor communication strategy. His observations about the presence of primitive traits are of greater interest. For instance, when he explains his proposal to privatize collective land—a reform that in his opinion would benefit the poor—he notices that his peasant audience, "above all the most primitive of them," refuse to be convinced "because of centuries of mistrust and frustration, doubtless" (359). What never crosses Vargas Llosa's mind is that someone could reject his proposals *rationally* due to their different way of looking at things.

In the two examples given we have seen how the author has gone from describing as immature those who reject his liberal ideology to classifying them as primitive. Nevertheless, on occasion, he presents this regression in even more radical terms, as evidenced in a surprising passage found toward the end of the book:

> My grimmest memory of those days is that of my arrival, one torrid morning, in a little settlement . . . in the valley of Chira. Armed with stick and stones and all sorts of weapons to bruise and batter, an infuriated horde of men and women came to meet me . . . who appeared to have emerged from the depths of time, a prehistory in which men and animals were indistinguishable, since for both life was a blind struggle for survival. Half-naked, with very long hair and finger nails never touched by a pair of scissors, surrounded by emaciated children with huge swollen bellies, bellowing and shouting to keep their courage up, they hurled themselves on the caravan of vehicles as though fighting to save their lives or seeking to immolate themselves, with a rashness and a savagery that said everything about the almost inconceivable levels of deterioration to which life for millions of Peruvians had sunk. (514)

Vargas Llosa is perturbed by the abjection of the group that attacks him. When I refer to "abjection," I am not referring to the group's degradation, filth, or sickliness, but rather to the condition concomitant with a collapse of sense and the liberation of all that rejects limitations or rules: that which is liminal, hybrid, ambiguous, everything that perturbs identity and the borders that protect it.[7] This seems an inescapable reading of the author's rejection of that horde, which resembles a human grouping but is, in some manner, less than human, a hybrid that causes fear and repugnance in the author. This fear and repugnance originate not so much in their misery and nakedness as in their long hair and nails and their lack of culture. (I cannot help wonder what Vargas Llosa would have thought if he had had the chance of shaking hands with the French philosopher Gilles Deleuze). This is not the first moment in which long nails and hair appear as markers of antimodernity in *A Fish in the Water*. There were the members of the Iglesia Israelita del Nuevo Pacto (Israelite Church of the New Covenant) who practice a religious communitarianism and abstain from cutting hair and nails so as not to interfere with natural states of being. Mario Vargas Llosa interviewed the prophet and leader of the sect, Ezequiel Ataucusi Gamonal, and the head of the "apostles," Jeremías Ortiz Arcos, who had "tangled braided dreadlocks," in the home of the anthropologist Juan Ossio, who was studying this group at the time (435). The prophet seemed sympathetic toward Vargas Llosa and, during a moment in the meeting, grabbed his arm "with his black talons" and offered his support for the novelist's candidacy (435). This support did not materialize since Ataucusi decided to become a candidate himself.

The two episodes mentioned previously repeat an old reflexive gesture characteristic of Spanish American liberalism: primitivism as a repository where all elements resistant of their political projects, all groups that reject any type of insertion into market-based society, are assimilated. From this perspective, humanity is present only if a position within schemes of production is accepted. Moreover, an old romantic topos is actualized: the writer as epic hero.[8] He is the bringer of culture, the embodiment of the highest social values, who helps lead the people toward utopia.[9] A utopia elected—"countries today can *choose* to be prosperous" (44)—by means of the articulation of the country with international markets and that will bring development and promote advanced cultural values—"a culture based on success" (156).

The phrase "old reflexive gesture of Spanish American liberalism" needs to be stressed. Vargas Llosa constructs a narrative in which liberalism is presented as a new intellectual current within Peruvian society. According to the author, one of the virtues of the Encuentro por la Libertad (Encounter for Freedom) on August 21, 1987, at the Plaza San Martín consisted in that "it opened the doors of Peruvian political life to liberal thought that up until then had lacked a public presence, since all of our modern history had been, practically speaking, a monopoly of the ideological populisms of conservatives and socialists of various tendencies" (39). This is not correct. Liberalism has not been absent from Peruvian political life; nor does it lack responsibility in the manner in which Peruvian society has been designed.[10] To a great degree, the emancipation of Latin America found intellectual justification in the liberal creed, in particular its Eurocentrism and its belief that progress—a key notion—would be achieved by incorporating the nascent republics into the world industrial system. Liberalism introduced ideas of the Enlightenment: the need for a written constitution and the notion of citizenship; the rejection of authoritarianism; free markets in labor and goods; universal suffrage; equality of citizens before the state and law; separation of church and state. Liberalism also added to its intellectual repertoire ideas taken from thinkers such as Charles Darwin, Auguste Comte, and Herbert Spencer. This is not the place to recapitulate the history of liberalism in Spanish America, its contradictions, diverse manifestations, or achievements. What is important is to point out its decisive role in the creation of the models of identity upheld by the societies in which it was introduced. This role is not insignificant. Liberalism was one of the factors that, bolstered by the internal contradictions of a stratified society like that of Peru, contributed to stopping the dismantling of colonial class structures. The liberal constitutional models that were imposed in Spanish America excluded large sectors of the population, if not the majority, from citizenship, while, at the same time, the new social dynamics confirmed the privilege of few over the many. It is no accident, then, that race reappears in the center of the tumultuous electoral process in which Vargas Llosa participated, since his candidacy agglomerated precisely those sectors that, conscious or unconsciously, profited from the previously mentioned mercantilism of the skin. Vargas Llosa writes about a meeting that took place during the second electoral round:

> When I was shown the video of a rally in Villa El Salvador on May 9, in which Fujimori used the racial subject in this undisguised way . . . defining the electoral contest before a crowd of impoverished Indians and *cholos* from the city's squatter slums as a confrontation between whites and coloreds. I greatly regretted it, for stirring racial prejudice in that way meant playing with fire, but I thought it was going to bring him good results in the polls. Rancor, resentment, frustration of people exploited and marginalized for centuries, who saw the white man as someone who was powerful and an exploiter, could be wondrously well manipulated by a demagogue, if he continually repeated something that, moreover, had an apparent basis in fact: my candidacy had seemed to enjoy the support of the "whites" of Peru. (501–2)

That Vargas Llosa did not foresee that this element would sooner or later erupt in a campaign, such as the one in which he participated, can only be explained by a severe disconnection from the reality of the country he aspired to govern. In fact, Ricardo Belmont, a less-intelligent and less-sophisticated politician and communicator saw all of this clearly. In

1990, as head of a political movement named Movimiento Cívico Independiente OBRAS (Independent Civic Movement WORKS), he became Mayor of Lima, defeating the FREDEMO candidate. With great ease, Belmont noticed the connection between social position and race, as well as the potential rejection that a "white" candidate could arouse among an electorate of "color." Thus when, in July 1989, Belmont and Vargas Llosa have a meeting, the former declares, "My own class, the bourgeoisie, has nothing but contempt for me, because I talk slang and because they think I lack culture. However, even though *I'm a whitie*, mestizos and blacks from the shantytowns like me a lot and will vote for me" (132; my italics). Belmont has a populist style that allows him avoid being associated with the arrogance and exclusion that part of the Peruvian population attributes to the well-off white minority. This is why Vargas Llosa's use of Belmont's political success, as a counterexample that minimizes the import of his own whiteness, is particularly unsatisfying (315–16) given that, as he acknowledges in the last chapter of the book, "it is true that economic power has ordinarily been concentrated in the small minority with European ancestors, and poverty and wretchedness (this without exception) in aboriginal Peruvians or those of African origin. That miniscule minority which is white or can pass for white, thanks to money or ascending the social ladder, has never concealed its scorn for Peruvians of another color and another culture, to the point that expressions such as *cholo*, *mulato*, *zambo*, *chinocholo*, have in the mouth of this minority a pejorative connotation" (498–99).

Vargas Llosa notices *post festum* imaginary constructions that should have always been evident, given the experiences narrated. They problematize the coherence of his political alliances. In fact, it is difficult to understand why Vargas Llosa joined forces with that "miniscule minority which is white or can pass for white," (515) instead of with the informal entrepreneurs. The latter, *cholo* representatives of popular capitalism, had been identified and studied by Hernando de Soto in *The Other Path*; a text that had been enthusiastically championed by the Peruvian novelist. The explanation for his political alliances cannot be ideological affinity because, as is made clear in the fourth and twelfth chapters—"The Democratic Front" and "Schemers and Dragons"—many of those who supported his candidacy—the mercantilist entrepreneurs, the bosses, the mediocre, the opportunists—did not think like him or understand him. Therefore, their support can also be explained by means of the same irrationality that Vargas Llosa claims to find in those unwilling to grant him their votes (510) but that he does not stress when dealing with his supporters. The political opportunism of some of these sympathizers is confirmed in the "Colophon," when he analyzes the conduct of individual supporters.[11] Likewise, the explanation of these bad decisions on Vargas Llosa's part must be reviewed with care. While in some cases he admits to having made errors—such as his mistaken interpretation of the political meetings of April 1990 in Cuzco, Lima, and Arequipa before the first electoral round (439–40)—in other passages he seems to seek the understanding of the reader using, again, the strategy of self-victimization (the "child in politics"), as is evidenced in Chapter 18—"The Dirty War." Vargas Llosa's experiences never lead him to question the perspective from which he judges and evaluates events.

Despite his statements otherwise, this point of view does not differ substantially from the revolutionary ideals to which he ascribed when young. Instead of a grand socialist narrative, he now proposes an alternative metanarrative in which the protagonist is the economic rationalism of liberalism. In both cases, a univocal teleological emancipation is proposed, in which dissimilar experiences are made homogeneous under the hegemony of a universal trait understood as such from a logical and rational perspective. Vargas Llosa never questions the existence of a unitary criterion of rationality, nor notices the fact that he can determine irrationality as the explicative hypothesis for the misencounter between author and a large number of the voters only on the basis of a principle of exclusion. The liberalism of Vargas Llosa proposes at its core a rational and free subject, self-defined on the basis of its market choices in its attempt at maximizing personal benefit. However, it happens that the globalized world in which we live (and in which arguably we already lived in 1990), is one in which corporations are the main agents, where there is no place precisely for the pioneering individualism of primitive capitalism.

Moreover, is not this liberal confidence in the rationality of a centered and free subject too simple in conceptual terms? After all, as poststructuralist thought has shown us, the unity of the subject is, in reality, a fiction derived from a metaphysic of presence, incomprehensible without the mediation of signs. In the same vein, could not one think that, by means of technologies of the self and of self-control, the modern state forms the subjects that fulfill these predetermined roles?[12] These are just two questions that come to mind after finishing reading *A Fish in the Water*; a memorable text that provides us throughout its pages a much more complex individual than the ideological self the writer overtly defines.

NOTES

1. The borders between autobiography and memoir are not clear. Nevertheless, one may conclude that the first assumes the totality of an individual, while the second concentrates on one aspect of the individual's life in which what is determining are social circumstances that both include and exceed it (Lecarme 49–50). In fact, memoirs are a didactic-essayistic genre which gains importance from the eighteenth century on as a means for the recovery of history by means of testimony or chronicle (García Berrio 227). *A Fish in the Water* manifests a tension between both modalities (autobiography and memoir). The text claims the condition of memoir but one of its two narrative lines deals with the author's formative process.

2. See Archard 30–33.

3. There are numerous writings on the subject of autobiography and memoirs. In this article I follow the ideas of De Man ("Autobiography as De-Facement"), Gilmore and Lecarme-Tabone.

4. On the role of race in Peru and Spanish-America, see Manrique (*La piel y la pluma*) and Quijano.

5. I take the concept of "mercantilism of the skin" from Carlos Iván Degregori, author of the best analysis of the Peruvian elections of 1990 that I know of: "El aprendiz de brujo y el curandero chino. Etnicidad, modernidad y ciudadanía." Writing about the *criollos*, Degregori describes them as follows: "upper and middle classes, of white and mestizo skins colors, mostly descendants of Spaniards, even though from the end of the [nineteenth century] immigrants from other European countries join their ranks." He also adds to these groups, "popular *criollo* sectors, especially from Lima, that share in the codes of the dominant *criollos*" (88).

6. On Vargas Llosa's (temporary) closeness to social democratic ideas, see "La falacia del tercermundismo," his review of Carlos Rangel's *El tercermundismo*.

7. See Kristeva 1–10.

8. At the height of the electoral campaign, Vargas Llosa looks ironically at his predicament by writing a poem on Hercules and his labors. It is of interest that the poem, titled "Alcides," privileges the maternal line of the hero's genealogy, since Alcides as a name is derived from Alcmene, Hercules's mother. It is surprising that this poem, the first published by the author, has received no critical comments till now.

9. See Vidal 50–56.

10. See Romero, 155–71.

11. Alma Guillermoprieto has argued in favor of explaining Vargas Llosa's inability to judge his supporters by "the possibility that, as an adult, he never ceased feeling illegitimate and deferential in the presence of the moneyed class, and willing to suspend disbelief" (177).

12. These arguments are based on Foucault ("The Subject and Power") and Jameson ("Postmodernism and Consumer Society").

PART III

MARIO VARGAS LLOSA IN THE TWENTY-FIRST CENTURY

CHAPTER 8

SEX, POLITICS, AND HIGH ART

VARGAS LLOSA'S LONG ROAD TO *THE FEAST OF THE GOAT*

GENE H. BELL-VILLADA[1]

THE LAUNCHING OF VARGAS LLOSA'S *THE FEAST OF THE Goat* (2000) in Spain unleashed something of a cultural whirlwind. Indeed, the coming-out of the *Goat* may well become a legend in the annals of book publishing, comparable to that we associate with, say, *One Hundred Years of Solitude*. The initial print run of ten thousand copies sold out in a day. In Santo Domingo, the Dominican capital, *The Feast of the Goat* was presented at the Hotel Jaragua (the place where the character Urania Cabral stays and the setting for her first and final scenes) before an audience of a thousand (Armas Marcelo 443). A local supermarket chain called La Cadena ran full-page ads offering a free bottle of wine with each purchase of *The Feast of the Goat* (Gewecke 152). Meanwhile some high-placed Dominicans, feeling unfairly singled out as Trujillistas in the novel, protested angrily about the alleged literary injustice done them.

Vargas Llosa, on a book tour, arrived at Santo Domingo airport with bodyguards for himself and for his family. The author's literary excursion would go on to include stops in Buenos Aires, Lima, Mexico City, and even Miami. Elsewhere, in the UK and Switzerland, reviews appeared in the press even before the respective translations were out (Köllmann, "*La fiesta del chivo*" 135).

The publishing event next became a mass reading event. Spanish critic J. J. Armas Marcelo remarks on the possibly hundreds of thousands of Hispanic readers who were possessed by Vargas Llosa's book, reading it at top speed and then passionately discussing it with others (Armas Marcelo 135). As we all know, it's not every day that a serious, complex work of literary *and* political fiction arouses such broadly based interest.

I was a minor participant in that literary wave. As a casual reader, I gobbled up the novel's five-hundred-plus pages in just two sittings while on vacation in New Mexico, just months after its appearance in print, and was subsequently invited to review the English version for *Commonweal* magazine a year thereafter. Later, on November 14, 2002, I saw Mario Vargas Llosa read aloud from the *The Feast of the Goat* (in the fine translation by Edith Grossman) to a packed audience at Skidmore College. His selection came from chapter 2, the first of six strategically placed close-ups portraying the sordid doings of real-life General Rafael Leónidas Trujillo, dictator of the Dominican Republic, 1930 to 1961 (and still widely regarded as one of the worst despots in Latin America's history). These chapters depict the tyrant during the last day of his life as he goes through his ordinary, vicious routines while at the same time reminiscing about his brutal triumphs and occasional defeats.

The Peruvian novelist's recitation was only the first in a series of events connected with Skidmore's awarding him an honorary doctorate later that evening. Next day, Robert Boyers (editor of *Salmagundi*) and I paired off doing a public interview with Vargas Llosa before a large gathering that included my senior-seminar students and colleagues from Williams. The conversation eventually appeared in the Summer–Fall 2007 issue of that respected journal.

A RETURN TO FORM

This massive, international response was a vindication of the author's efforts. An indefatigable researcher, Vargas Llosa had spent three and a half years on the *The Feast of the Goat*. He combed Dominican dailies of the time, perused every book he could find about the period, dug into the country's national archives, and conducted countless interviews, some with Trujillista collaborators, even and including three encounters with Joaquín Balaguer, Trujillo's successor and the wily protagonist of the last third of *The Feast of the Goat*. In one unsettling comic incident, the Peruvian author attended a dinner with some erstwhile secretaries and supporters of Trujillo, all of whom referred to the dictator in the present tense, as if he were still living, reverentially calling him "The Chief" and "His Excellency" (López-Calvo 34). This living presence after death is an extreme instance of Vargas Llosa's larger theme: namely, Trujillo's total sway over his compatriots "not only over their conduct but also over their minds and even their dreams," or their "spiritual vassalage," in the author's own words (*The Feast of the Goat* 434).

The book is a technical tour de force on a grand scale, a return to those vast, "totalizing" novels the author Vargas Llosa painstakingly composed in the 1960s—*The Green House* (1966), *Conversation in the Cathedral* (1969)—and achieved yet again in 1981 with *The War of the End of the World*. As he does in those earlier works, the author skillfully juggles a number of equally important plotlines. At the center of it all is Trujillo himself, a foul-mouthed lout and frankly loathsome. Vargas Llosa takes on the enormous risk of painting the dictator from up close, albeit in third person, and succeeds in doing so with mastery and flair.

Actively opposing the vile despot are seven coconspirators, disaffected army officers who, for the first half of the novel, sit secretly in two cars parked on the Malecón, the city's seaside boulevard. Waiting tensely for the despot, who is expected to be bound for his country mansion in his limousine, they're itching to assassinate him and thereby avenge past hurts inflicted on them and their kin by Trujillo.

As really happened in 1961, the conspirators are victorious—but only in phase one of the total plot. They down the old dictator in a torrent of gunfire. Then everything goes afoul. A top army general named "Pupo" Román, who was slated to seize power on their behalf, gets hopelessly caught up in the machinery of rules and hierarchy, and proves unable to take decisive action. The Trujillista system continues to function of its own accord. Most of the plotters are captured ("Pupo" Román included) and, in some horrific scenes, are subjected to blood-curdling tortures and then death.

Amid this turmoil we witness the rise of Joaquín Balaguer, Trujillo's right-hand man and a most unlikely politician. Round-faced and squat, a mellifluous man of letters with no military experience, he is the palace politician extraordinaire. A master of discretion and protocol, sublimely uninterested in money or sex, he never once loses his composure and slowly succeeds in besting Trujillo's closest retainers—the late dictator's own wife and son Ramfis included. If Balaguer had not existed, his character may well have strained credulity.

Framing the historical portions of *The Feast of the Goat* is the only purely fictional material and the sole subplot focused on family life and feelings. It tells of Urania Cabral, a successful, forty-nine-year-old spinster-lawyer who lives in Manhattan and has returned to the island nation for the first time in three decades. Her father, a onetime Trujillista senator, had sent her off to 'El Norte' after the dictator's failed attempt (due to impotence) at seducing the pubescent virgin. Despite Trujillo's going limp with her in bed, she nonetheless suffered some chilling indignities, the result both of the despot's sick salaciousness and the spineless opportunism of her dad, who'd actually offered her to the tyrant simply to regain political favor. Following some long, painful conversations with her relatives and her now-mute, paralyzed father (through which Vargas Llosa shows us the more emotional, spiritual damage caused by the régime), Urania will return to New York City with some slight balance restored to her skewed and painful life.

Vargas Llosa brilliantly depicts a political system in which sadism has become the ordinary, everyday norm. Yet the book's pages show not a hint of preachy didacticism. *The Feast of the Goat* is primarily a story, driven by certain narrative principles to which the novelist has steadfastly adhered over the course of his writing career. First, there is the example of the novel of adventure. From his most youthful scribbling days, Vargas Llosa found a model to emulate in Dumas's musketeers and Monte Cristo, those action-packed tales that keep readers in suspense, avidly turning pages just to see what happens next. Some of the Peruvian's most complex works function precisely this way, and such is the immediate strength of *The Feast of the Goat*.

Second, there is Flaubert, admired from early on by the young novelist for his "works that are rigorously and symmetrically constructed" (*The Perpetual Orgy* 10). Flaubert's letters—Vargas Llosa notes in *The Perpetual Orgy*, an in-depth study of the French author—show us the latter's "fanatic concern for form" (37), the "inch-by-inch conquest" (34) through which he succeeded in perfecting his craft. Add to this formal rigor Flaubert's famous objectivity, his making every effort to be in his novels "like God in His creation—invisible and all-powerful . . . everywhere but never seen," as the hermit of Croisset remarked in a missive to his mistress Louise Colet (qtd. in Kristal *Temptation of the Word* 209).

Besides these triumphs of high artistry, the raw, human content in Flaubert has always captivated Vargas Llosa. In contrast to Balzac's larger-than-life buccaneers or Dickens's vivid eccentrics, Flaubert's cast of characters is rather "the realm of mediocrity, the gray universe of the man without qualities" (*The Perpetual Orgy* 214). Last but not least, one must mention the heady brew of "rebellion-vulgarity-violence-sex" that, as Vargas Llosa points out, is the lifeblood of Bovary (30), along with the ways in which sexual and economic life intermingle. These literary *aperçus*, first published in Spanish in 1975, seem custom-made for the "rebellion-vulgarity-violence-sex" found in *The Feast of the Goat*, as well as for many of its characters, who—their uncontrolled cruelty, power lust, and sexual

appetites aside—are rather ordinary, unremarkable sorts. Vargas Llosa's
art gives flesh to the banality of evildoers.

Yet another key factor in *The Feast of the Goat* is the subjacent presence of Faulkner, "the first novelist I read with pencil and paper in hand,"
the author reflected in a 1989 interview with Ricardo Setti (Setti 34).
Faulkner, notes the Peruvian in his own essay on the making of *The Green
House*, "was always for me the paradigmatic novelist (he still is)" (*Historia
secreta de una novela* 58). Significantly, during his apprenticeship Vargas
Llosa was quite taken with *The Wild Palms* and its unique device: the
unfolding of two separate, parallel plots that not once intersect. Much
of *The Green House* operates in precisely this way, with, for instance, its
wholly self-contained subplot involving the Japanese adventurer, Fushía.
In similar fashion, in *The Feast of the Goat*, the divers accounts of the
conspirators, of Urania, and of Balaguer overlap but minimally and are
related only through the central, unifying matter of Trujillo.

As with many Latin Americans who started out in the 1950s,
Faulkner's nonlinear structuring of time and his organizing narrative as
a set of contending, unreliable narrators, helped Vargas Llosa reimagine
his homeland and its peoples from the ground up (and I mean that literally: from the jungle, the desert, the river, the city, the mansion, and
the slum all at once). In *The Feast of the Goat*, similarly, the flashbacks
furnished to us by the several plotters' recollections, by the returnee
Urania in her anguished family conversations, and by Trujillo himself
in his torrential ravings all set forth the antecedents to current actions—
the troubled past that has produced a horrendous present. By the year
2000, of course, Faulknerian technique had been all but normalized in
fiction writing (and in film editing) the world over, to the point where
many casual readers of *The Feast of the Goat* may well have been scarcely
aware of its "experimental" construction.

The meticulous structuring of *The Feast of the Goat* merits close attention. The novel divides precisely in half, both in terms of its two dozen
chapters (1 to 12; 13 to 24) and almost as neatly in its page numbers
(pages 11 to 251; pages 252 to 518). The cutoff line, as one expects,
is the dramatic assassination of Trujillo at the end of the book's twelfth
chapter. Perhaps not accidentally, the opening word of that first half is
"Urania" while, by contrast, the concluding Spanish noun, in chapter 12,
is "Maligno."[2]

The book's initial portion adheres to a fairly rigorous sequence: four
sets of three-chapter clusters (1 to 3; 4 to 6; 7 to 9; 10 to 12). Each set in
turn holds to a specific, recurring pattern, namely, (1) Urania, (2) Trujillo,

and (3) the coconspirators. As the dozen unfolds, the chapters evolve as follows:

- *Chapters 1, 4, 7, and 10.* Urania's return to Santo Domingo and visit with her relatives, alternating with flashbacks to her father and his political career.
- *Chapters 2, 5, 8, and 11.* Trujillo in his final days. Alone with his routines, or in the company of his closest allies (Johnny Abbes, Chirinos, Simon Gittleman), and with the bothersome memory of "the girl" (revealed in the last chapter to be an adolescent Urania). Relevant flashbacks to the dictator's past.
- *Chapters 3, 6, 9, and 12.* The quartet of midlevel army officers, coconspirators in tyrannicide, waiting tensely inside a car on the Malecón: they are Salvador García Sadhalá ("el Turco"), Amado García Guerrero ("Amadito"), Antonio de la Maza ("Tony"), and Antonio Imbert. Each of these chapters centers in part on a select member of the foursome, evoking via flashbacks his background and recalling his soured ties to the regime. Somewhere behind the group, in another car, sit an additional three coconspirators; one of them, Pedro Livio Cedeño, will end up accidentally wounded in the rain of bullets, with tragic consequences.

As the latter half of *The Feast of the Goat* unfolds, the narrative pattern undergoes a gradual change, is ultimately disrupted and scrambled. Such formal shifts are appropriate, given that the stable but brutal Trujillo order has been shattered, and in its stead an unpredictable chaos now grips the (political and literary) system. Were the original sequence to be retained, the next three-chapter bundles would have been 13 to 15, 16 to 18, 19 to 21, and 22 to 24.

Not so, however. While chapters 13 and 16 still maintain the focus on Urania, the sequence is totally abandoned in chapters 19 and 22, which would "normally" be hers. Urania will only resurface in the concluding chapter, number 24, where we at last read of her sordid, skin-crawling, bedroom episode with 'El Jefe.' Coming not long after the horrendous bodily tortures of chapters 19 through 21, the young girl's sexual-psychological abuse may arguably pale by comparison, yet it builds up as an event as horrific and morally offensive as are the physical ordeals and death endured by the adult officers.

The tripartite cluster just after the halfway point repeats the familiar template, though with certain subtle differences. Following Urania's evolving tale in chapter 13, number 14 remains a chapter about Trujillo, yet in this case depicting him, for the first time, in a tense private meeting with Balaguer—and thereby preparing us readers for the impending "succession." The fifteenth/third chapter does stick with the conspirators-turned-tyrannicides, but now moves away from the original quartet in the front car to trace the aftermath of the wounding of rear-vehicle passenger Pedro Livio Cedeño—his transfer to a clinic, and his detention, interrogation, and torture at the hands of Johnny Abbes.

The set 16 through 18 again starts with Urania; the next couple of chapters, however, break with the established arrangement. Number 17 drops Trujillo temporarily and relates instead the precarious situation, flight, and murder of conspirator Amadito. And the eighteenth/third chapter brings about a kind of fusion, or a reversal: it now portrays the dictator in his final hour, riding in his limousine, with his brief visit to his mother, his last perceptions (the familiar houses that pass by on the Malecón), his dashed hopes (the aborted encounter with Moni), his other preoccupations, and as ever, appropriate flashbacks. In the last paragraph, Trujillo hears shots, reaches for a gun, and feels bullets in his arm. It is thus the Malecón scene, this time narrated not from the viewpoint of the four anxious junior officers but from that of their feared, despised target and top-dog villain.

The pattern is all but gone in chapters 19 to 21, a set focusing exclusively on state terror, repression, murder, and sheer sadism. Number 19 depicts Tony de la Maza and (from the second car) Juan Tomás Díaz relentlessly on the lam and eventually brought down by gunfire. The twentieth tells of high conspirator General "Pupo" Román's fatal indecision and paralysis, culminating in his final torture and death by Trujillo's son Ramfis. The twenty-first/third chapter in a sense folds back and again gathers the surviving coconspirators as a group, though now as hapless detainees who are imprisoned, racked, and in the end brutally murdered (along with a trio of innocent rookie guards) by the security forces over some seaside cliffs. These hair-raising chapters, amazingly enough, stretch out over a period of more than three months.

Yet one more sequence emerges in 22–24, the final bundle and, structurally, the novel's dénouement. The first in the cluster tells of the astounding ascendancy of the crafty conniver and phrasemaker Joaquín Balaguer. Accordingly, the chapter's style at times takes on the wily courtier's flowery speech, his pseudoreligious and patriotic rhetoric, often paraphrasing him sans quotation marks and employing such high-sounding technicisms as "consubstantially" and "dialectically." By contrast, number 23 contains what are the most serene moments in the book, showing Antonio Imbert securely hiding in the home of the Cavaglieris, the

Italian husband of the couple being a fortunate employee of his country's embassy. Narrated in a straight, simple, direct prose, the episode offers a distinct foil to the insidious artifice and ornate falsehoods that typify Balaguer's previous chapter. The finale, number 24, brings things full circle with Urania's remembrance of her past sexual abuse and its enduring effects up to the present, though the book ends on a note of possible reconciliation with her estranged female relatives.

In addition to the novel's large-scale architecture, there is a yet more subtle geometry holding these disparate elements together. I am referring to certain narrative cross-references and verbatim repetitions that help bind the later chapters into a fully integrated totality. The most extensive instances thereof can be found between Chapter 20, which concentrates on the erratic behavior of Pupo Román, and Chapter 22, on Balaguer's steady rise to power. In the earlier episode, Pupo wakes up the civilian president with a nighttime phone call, informing him of an urgent meeting at a military location. After a long silence, Balaguer proffers this measured, emotionless reply: "If something so serious has occurred, then as President of the Republic my place is not in a barracks but at the National Palace. I am going there now. I suggest the meeting be held in my office. Goodbye." The statement appears halfway through Pupo Román's chapter (317) and also in the opening paragraph of Balaguer's (346) and in each case is followed by the president's abruptly hanging up on a nonplussed Pupo.

Many of the minutiae of plot and dialogue from the Pupo-Balaguer face-off are then relayed in the president's chapter, though indirectly and with altered phraseology, and from the erstwhile puppet's point of view. In a revealing instance, the general has just given the civilian chief of state a lengthy tongue-lashing that ends, "Who the hell do you think you are?" And we read, "The little man looked at him *as if he were listening to the rain.* After observing him for a moment, he smiled amiably" (324, emphasis added). Pupo's scolding reappears in chapter 22, yet much abbreviated and this time with the army officer waving a submachine gun at Balaguer. At this point the narrative proceeds, "The President remained imperturbable, looking him in the eye. *He felt invisible rain in his face, the general's spittle.* This lunatic would not fire now" (353, emphasis added). The seeming rain was thus actually an excited, uncontrolled Pupo's saliva—though the latter didn't realize it—and here comes off as part of his gradual defeat.

Numerous other hidden parallels exist between these two chapters, all of which serve to offer differing, Faulknerian perspectives on the same event. An entire analytical essay could indeed be written about this network of cross-references in Vargas Llosa's novel. In a comparable if briefer example from another episode, we find out at the end of chapter 20 that coconspirator Luis Amiamá had been hiding in a closet at the home of the Health Minister; fifty pages hence, as Imbert's quiet chapter 23 comes to an end, the lucky fugitive hears over the airwaves the news about the survival of colleague Amiamá.

It is this intricacy of design that makes *The Feast of the Goat* both a compelling read and a satisfying artistic experience. I would further argue, moreover, that the strict geometric framework of Vargas Llosa's novel furnishes for its torture episodes a key prop and scaffold that renders more bearable their infrahuman evils, saves those chapters from degenerating into a catalog of horrors. When we read comparable nonfiction—say, a *testimonio* by Jacobo Timerman or Alicia Partnoy—the simply assumed fact that the story being told is personal and true lends it an immediate solidity and legitimacy, and we thus expect less in the way of structural, narrative, or stylistic artifice. In a novel about evil and suffering, however, even a historical one, simply to string accounts of misdeeds and atrocities will not suffice. Some organizing principles are necessary—and the more of them, the better. To bring in another analogy, what distinguishes *King Lear* from many a second-tier, blood-soaked Jacobean drama is Shakespeare's elaborate yet precise plotting, along with his highly distilled poetic language. Tragic pity and fear are by no means a given; they must be earned and can be evoked only via artistry and craft.

IDEOLOGICAL SHIFTS

The combined legacy of Dumas, Faulkner, and Flaubert helped shape Vargas Llosa's narrative practice from his very first novel, *The Time of the Hero* (1962), and on to his most ambitious ones: *The Green House, Conversation in the Cathedral,* and *The War of the End of the World.* Indeed, *The Feast of the Goat* in many ways is a return to his bold and wideranging experiments from the 1960s. In certain other ways, however, the Peruvian's account of Trujillo is a new kind of marker, a different sort of milestone in his personal literary history, for several reasons.

Following *The War of the End of the World,* the novelist had drastically narrowed his compass, concentrating rather on the smaller-scale landscapes of *The Storyteller* (1986), *Who Killed Palomino Molero?* (1989), and *Death in the Andes* (1993). The scope in these and other Vargas Llosa fictions of the same vintage is much reduced, and the writing not consistently among his finest. From almost any lesser-known author, such novels might be seen as good enough and promising, might even have been praised highly. In the case of Vargas Llosa, however, they stand in the intimidating shadow of his own early masterpieces. (Like Mailer, Vargas Llosa had the rare good fortune of producing some of his most innovative work while still barely thirty.) Even the greatest of fans might have concluded that the Peruvian's worthiest books were behind him.

And then there were the ongoing ideological shifts over three decades. In the 1960s Vargas Llosa, like most prominent, young, Latin American intellectuals at the time, was a convinced socialist, an ardent anti-imperialist, and a committed supporter of the Cuban Revolution. His literary model then was the leftist Jean-Paul Sartre. And in his fiction as well as his essays, he was not averse to citing Marx, Engels, and Lenin. In *Conversation in the Cathedral* about the only positive (indeed heroic) characters are the left-wing activists and Marxist youths whom the disaffected protagonist, Santiago Zavala, befriends while enrolled at San Marcos University.

Vargas Llosa's socialist faith was shaken in 1971, when the Castro regime arrested the Cuban poet Heberto Padilla and forced him to "confess" publicly to alleged counterrevolutionary sins In response, dozens of leftist intellectuals from Europe and Latin America—among them Sartre, Beauvoir, Enzensberger, Fuentes, and Vargas Llosa—signed letters of protest to Fidel Castro expressing their concern and, on one occasion, comparing the Padilla affair to "the most sordid moments of Stalinism" ("Carta a Fidel Castro" 250). The Padilla episode marked a dramatic end to the twelve-year honeymoon between Western socialists and the Cuban Revolution.

Most of those international protestors nevertheless would remain situated on the Left. Vargas Llosa by contrast broke with the Cuban project and moved to the center of the political spectrum, a shift that earned him much verbal abuse in Cuba and elsewhere. And so, during the 1970s and early 1980s he started identifying himself as equally opposed to Marxist caudillo Castro in Cuba and to the barracks tyrant Pinochet in Chile. Former literary hero Sartre was now replaced by Camus, whose humanistic conception of life and centrist dislike of all fanatics and dictatorships (French colonial rule in Algeria excepted) were now more in tune with the reinvented Vargas Llosa. (The Peruvian even published in 1981 a book of essays, *Entre Sartre y Camus* [*Between Sartre and Camus*].) The change is dramatically reflected in *The War of the End of the World*, in which virtually all political actors—religious rebels in Canudos, roving anarchist Galileo Gall, republican press publicists, Brazilian army officers—come off as deluded fanatics. Only the refined and civilized Baron of Cañabrava, who remains steadfastly aloof from all extreme positions, stands out as a positive figure.

And then, during the late 1980s, Vargas Llosa became an avowed conservative. His shift was partly in reaction to the horrors inflicted by the demented Shining Path guerrillas and the monumental incompetence of the left-leaning APRA government of President Alán García. One particular moment of truth for the author came when the García administration nationalized the banks. In response, Vargas Llosa joined in with the massive street demonstrations that reviled the move as state tyranny. This moment of activism eventually launched Vargas Llosa onto his brief career as party politician: in 1989 he ran a vigorous campaign for the Peruvian presidency on a conservative ticket. And then, at the eleventh hour, there arose the dark-horse candidacy of Alberto Fujimori, an agronomy professor who adopted a populist stance while attacking Vargas Llosa as a pretty-boy candidate of the rich.

Vargas Llosa lost. Ironically, Fujimori then went on to apply the same free-market formulas that Vargas Llosa had so passionately espoused. Disillusioned with political life, the novelist now returned to his strictly literary vocation and wrote eloquently about the presidential battle in the even-numbered chapters of his memoir, *A Fish in the Water*.

One might think that, following his experience with the political jungle, Vargas Llosa would mellow ideologically. But he would surprise his readers with yet another rightward shift. In the 1990s, the author emerged as an uncompromising libertarian, in the U.S. sense. (In Europe, it should be noted, "libertarian" means "anarchist.") His patron saints are now the all but merciless free-marketeers Ludwig von Mises, Friedrich von Hayek, Robert Nozick and Milton Friedman. He has dined with Baroness Thatcher. (On the other hand he is not above referring to Gabriel García Márquez as "a courtier of Castro" ["Vargas Llosa llama a García Márquez" 27]). His new Latin American heroes are the ubiquitous street vendors, whom he construes as carriers of the entrepreneurial future. And in his biweekly columns for the prestigious Madrid daily *El País*, he rails regularly against labor unions, state pensions, the European welfare state (of all things), and *any* form of government intervention in the market. He praises "labor flexibility" (i.e., absence of job security) as beneficial for all—including their employees. And, in "El futuro incierto de América Latina," an October 18, 2004 "Piedra de toque" article for *El País*, he hails South Korea, Taiwan, and Singapore as models because of their modernization and ability to integrate themselves into the world economy.[3] This meant turning a blind eye to their protectionism, their often-interventionist economic policies, and their early agrarian reform programs that had distributed large landholdings to local small farmers.[4]

As part of his evolving libertarianism, Vargas Llosa assumed a critical stance toward Latin American indigenist movements and their supporters abroad. For him, assimilation to Western ways is the only answer. In

an article he published on the eve of the 1992 Columbus quincenten-
nial, Vargas Llosa remarks, "If forced to choose between the preservation
of Indian cultures and their complete assimilation, with great sadness I
would choose modernization of the Indian population . . . Modernization is possible only with the sacrifice of the Indian culture ("Questions
of Conquest" 52–53). Replying to those activists who wish to legitimize
the indigenist past, the novelist routinely counters with the question: Oh,
then do you also wish to revive human sacrifice?

This latter possibility is actually raised in *Death in the Andes*, which
tells, among other things, of some hapless individuals mysteriously disappearing, in succession, from a remote Andean village. At first the Shining Path guerrillas are the prime suspects as kidnappers. In time, a more
macabre truth comes into view: a local tavern keeper, his wife, and some
allies of the couple have been secretly practicing human sacrifice and cannibalism in order to placate totem beasts and mountain spirits. Even *The
Storyteller*, a novel much more sympathetic to a group of forest-dwelling
Indians, has as its protagonist Saúl Zuratas, a voluble young Jew from
Lima whose adult decision to join the Machiguenga tribe is portrayed as
an eccentric, utopian impulse. In these middle-period books we see Vargas Llosa the avowed liberal, subtly putting "totalitarian" and "fanatical"
elements in a less than positive light.

Vargas Llosa's literary admirers often express private dismay at his
metamorphosis into an apostle for the libertarian creed. And no doubt
there is something rigid and unforgiving about the author's latter-day
position. As a political thinker he seems to have become almost as much
of a hard-line ideologue as the dogmatic leftists, meddlesome bureau-
crats, and assorted fanatics he is given to spoofing in fiction and bashing
in articles and speeches. Some of his opinion columns can on occasion
sound like extracts from a novel by Ayn Rand.

The born-again conservatism of Vargas Llosa, moreover, coincided
with the eighteen-year stretch of narrowed art that I've described earlier.
For his critics, great was the temptation to explain his artistic downturn
as bound up with his hardening in ideology. There are well-known precedents for this pattern, notably Wordsworth, Dos Passos, and cummings,
whose conversion to a crabbed conservatism was accompanied by a palpable decline in their respective literary art.

The Feast of the Goat thus came as a surprise. Among the book's immediate and most striking traits was its vast range, comparable to that of
the author's superb early works. The other salient characteristic was *The
Feast of the Goat*'s having absolutely nothing to do with Peru and its gut-
wrenching issues. Vargas Llosa seemed to have successfully distanced

himself from that personal/political tangle and its associated hurts. He had reinvented himself yet again.

The choice of a country and topic largely alien to Vargas Llosa's demons, moreover, allowed him to recapture the serene, Flaubertian objectivity that had been the hallmark of even his most disquieting early narratives. One could now distinguish the vital, innovative novelist from the dogmatic, libertarian propagandist—and with the author's explicit blessing: to a question from a member of an audience who had brought up precisely this disjunction, Vargas Llosa pointedly replied, "Read my novels, and avoid my articles, essays, lectures, and interviews" (Armas Marcelo 446). The critical ideal of separating the artist from the person became something miraculously realizable with *The Feast of the Goat*.

A NEW TWIST FOR A POLITICAL NOVELIST

From the outset of his writing career, Vargas Llosa has stood out as a powerful political novelist, or, if you will, as a novelist about politics. Whether the subject be life in a military school, or the abuses against both young girls and independent rubber tappers in the Amazon, or the sinister manipulations of the secret police under the eight-year bar-racks dictatorship (1948–1956) of General Manuel Odría, the Peruvian author has given verbal flesh to some highly disturbing sociopolitical facts in his homeland.

Latin America, of course, has an inordinately long history of political fiction, a great deal of which has sunk into oblivion—the sad fate of so much protest literature. This less-than-solid tradition was given a new artistic turn by the novelists of the so-called Boom. Authors such as Juan Rulfo, Carlos Fuentes, Gabriel García Márquez, and Vargas Llosa (among others) would learn from international Modernism and write under the assumption that a novel must be lovingly crafted and that, in fiction, complex political realities are best served by correspondingly complex techniques and structures. Simply pointing at, shedding light and opening a window on injustices was not enough, the novelists recognized; the pointers, the light, and the windows needed their own density and texture, too. Or as Vargas Llosa remarks in *The Perpetual Orgy*, "the choice of a 'realistic' subject does not free a writer of narrative of formal responsibility" (221).

For the young writers who came of age during the budding years of the "Boom," Faulkner was the indispensable teacher. His works dem-onstrated to budding novices that the horrors of war, slavery, and rac-ism can be effectively conveyed via thick prose, nonlinear organization, and a set of shifting narrators. Faulkner wasn't the sole master, however; Kafka, Joyce, Camus, Dos Passos, and even Virginia Woolf contributed to this literary transculturation and innovation. In many regards the Latin American Boom stands as the most consummate latter-day heir to the Euro-American modernist revolution.

Vargas Llosa, for his part, reinvents and represents all sorts of social injustice and human suffering via his own dazzling, modernist-inspired craft and formal wizardry. The Peruvian, let it be said, is among the most technically conscious authors in history. In his book-length studies of García Márquez and Flaubert, he spends many pages examining those authors' technical procedures. Vargas Llosa has also held academic positions on three continents, and as a teacher he is known for focusing large amounts of attention on narrative technique. Accordingly, some of the author's critics like to supplement their verbal analyses with diagrams that help us visualize the elaborateness of his novelistic scaffolds (see Oviedo, 132, 253).

This architectural rigor is perhaps all but necessary in works whose casts of characters can number several dozen and whose four or five plots and still more subplots alternately intertwine and separate and then meet and diverge yet again. One of his chief resources takes its cue from Flaubert: I am referring to the technique of freely intermingling conversations from different situations and/or time frames in the plotline of a novel. In the Peruvian's hands it becomes his own signature device, much as the fictive essay and invented author are for Borges, magico-realist folk events are for García Márquez, or one-way dialogue is for Puig.

To my knowledge, in prose fiction the technique had its premiere in part 2, chapter 8 of *Madame Bovary*: the famous scene in which Emma is being seduced by Rodolphe in Yonville's town hall, even as the outside sounds and public speeches of an eagerly awaited agricultural show mingle with the illicit, amorous goings-on inside. Vargas Llosa in turn first took up the device in the concluding ten pages of his debut novel, *The Time of the Hero*, when he presents the aftermath of graduation from the Leoncio Prado military academy. Erstwhile cadet Jaguar (the tough guy) and his former partner-in-crime Skinny Higueras are chatting about Jaguar's renewed courtship of and eventual marriage to Teresa.[5] Then, without transition, the setting shifts to actual scenes of the couple's romance and makeshift wedding. The dialogue and events move freely, seamlessly back and forth between the two situations.

Appearing as it does so late in the book, the newly found technique seems almost a last-minute inspiration, even an afterthought. Vargas Llosa will later expand vastly on this discovery in most of his major works (although it is notably absent from *The War of the End of the World*).[6] The device, moreover, will become increasingly complex as the author himself develops. José Miguel Oviedo remarks that, at one point in *Conversation in the Cathedral,* book II, chapter 4, there are as many as eighteen different dialogues being so interwoven (Oviedo 252); and Dick Gerdes, tallies up *nineteen* such simultaneous exchanges in a scene elsewhere depicting a political rally (Gerdes 92). Finally, in *The Feast of the Goat,* the montage of chatter encompasses entire episodes, with dialogue and actions both. Indeed, *The Feast of the Goat* and *Conversation in the Cathedral* are directly linked in their method. Both unfold as the result of a long dialogue—Santiago Zavala talking intensely to his father's former chauffeur in a bar (called "The Cathedral") and thence reliving his family's and country's history, and Urania Cabral recounting to gathered relatives her sordid misadventure with Trujillo (the "Feast" ironically alluded to in the title), which in turn expands into a portrait of the sexual and political baseness of the regime.

There exists as yet no generally accepted term to denote the distinctive technique (as there is for, say, "stream-of-consciousness" or "unreliable narrators"). José Miguel Oviedo refers to the tactic as "telescopic dialogues" (Oviedo 257), and Sara Castro-Klarén draws on the geometric analogy of the "polyhedron" (Castro-Klarén 70). Vargas Llosa's own occasional shorthand phrases for the device are "Chinese boxes" and "communicating vessels" (the latter a concept familiar to literary scholars from Russian formalism). I would modestly venture the terms "dialogue montage" or "montage of conversations," phrases that evoke film editing procedures, which these multidialogue assemblages strongly resemble. Whatever one chooses to call it, the technique is Vargas Llosa's trademark, and he will go down in history as the novelist who first brought it to full fruition (as Joyce did with the interior monologue).

The device, needless to say, is an extremely effective means of conveying narrative information as filtered through the statements of interlocutors and of mingling their several plots atemporally without need of ordinary chronology. In addition, the technique is of a piece with Vargas Llosa's own interest in outward action and surfaces rather than in inward consciousness and thought processes. As Luis Harss and Barbara Dohmann long ago pointed out, Vargas Llosa in his fiction scarcely goes beyond appearances; "the 'metaphysical dimension' or invisibility dimension' . . . is completely missing in his work" (360).

A TOTALIZING NOVEL?

Starting with his earliest days as a writer, Vargas Llosa wished to bring out "totalizing" novels that would take on all aspects of human existence. In this regard he is the conscious heir of the nineteenth-century French masters—Balzac, Flaubert, Hugo—whose subject matter was nothing less than the entirety of their nation's social order.

The Gallic novelists' omnivorous, panoramic outlook included sex. Unlike their counterparts across the English Channel, they dramatized the role of sexual desire in people's everyday lives. Correspondingly, in Vargas Llosa's most ambitious works he shows how power and injustice are not solely about guns and money, but also about brothels, whores, pimps, priapism, secret mistresses, closeted homosexuality, sordid amours, statutory rape, and more. Vargas Llosa's grandest fictions thus capture the erotics—the mostly down-and-dirty erotics—of political and economic power.

Had Vargas Llosa decided to emulate E. M. Forster and simply stopped writing fiction in, say, 1981, he would in all likelihood still be remembered as the author of "the most extraordinary novel of adolescence ever to have come from us" (Carlos Fuentes's assessment of *The Time of the Hero*, Fuentes 38) some remarkable big works (*The Green House, The War of the End of the World*), a couple of ingenious comic narratives (*Captain Pantoja and the Special Service, Aunt Julia and the Scriptwriter*) and, at the very least, one masterpiece.

Conversation is a book in which about a hundred characters and their myriad actions are held in a unique balance, in which the magma of content is thoroughly controlled by the massively engineered, precisely constructed and sculpted form. The upper-class Zavala family, the personality of secret police chief Cayo Bermúdez, the *lumpen* underworld of hooligans and prostitutes, the rural and urban poor and the domestics who barely get by, the shadowy yet inviting network of student activists, and Santiago's disaffection with the entire social order: it all adds up to a total picture seldom matched in narrative.

And it is, quite simply, an amazing read. I first devoured *Conversation* at high speed, on Trans-Europ Express train trips in 1975. I found myself hooked from the start and subsequently dazzled as its many plots thickened. Perusing it for my third time in preparation for this essay, I was struck, on reaching the final pages, by the book's classical balance and serenity. At the same time the work demonstrates a certain innocence, a glimmer of hope from the then just thirty-three-year-old novelist. As I've noted earlier, the only positive characters in *Conversation* are the young leftists whose ranks protagonist Santiago Zavala joins briefly. His attraction to Aída, the bright coringleader of the Marxist cell, blends erotic longing with his desire for a more authentic political-cum-family history; Aída's genuine pride in her father, a former activist, poses a neat foil to Santiago's disgust with his rich progenitor's corrupt ways. Zavalita's comrades-in-struggle show decided courage in their actions, and they endure imprisonment and exile for their principled dissidence. (Vargas Llosa, incidentally, assigns to them the acronym of the same leftist group—COAHUIDE—that he himself had been involved with as a student.) All this is seen through the eyes of Zavalita, who is otherwise something of a nauseated, existential, Sartrean antihero.

Never in his subsequent works will Vargas Llosa feature so full, precise, and convincing a moral counterweight to the dominant forces of injustice and corruption. The loss of his early socialist convictions no doubt had deprived him, at least temporarily, of a sufficiently capacious worldview; and the ensuing void is to be seen in the novels that follow. There is, in *The War*, an odd irony in his depicting the Baron of Cañabrava—a wealthy feudal lord, after all—as the only sane alternative to a gallery of half-crazed fanatics. I must further confess that, when reexamining *The War of the End of the World* for this piece, I found it less fully achieved, less wise than when I first encountered it as an outside evaluator for a New York publisher in 1981. Moreover, the scene in which the Baron beds down with his maidservant Sebastiana, under the willing gaze of his wife, now seemed to me gratuitous and jolting. In this reaction I am seconded by the great literary critic Angel Rama, who in his 1982 review-essay adjudges this scene "disconcerting" and considers its hedonism too "flagrant" an imbalance with "the epic actions," the rebellion, and repression unfolding in the backlands of Brazil ("*La guerra del fin del mundo*" 341). This is an instance in which the sex in Vargas Llosa fails to convince.

In other novels, some relief from all that is false, sordid, or ugly is offered either by romantic love (*Death in the Andes*), by salvation through art (*Aunt Julia and the Scriptwriter*), or by humor and satire itself (*Captain Pantoja and the Special Service*). In *The Real Life of Alejandro Mayta*, by contrast, about the only positive aspect is a kind of emotional, unspoken *Schadenfreude* on the part of the anonymous novelist-narrator. With a touch of the Joseph Conrad of *Under Western Eyes*, the author here seems to have fully distanced himself from and perhaps exorcised his youthful leftism. His band of Trotskyist rebels comes off as scarcely more than dogmatic and self-deceived, yet also pathetically inept. The actual historical revolt that took place in May 1962 (led by one Vicente Mayta Mercado) has been moved back to 1958, two years before the Cuban Revolution and its promises of hemispheric social change—presumably so as to make Mayta's "uprising" all the more pointless and futile (Kristal *Temptation of the Word* 124). The doubly fictionalized accounts of a Soviet-Cuban invasion of Peru from Bolivia (initially presented as narrative future fact, later on denied as novelistic invention) make *Mayta* very much a product of the mid-1980s, when "the Soviet threat" was a daily slogan, and when the very existence of a USSR seemed eternal and incontestable. At novel's end, Vargas Llosa's rebel leader has little to show in the way of tragic qualities or courage. He is simply an ice cream parlor clerk whose Marxist insights ultimately mattered but little.

The trend continues. Its own greatness notwithstanding, *The Feast of the Goat* is a book notably lacking in moral alternatives, in other possibilities. The plotters assassinate Trujillo more because of past outrages he'd visited upon them than out of any higher principle. Only toward the end do we read of an altruistic couple called Cavaglieri (Italian for "gentlemen") who give unconditional shelter to a fleeing Antonio Imbert, one of the seven original conspirators. There is also Sister Mary, a nun who in the last pages helps rescue adolescent victim Urania from the regime's clutches and spirits her off to a girls' school in Michigan. And finally, in the concluding pages, a forty-nine-year-old Urania rediscovers the sustaining role of family ties.

These moments aside, *The Feast of the Goat* gives us a bleak and claustrophobic picture (and, in that regard, no doubt an accurate one). Yet other authors, such as Manuel Vázquez Montalbán (*Galíndez*) and Julia Alvarez (*In the Time of the Butterflies*), have published novels memorializing the selfless efforts and tragic deaths of the courageous anti-Trujillo oppositionists Jesús de Galíndez and the Mirabal sisters; their books thus offer shreds of hope amid a thirty-year nightmare. Still, one must say of the novel that, in spite of its gaps, it inspires an intense pity and fear as few novels do.

Curiously, even though in his opinion pieces Vargas Llosa routinely extols entrepreneurs for "creating wealth" and singles out street hawkers as the carriers of a vibrant future society, in none of his latter-day novels does he venture to include such a figure either as a hero or as a passing if representative cameo character. Whereas in Vargas Llosa's later worldview, business people may have replaced the working class, in his fiction they do not take over let alone usurp the saving role of the left-wing militants in *Conversation in the Cathedral*.

Through a combination of verbal talent, clear intellect, formal exploration, vast energies for research, and a Flaubertian focus on sheer craft, Vargas Llosa has fashioned a literary legacy that is destined to endure. With *The Feast of the Goat*, moreover, he has demonstrated a capacity for self-renewal; and in *The Way to Paradise* he continues to tell stories that provoke and delight. He has sustained the initial promises of the 1960s; in his hands, the Latin American "Boom" of the novel lives on as one of the signal cultural events of the second half of the twentieth century. Readers of this volume can perhaps recall (as does this scribbler) the excitement being generated forty years ago by the likes of Borges and Cortázar, Fuentes and García Márquez. With Vargas Llosa, those literary energies happily remain.

NOTES

1. The author gratefully acknowledges major editorial assistance from Ignacio López-Calvo and Ronald Christ, both of whom helped make this a better essay.

2. It should be mentioned that, in the original Spanish version, chapters are numbered with Roman numerals. I have elected to use the Arabic numerals from the English translation, for the sake of easier readability.

3. In *A Fish in the Water*, Vargas Llosa stated that one of his principal campaign themes was to champion "the development that any country on the periphery that chooses economic freedom and joins the world's markets can achieve: Japan, Taiwan, South Korea, and Singapore. "They lacked natural resources, they were overpopulated and had started from zero, because of their colonial status or backwardness or because of a war that left them devastated. And the four of them, opting for development outward, had succeeded in becoming countries that exported and, by promoting private enterprise, brought about industrialization and a very rapid modernization, which ended mass unemployment and noticeably raised their standard of living. The four of them— but Japan in particular—were now competing in world markets with the most advanced countries. Were they not an example for Peru?" (255).

4. Lee Kuan Yew, the founding leader of Singapore, was, for instance, throughout his political career a member of the Socialist International, something Vargas Llosa would not have been likely to foreground

5. I am grateful to Clive Griffin of Trinity College, Oxford, for having noted and corrected a factual error in this line.

6. In interviews, the author explains that he strove to keep all dialogue in *The War of the End of the World* to a minimum, the reason being that reported conversations might have rung false within the original Brazilian-Portuguese context.

CHAPTER 9

HUMANISM AND CRITICISM

THE PRESENCE OF FRENCH CULTURE IN VARGAS LLOSA'S UTOPIA

ROLAND FORGUES

ON SEVERAL OCCASIONS, MARIO VARGAS LLOSA HAS WRITTEN AND spoken about his admiration for the culture, language, and philosophy of France, with which he had become well acquainted during his youth in Lima and early adulthood in Paris when he decided to become a professional writer. French literature and its great writers and thinkers have been at the core of his preoccupations as a dissident intellectual.

Alexandre Dumas's swashbucklers—*The Three Musketeers, The Queen's Necklace*, and *The Count of Monte Cristo*—have obviously had a great influence on a novel such as *Aunt Julia and the Scriptwriter*, in the exaggerated adventure of the young Vargas with Aunt Julia, on many episodes of *The War of the End of the World*, and on the tragicomic adventure of the Bad Girl and the protagonist and narrator Ricardo Somocurcio in *The Bad Girl*. Georges Bataille and the Marquis de Sade can be easily recognized behind the pages of several of Vargas Llosa's texts, as can be easily ascertained by looking at *In Praise of the Stepmother, The Notebooks of Don Rigoberto, The Way to Paradise*, and *The Bad Girl*. In *Captain Pantoja and the Special Service*, Vargas Llosa experiments with a new narrative technique that yet has a precedent in Rabelais's *Pantagruel*. Not only influenced by William Faulkner or James Joyce, the Peruvian writer is also indebted to Proust's introspection.

I will not analyze Gustave Flaubert nor his "perpetual orgy," which has been celebrated with great devotion by Vargas Llosa in his study on *Madame Bovary*. I study neither the short story writer Guy de Maupassant and his conception of realism in literature and of narrative art that the Peruvian writer will make his own nor Victor Hugo and *Les Misérables*—probably as great an influence on the formation of Vargas Llosa's critical conscience as his readings of Jean-Paul Sartre, Albert Camus, André Malraux, Maurice Merleau-Ponty, and others. Indeed, there is much of Hugo in Vargas Llosa's libertarian crusade and in his fight for freedom and human dignity. There is also much of Michel de Montaigne's cult of humanism and freedom in Vargas Llosa's writings. One cannot note the expression of a personal ethics on life and humanity in the Peruvian novelist's works and life without recalling the *honnête homme* of the sixteenth century portrayed by the author of the *Essais*.

I will center my reflection on three significant figures in twentieth-century French philosophy and letters: Sartre, Camus, and Malraux, in whom Vargas Llosa has admitted a permanent interest in his life as a writer and citizen.

At the beginning of Vargas Llosa's career as a writer and essayist, the influence of Sartre and Camus is evident in his famous theory of the "personal demons" and of the role of the creator as a "substitute for God," developed in his 1971 dissertation on the works of Gabriel García Márquez.

Let us remember that in this foundational essay, Vargas Llosa stated that to write novels was an act of rebellion against reality, against God, against God's creation, which is reality, that it is "an attempt to correct, change or abolish real reality and substitute for it the fictive reality that the novelist creates" concluding that "each novel is a secret deicide, a symbolic assassination of reality" (*Historia de un deicidio* 85). The words of Vargas Llosa echo those written by Sartre in his essay *What is Literature*, when the French philosopher confessed that "one of the chief motives of artistic creation is certainly the need of feeling we are essential in relationship to the world" (49).

The influence of Sartre, Camus and Malraux, though evident in the early works of Vargas Llosa, probably reaches its highest expression as autonomous thought integrated into his own system in his most recent novels, *The Way to Paradise* and *The Bad Girl*.[1]

If it is undeniable that Sartre's existentialism and his notion of commitment determine a good part of Vargas Llosa's literary practice, the discovery of Camus and the absurd probably constitute the starting point for his personal reflections and his elaboration of a philosophy of life that finds its highest point in his adhesion to Malraux's ideas of art conceived as an "antidestiny." In other words, art is considered a way to recuperate human presence beyond death, as the author of *The Human Condition* proudly proclaimed.

Although the influence of Camus was hidden at first by his strong and, originally, unconditional admiration for Sartre, nevertheless, in a review of *Carnets* written in 1965, Vargas Llosa praises Camus's will to "situate himself at a literary perspective, neither philosophic nor moral, to judge himself and justify his work." ("Camus y la literatura" 84). This judgment is fully compatible with Vargas Llosa's own attitude toward creation. Ten years later, as a consequence of a new reading of *The Rebel*, the Peruvian writer states his agreement with Camus:

> I did not read Camus again until a few months ago, when by chance, fol-lowing a terrorist attack in Lima, I reopened *The Rebel*, his essay on vio-lence in history that I had completely forgotten (or had never understood). It was a revelation. This analysis of the philosophical origins of terror that characterizes contemporary history astonished me with its lucidity and contemporary relevance and with the answers that it gave to many doubts and fears that I felt about reality in my country. I was also heartened that on several difficult, political, historical, and cultural questions, I had, on my own account, after a number of lapses, come exactly to the same con-clusions as Camus. ("Camus and the Morality of Limits" 107)

The presence of Camus and his philosophy is most strongly felt in *The Way to Paradise* and *The Bad Girl*, but in what could seem a contradic-tion, this presence is modified by Vargas Llosa's long contact with Sartre's thought and philosophy.

If *The Bad Girl*'s Ricardo Somocurcio's existential attitude reminds us of Antoine de Roquentin, Sartre's character in *Nausea*, Ricardo's is more fully rooted in the ideas of Camus in *The Rebel*, without completely dis-regarding the ideas proposed by Sartre through his character Anny, the companion of Antoine de Roquentin. One has just to reread the final dialogue of Sartre's characters, during the moment of the final encounter and farewell, to be convinced of this.

In the same manner that they summarize her relation with Antoine, the words Anny addresses to her companion could also summarize the relation of the Bad Girl and Ricardo: "You're a milestone . . . beside a road . . . You explain imperturbably and for the rest of your life you'll go on explaining that Melun is twenty seven kilometres and Montargis is forty two. That is why I need you so much" (*Nausea* 137). And similarly, Antoine's words could be Ricardo's: "She has caught me again, once more I have plunged into her strange universe, beyond ridicule, affectation, subtlety. I have even recovered the little fever that always stirred in me when I was with her and this bitter taste in the back of my mouth" (144).

Like Antoine de Roquentin, Ricardo could conclude the singular story of the Bad Girl with these suggestive words: "That's it. There are no adventures—there are no perfect moments . . . we have lost the same illusions, we have followed the same paths. I can guess the rest—I can even speak for her and tell myself all she has left to tell." (*Nausea* 47). While Sartre's character adds, "It's that we've changed together and in the same way . . . All that you've told me—I came to tell you the same thing—though with other words, of course" (144); his companion replies rubbing his weakness on his face with words that could in turn have been spoken by the Bad Girl: "Well, you're not thinking like me at all. You complain because things don't arrange around you like a bouquet of flowers, without your taking the slightest trouble to do anything. But I have never asked as much: I wanted action. You know when we played adventurer and adventuress: you were the one who had adventures; I was the one who made them happen. I said: I'm a man of action. Remember? Well, now I simply say: one can't be a man of action" (150). If disappointed by his adventures, Ricardo concludes, "In this life things rarely happen the way we little pissants plan them" (109); nevertheless he doesn't despair because, like Antoine de Roquentin, he did not expect much from life. Unlike the Bad Girl—like Anny—he comes to the conclusion that "one can't be a man of action," after having attempted to become one searching for power and wealth. The symbolism of the scene in which the Bad Girl destroys all her illusions of power and wealth, not only by deciding to marry Ricardo, but also by giving the *clochard* of the Pont Mirabeau all the money of her companion, cannot be more revealing. It signals the coming to conscience and recognition of the failure of her rebellion, made clear by the words that conclude the scene: "Thank you, Monsieur Clochard for saving the life of my happiness" (242).

This recognition is confirmed by the ending of the novel and the Bad Girl's final confession that sounds like a tragic mistake: "I came looking for you because I love you. Because I need you. Because I can't live with anybody except you. Though you may think it's a little late. I know this now. That's why, from now on, even though I die of hunger and have to live like a hippie, I'm going to live with you. And no one else" (270–71). But she has no regrets—as she confesses, except the conventional one of having made Ricardo suffer, because in reality, if the attitude of the Bad Girl can be partly understood by referring to Sartre's ideas, the starting point of her rebelliousness is linked to the ideas of Camus and his *Rebel*. In his attempt to affirm his identity, Camus will transform Descartes's formula "I think, therefore I am" into "I rebel, therefore I am." In this manner one can explain the constant rebelliousness of the Bad Girl, her permanent attempt to erase her identity in order to construct a new one as part of her exploration of the unknown, of her experience of limits, so dear to Georges Bataille, where the borders between reality and fiction, good and evil, sacred and profane, evaporate making life into a "wonderful adventure." "Peru"—Ricardo eloquently states about her—"was something she had deliberately expelled from her thoughts" (55).

If Ricardo resembles Antoine de Roquentin in his vital attitude and Meursault—the protagonist of Camus's *The Stranger*—in his disgust with existence and his apparent indifference, exemplified in Camus's protagonist's rejection of suicide, he is closer to Camus's justifications than to Sartre's:

> I had decided coldly, unmelodramatically, that this was, after all, a worthy way to die: jumping off the bridge, dignified by good modernist poetry and the intense voice of Juliette Gréco into the dirty waters of the Seine. Holding my breath or gulping down water, I would lose consciousness quickly—perhaps lose it with the force of my body hitting the water—and death would follow immediately. If you couldn't have the only thing you wanted in life, which was her, better to end it once and for all and do it this way, little pissant. (205–6)

But the hand of providence—incarnated in the *clochard* who grabs his legs, makes him trip and fall on the asphalt of the bridge, and then leaves stumbling as if nothing had happened, with a bottle of wine in his hand—saves him from death. And like the character of Paul Gauguin in *The Way to Paradise*, Ricardo returns home happy to be alive. Thus a romantic vision of life—literary and pessimistic—is superseded by an existentialist one, resolutely modern and optimistic: "I walked back to Rue Joseph Granier, laughing at myself, filled with gratitude and admiration for that drunken vagabond on the Pont Mirabeau who saved my life. I was going to jump, I'd have done it if he hadn't stopped me. I felt stupid, ridiculous, ashamed, and had begun to sneeze. All this cheap clownishness would end in a cold. The bones in my back ached because of my fall onto the pavement, and I wanted to sleep the rest of the night, the rest of my life" (206).

As is demonstrated in this final description, Vargas Llosa's character rejects suicide, not because he's "in the way," not because he is supernumerary, as Sartre argued through the mouth of Antoine de Ronquentin, but because it's not the solution, as Camus wrote in *The Myth of Sisyphus* (1942): "I draw from the absurd three consequences, which are my revolt, my freedom, and my passion. By the mere activity of consciousness I transform into a rule of life what was an invitation to death—and I refuse suicide" (64).

The "rule of life" will effectively be the final coexistence and solidarity with a woman physically mutilated, despite the fact that that mutilation also implies the mutilation of love and life.

After rejecting suicide, in reality, the novel exemplifies, by means of the common struggle on the different life paths of Ricardo and the Bad Girl, one of the key ideas that Camus would develop in *The Plague*: that in an absurd world salvation can only come from the fraternity and camaraderie that can be forged in a common struggle. Let us recall that in his play *Calígula* (1938), Camus's reflection on the absurd leads him to the conclusion that if in a world without God "everything is permitted," in the words of Ivan Karamazov, Dostoyevsky's hero, "does not mean that nothing is forbidden," as he will write later in *The Myth of Sisyphus* (67).[2] According to Camus no one can be saved alone; no one can be free against all.

In a world without God, characterized by the absurd, Camus refuses to sacrifice humanity in the name of the altar of History, or in the name of a sacralized future. In this sense, Sartre is correct when he comments on *The Stranger*: "The absurd man is a humanist; he knows only the good things of this world" ("An Explication of *The Stranger*" 116). This philosophy is in part what separated Camus from Sartre. And this is also what brought Vargas Llosa to the author of *The Rebel*, as he begun to distance himself from Jean-Paul Sartre, his early mentor.

In his essay "The Truth of Lies," Vargas Llosa declares that literature is a continuous theft of which the author is usually unaware, because it is a complex mass phenomenon. From this perspective, I would argue that *The Way to Paradise* and *The Bad Girl* are probably among the best thefts from Camus's literature, but reinterpreted from the perspective of the traces that Sartre has left on Vargas Llosa. In particular they are among the best thefts from *The Stranger*, in which Vargas Llosa sees "an argument against the tyranny of convention and the lie that social life is based upon" ("Camus and the Morality of Limits" 110).

Regarding Camus's character, Vargas Llosa states,

> Meursault is, in a certain way, a martyr to truth. What leads to his imprisonment, sentencing and presumably his execution is his ontological inability to disguise his feelings, to do what other men do: play a part. It is impossible for Meursault, for example, to affect at his mother's funeral more grief than he actually feels, and say the things that, in these circumstances, it is expected that a son should say. Nor can he—despite the fact that his life depends on it—show the judge more repentance than he actually feels for the death he

has caused. He is punished for this, not for his crime. ("Camus and the Morality of Limits" 110)

In their search for the chimera of the universal harmony of human beings reconciled with themselves, with the other, and with the cosmos, Flora Tristán and Paul Gauguin, the heroes of *The Way to Paradise*, Ricardo Somocurcio and the Bad Girl, protagonists of *The Bad Girl*, are certainly, like Meursault, the protagonist of *The Stranger*, martyrs to truth. Or more exactly, of their own truths. A truth can be contradictory—and is so in both the field of ideas and that of praxis, in both the conceptualization and the practice of sex—but they have decided to take truth to its final consequences.

Flora Tristán and Paul Gauguin *In the Way to Paradise*, as well as Ricardo Somocurcio and the Bad Girl, in *The Bad Girl*, are involved in a literary process of sacrifice and redemption that ought to lead them to their desired utopia.

This process is continuously threatened in *The Way to Paradise* by "that bullet lodged in her chest," (51) in the case of Flora Tristán, and "unspeakable illness," (260) in that of Paul Gauguin. To Flora Tristán's generous collectivist and social utopia of the union between women and all the oppressed of the world, Vargas Llosa juxtaposes her grandson Paul Gauguin's individual and solipsistic utopia of sex as creation and of the return to the primitive as a source of identity and life.

In *The Bad Girl*, the threat is constituted by the successive adventures that can change the path of the story and that lead to physical destruction. To Ricardo's conformism, Vargas Llosa counterposes the anticonformist madness of the Bad Girl, that leads to a final consensus and sacrifice.

Although it is true that certain of the characters of Vargas Llosa and Camus are "strangers" in their own world, I do not believe that Flora Tristán, Paul Gauguin, Ricardo Somocurcio or the Bad Girl are "martyrs" of exactly the same truth as Meursault: that truth that Sartre demystified in his brilliant and polemical essay on *The Stranger* in 1943. In that essay the young Sartre argued, "Camus's story is analytic and humorous. Like all artists, he *invents*, because he pretends to be reconstituting raw experience and because he slyly eliminates all the significant links which are also part of the experience" ("Explication of *The Stranger*" 118). And the philosopher added, "In literature, this method has proved its worth. It was Voltaire's method in *L'Ingénu* and *Micromégas* and Swift's in *Gulliver's Travels*. For the eighteenth century also had its own outsiders, 'noble savages,' usually, who, transported to a strange civilization, perceived facts 'before being able to grasp their meaning'" (118). And "the effect of this discrepancy was to arouse in the reader the feeling of the absurd" (118).

Although Flora Tristán, Paul Gauguin, Ricardo Somocurcio, and the Bad Girl live, like Meursault, in an absurd world, unlike Camus's antihero, they are not reconciled with it. Each one in his manner fights to transform it; even Ricardo Somocurcio whose attitude seems at first somewhat conformist, never stops believing in realizing his union with the Bad Girl. In "La literatura y la vida" ("Literature and Life"), Vargas Llosa states clearly that "a democratic and free society needs citizens who are responsible and critical, aware of the need to continuously examine the world in which we live in order to attempt to bring it closer to that in which we desire to live—an always chimerical goal; but thanks to whose insistence in attempting this unrealizable dream—of making reality congruent with our desires—civilization was born and has progressed, permitting humanity to defeat many—though obviously not all—the demons that haunt it" (38).

Despite the will to continue fighting, it is also true that the ultimate failure of Vargas Llosa's protagonists is due to the futility of the struggle, a kind of a posteriori justification of Meursault's attitude.

One of the best examples of Vargas Llosa's characters' declared but frustrated will to construct their own destinies is Paul Gauguin's justification for his suicide attempt, which, of course, will fail: "Your death would come as you had planned it, not where and when the unspeakable illness decided" (*The Way to Paradise* 221–22). This failure, demonstrates the futility of suicide—and, therefore, its rejection as previously argued by Camus. Thus, following Camus, by having Paul, return to his creative task, Vargas Llosa transforms "into a rule of life what was an invitation to death":

> Although he was tortured by thirst—his tongue was as petrified as a lizard's—he didn't feel bad in body or in spirit, as he headed down the mountain toward the valley; rather, he was filled with eager anticipation. You were anxious to be home, to plunge into the river Punaauia where you bathed each morning before starting work, to drink plenty of water and some nice hot tea with a dash of rum (was there any rum left?). Then, lighting your pipe (was there any tobacco left?), you would go into the studio and immediately paint the title that had come to you thanks to your frustrated suicide attempt, in black letters in the upper-left corner of that thirteen-foot-long stretch of sack-cloth to which you have been riveted these last few weeks. Was it a masterpiece? It was Koké. In that upper corner, those tremendous questions would preside over the canvas. You hadn't the slightest idea what the answers would be. But you were sure that anyone who knew how to look could find them in the painting's twelve figures, which traced, in a counterclockwise arc, the human trajectory from the beginning of life in infancy to its end in ignominious old age. (225)

The failure of the suicide attempt returns the character to the Judeo-Christian world of the twelve apostles he is painting now through the creation of a sacred space.

In this sacred space of myth the utopias of Flora Tristán and Paul Gauguin meet, based on the rejection of sexuality and the exaltation of spiritual love in the case of Flora Tristán and in the celebration of sexuality and the rejection of spiritual love in that of Paul Gauguin. And one may add, Vargas Llosa's utopia is also included in this space. As Octavio Paz states in *The Bow and the Lyre*:

> What is sacred transcends sexuality and the social institutions in which it is crystallized. It is eroticism, but also something that surpasses sexual desire; it is a social phenomenon, but it is also something else. What is sacred escapes us. When we try to grasp it, we find that it has its origin in something that predates us and becomes confused with our own being. The same happens with love and poetry. These three experiences are manifestations of something that is at the core of man. In the three beats the nostalgia for an earlier state. And this state of primordial unity, from which we were separated, from which we are being constantly separated, constitutes our original condition, to which we time and time again return. (119)

One can conclude that, beyond anecdote, Flora Tristán and Paul Gauguin in *The Way to Paradise* and Ricardo Somocurcio and the Bad Girl in *The Bad Girl* are, in the last instance, a kind of synthesis—a kind of cryptic testimony on the alliance between the greatness and tragedy of the human condition as conceived and lived by André Malraux, another of the great writers admired by Vargas Llosa:[3] "I know now—wrote André Malraux—that an intellectual is not only a man to whom books are necessary, he is any man whose reasoning, however elementary, affects and directs his life" (22–23). Would Vargas Llosa recognize himself in this definition? I do not doubt it for a moment.

For Vargas Llosa, as for André Malraux, a human being is defined by his actions, not by his words. Both writers share this epic vision of life and of artistic creation, seen as rejecting fate, as the means by which to preserve life beyond death.

Not in vain does the conclusión of *The Bad Girl* propose transforming the adventure of Ricardo and his companion into the plot of a novel, therefore, assigning to it the sacred condition of myth:

> One afternoon, when we were sitting in the garden at twilight, she said that if it ever occurred to me to write our love story, I shouldn't make her look too bad, because then her ghost would come and pull on my feet every night.
> 'And what made you think of that?'

'Because you always wanted to be a writer and didn't have the courage. Now that you'll be all alone, you can make good use of the time, and you won't miss me so much. At least admit I've given you the subject for a novel. Haven't I, good boy?' (276)

In a speech titled "Ganar batallas, no la guerra" ("To Win Battles, not the War") read on December 10, 1978, during his reception of the Award for Human Rights granted to him by the Latin American Jewish Congress, Vargas Llosa, after lamenting the "universal and flagrant" divorce between ideas and actions, stated,

> André Malraux expressed it thus, with his beautiful rethoric: 'Historians of the future will say that ours is a curious time, in which the left is not the left, the right is not the right, and the center is not in the center.' This is what we lucidly have to admit: we are mired in confusion. The morality that the diverse regimes and political parties practice has mixed and matched them to the point that contemporary history is a jungle where pre-existing political concepts, instead of guiding, confuse us. If at some time it was possible to differentiate good from evil—or in less metaphysical terms, progress and reaction—through the platforms and programs that each defended, today this is impossible because ideas— or better said, the words that formulate them—serve more to obscure reality than to describe it, especially in the political field. Notions of justice, democracy, legality, liberty, progress, reaction, socialism, revolution, mean so many different things depending on the person, party, or institution that use them that they no longer mean anything. This is why it is more important to observe what they do than to listen to what they say and, therefore, to applaud or reprehend them not for their noise but for their actions. (100–101)

Sartre, Camus, and Malraux, each in his own manner, have determined Vargas Llosa's philosophical formation and ontological reflection, not in a contradictory but in a complementary manner, guiding his writing toward an indivisible totality in which humanity, both as individuals and social beings, is at the center. If Sartre's reflections in *Being and Nothingness* on conscience as subject and freedom, on the encounter with the other, have taught Vargas Llosa the absolute necessity of commitment as creator and citizen, and the need to struggle to enter the roads of freedom, because human beings whose freedom is absolute are completely responsible for their actions, Camus and Malraux have helped him reflect on the absurd, fate and utopia, on rebellion and the human condition, on epic and art as the permanent creation and recreation of being.

It is through the influence of these three authors, in particular, that Vargas Llosa has developed his own conception on ethics and creation as inseparable and joined forms of existence and of their perdurability in myth.

NOTES

1. On *The Way to Paradise*, see my *Mario Vargas Llosa: ética y creación*. The most recent edition (2009) includes a chapter on *The Bad Girl*.
2. "The absurd does not liberate; it binds. It does not authorize all actions. 'Everything is permitted' does not mean that nothing is forbidden. The absurd merely confers an equivalence on the consequences of those actions. It does not recommend crime, for this would be childish, but it restores to remorse its futility" (Camus 67).
3. On this, see the interview "El Intelectual, el Poder y la Política," in *Vargas Llosa, Ética y creación*.

PART IV

MARIO VARGAS LLOSA, MAN OF LETTERS

CHAPTER 10

VARGAS LLOSA'S SELF-DEFINITION AS "THE MAN WHO WRITES AND THINKS"

SABINE KÖLLMANN

"LOVE HIS FICTION, HATE HIS POLITICS"—THIS STATEMENT COULD SUM up the attitude held by many readers of Mario Vargas Llosa's novels on the one hand and, on the other, his comments on current affairs that he publishes in journals in Europe and the Americas. Or in the words of the official Cuban newspaper *Granma*, "Vargas Llosa sigue siendo un canalla que escribe bien" ("Vargas Llosa is still a rogue who writes well") (*"Diario Granma*: 'Vargas Llosa sigue siendo un canalla que escribe bien'").[1] There was a time when Vargas Llosa vigorously defended what he saw as a necessary split, or indeed a vital tension, between the two roles he ascribed to the writer: his total freedom in creating a fictional world that would reflect his own inner conflicts with the world (his "demons," as he used to call them), regardless of any moral or political restrictions; and his responsibility toward society as an intellectual whose duty it is to question preconceived ideas, to encourage debate, and to provide some kind of guidance on social and political, cultural and moral issues by his comments. These are two rather old-fashioned concepts, some might object—they will indeed require further comment. They represent, however, the most consistent ideas throughout Vargas Llosa's fifty years of writing on literature, the creative process and the role of the writer. All through his career he has assumed both roles in parallel, always claiming that they are two sides of his vocation that do not necessarily have to be in tune with each other at all times. Discrepancies between his fictional creations and his ideas outside literature are unavoidable, according to this theory, due to the irrational, uncontrollable elements that he sees involved in creating an authentic work of fiction: "That element which rushes out spontaneously from the most secret corner of one's personality imposes a special colouring upon the story one is trying to write, establishes hierarchies among the characters which sometimes subtly overturn our conscious intention, adorns or impregnates that which we are narrating with a meaning or symbolism which, in some cases, not only does not coincide with our ideas but can even go so far as to substantially contradict them" (Vargas Llosa, "Literature and Freedom" 4).

More recently, however, we have heard Vargas Llosa complain about the fact that he is now indeed being perceived as a writer of admirable fictions, but of objectionable economic ideas and dubious political alliances. He has expressed his irritation at the "schizophrenic process" by which critics pay tribute to his novels or literary essays but feel the need to qualify their praise by distancing themselves from his opinions in public debates. He claims the right to be viewed "as a unified being, the man who writes and thinks," since he "believe[s] that both activities form part of a single, inseparable reality" ("Confessions of a Liberal"). What has brought about this change of attitude? Has what he wrote, back in 1970, about Balzac, the French author whom he admires as one of the greatest creators of "total realities" in fiction, come to haunt him: "Supporter of absolute monarchy, anti-Semite, conformist, and the creator of a novelistic oeuvre that today appears to us as a major example of critical realist literature"? ("Luzbel, Europa y otras conspiraciones" 83) It seems ironic that Vargas Llosa suddenly finds himself in that role of a writer whose fictions gain approval because they do *not* reflect his opinions outside literature. In the 1970 controversy with his critic Oscar Collazos he wrote, "Of course, one could mention many writers who declared themselves to be staunch conservatives but who wrote progressive works, or dedicated progressives, whose works promoted values totally opposed to those their authors professed" (83).

This is not far from some of the statements made by critics after the publication of *The Feast of the Goat*, Vargas Llosa's dictatorship novel of 2000, which surprised many by its old-fashioned commitment to denouncing political evils, an attitude clearly linked to early novels such as *Conversation in the Cathedral*. Whereas some of his work of the 1980s and '90s was simply dismissed because of the author's political stance, this novel could not easily be categorized as the work of a "neoliberal" author.[2] In an interview for the journal *Iberoamericana* the Spanish writer Manuel Vázquez Montalbán reiterated his opinion of Vargas Llosa as "prophet of neoliberalism and North American capitalism who cannot differentiate between victims and persecutors," but he conceded that this does not apply to *The Feast of the Goat*: "Not in this novel, here he seems to be the liberal novelist who is opposed to a dictator. He reclaims a progressive position" (177).

But is it true that Vargas Llosa's fiction and his literary essays bring out the best in him, whereas his political and economic statements are right-wing, neoliberal tirades, always in favor of U.S. capitalism? Do we have to love his work, hate his opinions? And is he really not recognized as a unified being?

The place to seek an answer to this last question is the meticulously assembled official website (by Rosario de Bedoya, *Página Web Oficial Mario Vargas Llosa*), which lists—well, basically everything he has ever done, said, and written; every honor he has ever received (and there are many of them: honorary doctorates from the world's most prestigious universities, state honors such as the Premio Cervantes, the French Légion d'Honneur, the Jerusalem Prize, the Peruvian Gran Cruz con Diamantes "El Sol del Perú"; as well as membership of the Real Academia Española, all carefully listed alongside prizes such as "Su peso en Miel de La Alcarria" ("His Weight in Honey from La Alcarria"), the title "Bodeguero Mayor del Reyno de Navarra" ("Chief Tavern Keeper of the Wine-Growing Region of Navarra"), as well as a star on the Puerto Banús Walk of Fame. The Web site also contains records of every edition and translation of his own work that he has in his personal library (with photographic documentation); every book and article that has been written about him that is in his archive; every place he has travelled to in order to participate in conferences, give papers, receive honors, do research or teach courses—a truly exhaustive documentation of Vargas Llosa's positively exhausting range of activities! It also provides ample proof that, for many years already, he has gained worldwide recognition for his dual role as novelist and intellectual. To mention only a few examples, from very different political and ideological backgrounds, in 1996 he was awarded the Peace Prize of the German Book Trade in honor of "his narrative and essayistic work that revolves around the idea of justice, freedom and equality as basis for a peaceful existence of the individual in society" and for his "courageous interventions in the conflicts of our time," always "committed to the inseparable link between politics and ethics" (*Friedenspreis des Deutschen Buchhandels 1996* 5);[3] in 2000 his birthplace Arequipa awarded him the "Patrimonio Cultural de La Humanidad" medal in recognition of his literary career and his courage in defending democracy and human rights; the American Enterprise Institute for Public Policy Research awarded the 2005 Irving Kristol Award to the writer "whose narrative art and political thought illumine the universal quest for freedom"; in the same year the municipality of Madrid honored Vargas Llosa with its "Medalla Interna-cional de las Artes" for "his exemplary creative career, as well as for his personal commitment to freedom"; a year later, the President of Nicara-gua decorated Vargas Llosa with the "Orden Rubén Darío en el Grado de Gran Cruz," "in recognition of his multiple merits as a writer, novelist, essayist and active and proven defender of democracy in the world and, especially, in Latin America"; 2007 saw him accepting the "Premio de la Tolerancia" in Barcelona, for the defense of freedom, human rights, and constitutionalism in his life and work,[4] and in November 2008 he was awarded the Peace Prize of the German "Friedrich-Naumann Stiftung für die Freiheit," an organization close to the country's Liberal Party (FDP), which honored him "not only for his literary work, but also for his com-mitment to liberal values and civil rights in Latin America" (*Página Web Oficial Mario Vargas Llosa*).[5]

This is an impressive range of awards by institutions and organiza-tions reaching across the political spectrum, from the neoconserva-tive U.S. Right to the German Publishers and Booksellers Association, which, since the 1950s, honors independent intellectuals committed to "peace, humanity and understanding among all peoples and nations of the world" (*Boersenverein des Deutschen Buchhandels*) (previous win-ners have included Albert Schweitzer, Václav Havel, Susan Sontag, Jorge Semprún, Octavio Paz and Ernesto Cardenal). One might wonder what makes Mario Vargas Llosa such a controversial figure that people feel they have to distance themselves from the opinions of a man who is, again and again, praised in these or similar words: "For his strong commitment to the defense of freedom, human rights and constitutionalism; for his intel-lectual independence when studying with rigor and depth the great topics that affect us as individuals and citizens, preferring solid argumentation over intellectual fashions; for his empathy with the downtrodden; for his courage in assuming commitments dictated by his conscience even if they lead to personal disadvantage" (Rodríguez).

A number of different issues are in play here. To begin with, Vargas Llosa is not easy to categorize in his literary production, where dictatorship novels stand next to erotic fiction; where parody, melodrama, and playful metafic-tion exist alongside novels about political and religious fanatics; and where the fictionalization of a famous artist and his radical feminist grandmother has recently been followed by a theatrical retelling of the *Odyssey*. Nor is Vargas Llosa easy to categorize in his political and economic statements: at the same time that he attacks Latin American left-wing populist leaders, he denounces U.S. plans for an anti-immigration wall on the border of Mexico. His promotion of neoliberal free-market economics coexists with a consistent defense of gay rights. His appeal to welcome immigrants of every color and creed for the culture, energy and life that they bring to their host nations does not prevent Vargas Llosa from declaring the politics of unconditional multiculturalism a failure. His fight against regional separatism in Spain has an uneasy echo in his belief that the indigenous cultures of Latin America will have to give up their separate identity in favor of progress. His support for the state of Israel and his acceptance of the Jerusalem Prize in 1995 do not keep Vargas Llosa from writing a passionate denunciation of Israeli settlements in Palestinian territory. His ongoing campaign for civil rights, democracy and a free judiciary included his support for a cross-border prosecution of Pinochet and other dictators.[6]

However, the fact that Vargas Llosa utters his opinions with great polemical verve, giving them an appearance of absoluteness, has provoked strong reactions of support or rejection.[7] In my view there is no evidence for the claim by John King, paraphrasing Efraín Kristal, that Vargas Llosa's utterances on current affairs have mellowed since the lost election in 1990. King speaks of a "recognition of the frailties of those with whom he disagrees," of "wistfulness" and a conciliatory, "elegiac tone" ("Editor's Preface" xvii–xviii). In fact, Vargas Llosa continues to use emotionally rousing rhetoric and can be acidic or sarcastic in his judgments. Consider this 1998 article about "good and bad dictators," in which he criticizes the King of Spain's visit to Fidel Castro's Cuba with the following sarcastic description:

> The Spanish government of José María Aznar—having maintained a critical distance from Castro in the past, but having recently, and inexplicably, developed a pornographic passion for the Caribbean dictatorship—will send them King Juan Carlos on an official visit. The Spanish monarch—who doubts it?—will receive the gift of a ration of [political] prisoners, too. And while in the Plaza de la Revolution, full to the brim, the good dictator [Fidel Castro] will whisper to the courtesan closest to him, perhaps even a Nobel Prize winner [side swipe to García Márquez], that these class enemies are even more foolish than he thought. And for once he will be right. ("El bueno y el malo")

The spiteful picture that Vargas Llosa evokes here does not live up to his often promoted ideal of a cultured debate, nor does an absolute rejection of any dialogue with Cuba agree with his own politics of forming alliances with former adversaries in order to achieve a higher goal.[8]

Whereas his defense of a favored cause, or his denunciation of an evil, is always extremely vigorous, he reserves the right to change his opinions according to his conscience. This happened for example when he modified his critical attitude to the Iraq invasion during a visit to the country in the summer of 2003, documented in his "Iraq Diary."[9] Vargas Llosa insists that this ability to reexamine one's opinions and attitudes in the light of additional information, new developments, or more convincing arguments is crucial: "I believe that the possibility of error is, precisely, what defines a liberal intellectual, one who accepts the possibility of being mistaken in what he defends and who, therefore, has to concede that opinions contrary to his own, antagonistic views, have an equal right to exist" (*Semana de autor* 67).

But the belief in a coexistence of diverging opinions is not always obvious in a writer who chooses titles for his essay collections that evoke the image of him in a battle against all odds: *Contra viento y marea* (Against Wind and Tide), *Carta de batalla* . . . (Order of Battle . . .), *Desafíos a la libertad* (Challenges to Liberty). This goes back to Vargas Llosa's notorious acceptance speech for the Rómulo Gallegos prize in 1967, titled "La literatura es fuego" ("Literature Is Fire"), which set out his ideas of the writer and the role of literature in society. A masterpiece of incendiary rhetoric,[10] this speech founded his reputation as a socialist writer and Castro supporter,[11] who later went on to renounce the Cuban model for its lack of freedom—a "betrayal" for which leftist intellectuals have never forgiven him. (All this despite the fact that Castro was widely criticized during the Padilla affair of 1971 and that Vargas Llosa's famous letter of protest against the Stalinist self-denunciation imposed on the Cuban writer Heberto Padilla was signed by a whole range of high-profile left-wing intellectuals.)[12] But it was Vargas Llosa's continuing criticism of the abuses of autocratic power in Cuba, and more recently in Venezuela under Hugo Chávez, that made him the hate figure of the Latin American left—so much so that Gustavo Faverón Patriau, in a review of Herbert Morote's *Vargas Llosa, tal cual*, could state, "To write against Vargas Llosa is, by now, a national sport, a common practice, and, of course, a literary genre in itself" (qtd. in Faverón). In reality, Vargas Llosa's ideas about literature and the writer in society have changed little over the course of the years. His call for freedom—especially freedom of speech, which he has always regarded as the basis of a free society—and his denunciation of the lack of freedom in countries or organizations, is as vigorous as it was when he began his career. One of his early programmatic texts (1966), which formed the basis of the notorious "Literature Is Fire" speech, set out what would become the motto of his life of writing:

> There is no artistic creation without nonconformity and rebellion. The *raison d'être* of literature is protest, disagreement and criticism. The writer has been, is, and will continue to be, dissatisfied. . . . literature is a form

of permanent insurrection . . . Literature contributes to human improvement, preventing spiritual atrophy, self-satisfaction, stagnation, human
paralysis and intellectual or moral decline. Its mission is to arouse, to disturb, to alarm, to keep men in a constant state of dissatisfaction with themselves; its function is to stimulate, without respite, the desire for change
and improvement, even when it is necessary to use the sharpest weapons to
accomplish this task . . . literature . . . will always be *in opposition*, it cannot
be otherwise. ("Una insurrección permanente" 109)

This idea of literature as a subversive force, widening the perspective on
reality and thus encouraging a more critical attitude, is still present in his
more recent texts, such as *Letters to a Young Novelist* (1997), where he writes
that "the unease fomented by good literature, may, in certain circumstances,
even translate itself into an act of rebellion against authority, the establishment, or sanctioned beliefs" (9). There is not much difference between the
proclamation of intent of the young leftist author and that of the "neoliberal" writer thirty-one years later, who has nevertheless come under attack
by a number of leftist critics for the betrayal of his ideals and for his ideologically conservative, "reactionary" attitudes in politics *and* in fiction.[13]

In the climate of the 1960s and '70s, however, the rebellious nature
that Vargas Llosa ascribes to literature was understood in political terms,
a misunderstanding that was supported by his use of politically charged
terms such as "militancy," "insurrection," and "dissidence" ("La literatura
es fuego" 177, 179; "Resurrección de Belcebú" 276).[14] But the unhappi-
ness with the real world that literature creates must be seen in the context
of Vargas Llosa's dichotomy between "real reality" and "fictitious reality,"
concepts by which he has tried to explain the creative process of transforming reality into fiction—or "truth" into "lies"—and the effect that fiction
then has on the "real" world. Starting from a rebellion against something
lacking in reality, the writer creates a fiction that is, so to speak, truer than
life—what he calls the "truth of lies" or "truthful lie." By revealing the
insufficiencies of life this fictional world has an active effect on reality,
nourishing, as he puts it in a 2008 essay for *Letras Libres*, the impulse to
bring about change: "From this imbalance, from this abyss between the
truth of our lives as we live them and the life which we are able to dream
and to live in our imagination, originates that other essential human characteristic which is nonconformity, dissatisfaction, and rebelliousness; the
recklessness to defy life as it is, and the willingness to fight in order to
transform it, so that it comes closer to the one we construct according to
our fantasies" ("El viaje a la ficción" 14).

Vargas Llosa explained early on that the writer's rebellion can be
roused by many things, some of which might be very personal issues (the

"demons" of his theory): a disagreement with politics, society, ethics, family, sexuality, taboos, and so on. Literature expresses human nature in all its dimensions, good and bad. Hence his fiction deals with such diverse topics as politics, sex, the military, art, melodrama, fanaticism, religion, ideology, dictatorship, with the recurring themes of human suffering, injustice, machismo, authoritarianism, the father, journalism, storytelling, and the creative process itself.

In the 1970s, however, Vargas Llosa became involved in a number of debates over his "irresponsible" and "individualistic" concept of the personal "demons" in literature.[15] At that point he introduced into his theory the divide between the literary and the public side of the writer—and overemphasized the *total* freedom of the writer in his fiction. The author of fictions, so he claimed for a long time, has one obligation only: to write good literature, capable of reflecting the whole range of human concerns and obsessions by giving them form, order, and coherence in a unified work of art. *In parallel to that*, the writer as intellectual has a social responsibility to help shape public opinion by engendering debates, commenting on social issues, and taking a stance in current affairs.[16] However, when the two areas become intertwined and the writer tries to fulfill the public's expectation of "useful" fiction, literature is in danger of becoming inauthentic. Vargas Llosa made this claim above all in the 1970s and 1980s and illustrated it with a number of essays on the Peruvian indigenist writer José María Arguedas:[17]

> The "commitment" of a writer, understood as the obligation to take account of the injustices in his world and to think in terms of solutions, is no guarantee that his work has artistic value . . . But on the other hand, once this conception of literature is established in the minds of the public, it makes it more difficult to dissociate the one from the other: literary merit and the social and political effectiveness of a text. A society convinced that literature must be useful—that it must serve the present—will find it difficult to understand or accept those works which instead of reproducing reality, seek to order it or deny it. Nevertheless, the latter constitutes true literature. ("The Writer in Latin America" 36)

Over the years, in a number of essays Vargas Llosa has cited Jorge Luis Borges as an example of this kind of "true" literature, defending the Argentinian's literary merits despite his links with the worst dictators and his despicable statements about politics. An indicator that Vargas Llosa modified his opinion about the possible split between the writer as author and as intellectual is an article titled "Borges, político" from November 1999, in which he comes to this surprising conclusion:

It is not true that the work of a writer can be completely separated from his political ideas, his beliefs, his ethical and social likes and dislikes. On the contrary, all this is part of the clay out of which his imagination and his words model his fictions. Borges is, perhaps, the greatest writer of the Spanish language since the classics, since a Cervantes or a Quevedo. All the same, his genius, as in the case of the latter whom he admired so much, suffers from a certain inhumanity—despite, or perhaps due to its pure perfection; it lacks the vital fire that makes Cervantes, on the other hand, so human. This limitation did not show itself in the flawless style of his prose or in the exquisite originality of his inventions; it was there in the way he saw and understood the life of others, and his own life caught up in that of the rest; in that activity he disdained so much (and that is so often worthy of disdain): politics. (26)

Here Vargas Llosa takes into account the lack of empathy in Borges, which he sees reflected in his impeccable prose and his perfect works of fiction. In another article on the Argentinian writer, he explains that Borges could never have written novels: "Because the novel is the territory of totalized human experience, of integral life, of imperfection. In it are combined intellect and passion, knowledge and instinct, sensation and intuition, unequal and polyhedric material which ideas, on their own, are not able to fully express. That is why the great novelists are never perfect prose writers" ("Borges en París").

In his 1996 acceptance speech for the Peace Prize of the German Book Trade, Vargas Llosa declared that a writer cannot remain at the margin of society, merely observing: "Literature must plunge into the life of the streets, into common experience, into history in the making, as it has done during its best moments. It is only in this manner, without arrogance, without claiming omniscience, accepting the risk of being wrong, that writers can provide a service to their contemporaries and rescue their profession from the watered-down state into which it seems on occasion to be falling" (*Friedenspreis* 39).

We can see that, for some time already, Vargas Llosa's statements on the profession of the writer and the nature of fiction have shown a desire to recuperate the split between the author of fictions on the one hand and the public figure commenting on current affairs on the other, thus trying to reintegrate the two aspects of his vocation—hence his recent bitter remarks about the "bifurcation" of his personality, which formed the starting point of this essay. In a number of essays from 2000 onward, he has asserted that, by showing the "most profound truths of human reality" ("Literature and Life" 147), the lies of literature help to form critical and free individuals who feel that they are part of a larger community of human beings that transcends time, space, and ethnic or cultural boundaries.[18]

Those of us who read Cervantes, Shakespeare, Dante or Tolstoy understand each other and feel part of the same species because, in the works
that these writers created, we learn what we share as human beings, what
is common to all of us beneath the wide range of differences that separate
us. And there is no better defence against the stupidity of prejudice, racism, xenophobia, religious or political sectarianism or autarchic nationalism than this invariable truth that appears in all great literature: that men
and women across the world are equal, and that it is unjust that they are
subject to discrimination, repression and exploitation. ("Literature and
Life" 137)

This statement reveals the clear link between Vargas Llosa's role as
intellectual commentator and his ideas about the writer and the nature
of fiction. "Prejudice, racism, xenophobia, religious or political sectarianism or autarchic nationalism" are recurring topics of his many public
statements. In his role as newspaper columnist he attacks prejudices of
all sorts and defends the rights of the individual against collectivist doctrines, whether based on ethnic or national identity, religion, or ideology. This is the area where, it seems to me, there is indeed a coherence
between Vargas Llosa's political commentaries and his fiction. His novels,
as well as his essays, show an interest and compassion for everything that
affects human beings, their sufferings and their pleasures, always within
the context of a society that sets the rules and conditions that influence
an individual's life. In his erotic novel *The Notebooks of Don Rigoberto*
(1997), Vargas Llosa gives us a self-mocking reference to his views in the
polemical letters that Don Rigoberto writes to "collectivist" institutions
or groups, such as feminists, ecologists, Rotarians, patriots, and so on (in
the second subdivision of each chapter). This is an amusing self-parody
of the author's own polemical tendencies, his extreme dislike of collective
identities, and his strong individualistic credo—written in a style that is
only a shade more outrageously polemical than some of Vargas Llosa's
own articles. In the following diatribe Don Rigoberto addresses the type
of flag-waving patriot that Vargas Llosa felt so uneasy about during his
electoral campaign:[19]

The umbilical cord that connects you across centuries is called fear of the
unknown, hatred for what is different, rejection of adventure, panic at the
thought of freedom, and the responsibility it brings to invent yourself each
day, a vocation for servitude to the routine and the gregarious, a refusal to
decollectivize so that you will not be obliged to face the daily challenge of
individual sovereignty . . . I assure you this may be one side of the patriotic coin, but the other side of the exaltation of one's own is the denigration of what belongs to someone else, the desire to humiliate and defeat

others, those who are different from you because they have another skin color, another language, another god, another way of dressing, another diet. (169)

Vargas Llosa's fiction also reflects the social function that he ascribes to writing and storytelling.[20] The protagonist at the center of *The Storyteller* (1987) is shown to be the memory, conscience and integrating force of his society. In *The War of the End of the World* (1981) it is the myopic writer-character—a blind seer—who, at the end, survives the bloodshed and, by intending to establish the true story of Canudos, sets out to write against oblivion in order to give history a meaning. In *The Feast of the Goat* (2000), Urania returns to the country where she was raped as a child by the dictator and tells her true story to her family so that the horror of the authoritarian regime will not be forgotten.[21] The search for truth is a recurring motive of Vargas Llosa's fiction ever since his first novel. (Who killed the "Slave" in *Time of the Hero*, who killed "La Musa" in *Conversation in the Cathedral*, and who killed Palomino Molero in the novel of the same title? What happened to Meche in *La Chunga*, to the vanished people in *Death in the Andes*, and to the main character in *The Bad Girl*?) But as in real life, the truth often remains obscure or ambiguous.

The one area we do not find reflected in Vargas Llosa's novels is his rather dogmatic defense of economic liberalism and a globalized free-market ideology as the solutions to poverty and injustice. Whereas his newspaper columns and conferences since the 1980s display a zealous belief in the functioning of the free play of market forces for the common good, his fiction doesn't seem to lend itself to illustrate this "truth." The ambiguous nature of the "truthful lie" that is Vargas Llosa's fiction, according to his own definition, would indeed be at odds with a messianic message of the kind that he spreads in his public statements promoting "the basic precepts of liberalism, which are political democracy, the market economy and the defense of individual interests over those of the state" ("Confessions of a Liberal"). Following the model of Hayek and von Mises, he regards the free market as guarantor of progress, "not only in the economy, but also in politics and culture, the system that can best harmonize the almost infinite diversity of human expectations and ambitions, within an order that safeguards freedom" ("Sabio discreto y liberal"). His rejection of state interventionism and his message of a "liberal revolution" that would bring peace, justice and freedom to the world is absent from his fiction (*A Fish in the Water* 430).[22]

Vargas Llosa's novels have always included subconscious distortions of his own views, such as the skepticism about political commitment that set the underlying tone for *Conversation in the Cathedral*, at a time when his public statements were still full of optimism about the socialist model.[23] In *The Feast of the Goat* the subliminal theme of revenge, retribution and poetic justice emerges as a disturbing but basic characteristic of human nature.[24] Within the dual structure of *The Way to Paradise* (2003) the political campaigning of Flora Tristán, in the unevenly numbered chapters, is nowhere near as interesting as the fictionalization of Paul Gauguin's sexual/creative energies, in the evenly numbered ones. Vargas Llosa's novels are full of failures, self-doubters and skeptical outsiders. Even the hybrid *A Fish in the Water*, a memory of his electoral campaign juxtaposed with a retelling of his making as a writer, brings out his fundamental skepticism about politics and his aversion to power.

> Real politics . . . has little to do with ideas, values and imagination, with teleological visions—the ideal society we would like to create—and, to put it bluntly, little to do with generosity, solidarity, and idealism. It consists almost exclusively of maneuvers, intrigues, plots, paranoias, betrayals, a great deal of calculation, no little cynicism, and every variety of con game. Because what really gets the professional politician, whether of the center, the left, or the right, moving, what excites him and keeps him going is *power*, attaining it, remaining in it, or returning to it as soon as possible. (87)

Yet even after these disillusioning experiences, Vargas Llosa continues to play a role as an influential opinion maker who attempts to directly effect policymaking, using his fame and prestige as a powerful tool—and gets ensnared in exactly the kind of politics that he has described previously. This happens in two ways: First, he throws his weight behind political parties in elections in Peru as well as in Spain and thus tries to influence the political direction a country takes. (His recommendation to vote for his old foe Alan García in Peru, "holding one's nose," is an example of this ["Razones para una alianza"]). Second, he presides over the "Fundación Internacional para la Libertad," an organization that promotes a free-market doctrine, founded to counteract the resurgence of populism and the politics of a strong and protectionist state in Latin America.[25] It is part of an international network of organizations such as the American Enterprise Institute, the Heritage Foundation, the Hispanic-American Center for Economic Research, an so on. Vargas Llosa's association with these think tanks is quite at odds with the empathy inherent in his fiction for everything human, including human weaknesses, illusions and hubris. It is strange to find Vargas Llosa the vociferous enemy of nationalism, defender of gay marriage and the separation of state and church linked to, for example, the Heritage Foundation, with its declared strategy to "restore the family as the primary institution of civil society, and reclaim the fullness of religious liberty in America's civic life"; its promotion of abstinence education for teenagers; its strong emphasis on border control and national security, in favor of a leading role for the U.S. military in the world, in order to "protect the liberties of American citizens, and win the war of ideas" (*Heritage Foundation*).[26] It is hard to understand why Vargas Llosa, the independent liberal intellectual whose articles can be stimulating or infuriating[27] but are always worth reading, allows himself to be associated with ideas that are in strong opposition to some of his own convictions.

His acceptance speech for the Irving Kristol Award did actually contain remarks that will not have pleased some of his hosts, such as economics not being the field through which all problems are resolved, an idea that has "sometimes generated more damage to the cause of freedom than did the Marxists." He said that "ideas and culture are what differentiate civilization from barbarism, not the economy." But one wonders how many of his readers have actually read and reread these "Confessions of a Liberal" and discovered the finer points of a critical debate he is trying to encourage within a staunch right-wing organization. But his readers will have heard about this award for Vargas Llosa, named after the man who coined the expression "neoconservative," and might well want to dissociate the admired author of fiction from the political opinion maker.

Vargas Llosa would like to be seen as "the man who writes and thinks," fulfilling a vocation that he calls, in an article on the German writer Günter Grass, "the most formidable of functions because [the writer], in addition to entertaining, also informs, teaches, guides, provides orientation and lessons" ("Günter Grass en la picota"). But there is a fine line between the credibility of an intellectual and a writer who, through his independent position, is able to critically evaluate society and give some kind of guidance on political, economic, cultural and moral issues, and an activist in the service of a "liberal offensive" in favor of free market economics and against state intervention.

To come back to our initial question, no, Vargas Llosa is not a rogue ("*un canalla*"), and he does not always write well. In a writer whose career spans more than fifty years, it is perfectly legitimate to agree with some of his statements—and those who like his fictions, I dare say, are likely to favor his ideas about democracy, freedom and an independent judiciary—and disagree with others, while admiring some of his fictions and feeling disappointed by others.[28] We can enjoy his polemics, or detest his *ad hominem* style. But he has certainly enriched public debate and seldom leaves anybody indifferent. Thus Vargas Llosa continues to fulfill the role of the writer as a contrarian, an awkward "agitator of consciences" as he has always described it. In his comment on the Günter Grass affair he praises him for being one of the last authors and intellectuals who still believe in a commitment toward literature *and* society:

> Günter Grass is the last in a line of writers to which a Victor Hugo, a Thomas Mann, an Albert Camus, a Jean-Paul Sartre, belonged. They believed that, in addition to imagining fictions, dramas or poems, being a writer consisted of agitating their contemporaries' conscience, leading them to action, defending certain options while rejecting others. Like him, they were convinced that, when it came to the great social, political, cultural, and moral topics; the writer could serve as a guide, advisor, animator or ideological incendiary and that, thanks to their intervention, political life could be more than mere pragmatism, and become an intellectual feat, a debate of ideas, a creation. ("Günter Grass en la picota")[29]

In fact, Vargas Llosa himself belongs in this line of "incendiaries" and continues this tradition with great enthusiasm "against wind and tide."

NOTES

1. Quoted in "Diario Granma: 'Vargas Llosa sigue siendo un canalla que escribe bien'." *Expreso* (Lima), July 9, 1997; the article goes on to explain that this statement justifies the presence of Vargas Llosa's literary work in Cuba, despite his conservative and anti-Castro views.
2. This is an attribute used by Efraín Kristal to categorize Vargas Llosa's life and work in his *Temptation of the Word: the Novels of Mario Vargas Llosa*. See my comment on this and other attempts at categorization in *Vargas Llosa's Fiction & the Demons of Politics*, 242ff.
3. My translation of the German dedication.
4. http://www.tolerancia.org
5. http://www.fnst-freiheit.org
6. Articles on these topics can be found among Vargas Llosa's regular journalistic contributions to the Spanish newspaper *El País*, the Peruvian magazine *Caretas*, and the Mexican *Letras Libres*. Some of them are also contained in his collections of articles *La verdad de las mentiras. Ensayos sobre literatura, Desafíos a la libertad, El lenguaje de la pasión, Touchstones. Essays on Literature, Art and Politics, Wellsprings*, and *Sables y utopías. Visiones de América Latina*.
7. See also William Rowe, who describes how many critics seem to loose their critical distance due to Vargas Llosa's categorical statements and his polemical *ad hominem* arguments. "Liberalism and Authority: the Case of Mario Vargas Llosa."

8. As, for example, his support for his old adversary Alan García in the 2006 Peruvian elections in order to stop the populist Ollanta Humala and "save democracy," see "Razones para una alianza."

9. First published as a series of reportages in the newspapers *El País* and *Caretas*, then published as a book, *Diario de Iraq*; now available in English in *Touchstones* (266–319); see especially 318f. where he gives reasons for his change of opinion.

10. See the chapter on "Vargas Llosa's rhetoric of radicality" in my study *Vargas Llosa's Fiction & the Demons of Politics* 39–45.

11. "But within ten, twenty, or fifty years, the hour of social justice will arrive in our countries, as it has in Cuba, and the whole of Latin America will have freed itself from the order that despoils it, from the castes that exploit it, from the forces that now insult and repress it" ("Literature is Fire" 73).

12. See "Carta a Fidel Castro."

13. In addition to the already mentioned book by Morote, see Omaña and also Rowe. For an interesting evaluation see Larsen.

14. The English version of "La literature es fuego," "Literature Is Fire" omits the word *militancia* from its description of literature.

15. See, e.g., the controversy with Oscar Collazos et. al. *Literatura en la revolución y revolución en la literatura*; and the one with Angel Rama: *García Márquez y la problemática de la novela.*

16. These ideas about a possible split between writer and public figure became an issue in itself when Vargas Llosa ran for the presidency of Peru in the 1990 elections. During the campaign, his erotic novel *In Praise of the Stepmother* (1988) was read out in installments on national television, in order to denounce him as a pervert, a sign that the total freedom he claims for the author in literary matters certainly does not go together with a writer's direct involvement in politics.

17. "José María Arguedas experienced this terrible dilemma and one finds traces of this disjunction in his work and in his behavior as a citizen" (*La utopía arcaica* 28). Vargas Llosa's fascination with the life and work of Arguedas goes back to the 1950s, when his first articles on the indigenist writer appeared.

18. See "Un mundo sin novelas" 39.

19. See the descriptions of patriotic meetings during the 1990 presidential campaign in Peru and Vargas Llosa's uneasiness during these displays of nationalism in *A Fish in the Water.*

20. See my study *Literatur und Politik – Mario Vargas Llosa* 265–378.

21. See Köllmann, *Vargas Llosa's Fiction* 290–301.

22. In *A Fish in the Water* he speaks of the "liberal offensive that was traversing the world" and of hopes for a "liberal revolution" (429, 430).

23. See Köllmann, *Vargas Llosa's Fiction* 81–137.

24. Köllmann *Vargas Llosa's Fiction* 239–301.

25. http://www.fundacionfil.org.

26. http://www.heritage.org, only a click away from the website of Vargas Llosa's Foundation.

27. One just has to look at some of the newspaper blogs reacting to his articles to see how provocative Vargas Llosa can be.

28. His latest novel, *The Bad Girl*, is strangely lifeless and unengaging, and reads a bit like a travelogue—perhaps a consequence of his restless lifestyle? (See the chronology on his official website. But this would be the topic of another essay).

29. In his autobiography *Beim Häuten der Zwiebel* (2006), Grass revealed that, as a seventeen-year-old soldier toward the end of World War II, he became a member of the SS for a couple of months. This caused a scandal because of his always hotly disputed role as social conscience in post-war West German society. In his article Vargas Llosa defended Grass with whom he had previously exchanged heated arguments about left-wing European attitudes to Latin America.

CHAPTER 11

VARGAS LLOSA AND THE HISTORY OF IDEAS

AVATARS OF A DICTIONARY

WILFRIDO H. CORRAL

THE BATTLE OF IDEAS HAS NOT LOST ITS CENTRAL importance in the twenty-first century. It is and will always be the subtext of the world of letters. In particular since the Dreyfus Affair, novelists have rarely been absent from these intellectual skirmishes. Few Latin American writers have been as committed to them—in their essays, novels, reviews, journalistic texts and other writings—as Mario Vargas Llosa. Nevertheless, these categories are paltry when it comes to defining an intellectual's course. This ubiquitous author has also become, in the last and present centuries, the conductor of an international nongovernmental campaign in defense of freedom in literature and the ideas that nurture freedom in society. As is the case with all good conductors, he exerts his authority if needed; but then he becomes the antagonist of all enemies of freedom.

The following analysis deciphers the individual and international contexts underlying the thought of this one-man orchestra. If, as has been argued from different critical perspectives, his writings raise numerous questions, it is also true that he has provided many answers. He has become an indispensable author and it is therefore pertinent to investigate why some think otherwise. Thus this article is not, nor could it be, a hagiography—which is, moreover, the last thing Vargas Llosa would want. Let me then exemplify his practice with a development in his production during this century. Despite the fact that *The Feast of the Goat* (2000, English 2001) was a bestseller for more than a year, it is significant that Vargas Llosa followed it with the publication of the essay collection

The Language of Passion (2001, English 2003). It is as if he wanted to nourish his narrative with the ideas that always contextualize it.

This symbiotic relationship continued with *The Way to Paradise*, published in Spanish and English in 2003, *The Temptation of the Impossible: Victor Hugo and Les Misérables* (2004, English 2007) and is brought to date with *The Bad Girl* (2006, English 2007) and *Diccionario del amante de América Latina* (Dictionary of the Latin American Lover, 2006). One can even argue that *El viaje a la ficción. El mundo de Juan Carlos Onetti* (The Voyage to Fiction: The World of Juan Carlos Onetti, 2008) is a summary of his long-lasting concern with how personal authorial nuances can be projected in fiction; as well as of his long admiration for the Uruguayan Onetti. As a perceptive reviewer of *Touchstones: Essays on Literature, Art and Politics* (2007), a collection of his nonfiction from 1987 to the present, notes, Vargas Llosa has the energy of a Victor Hugo, and the essays and articles reviewed illustrate "how much his literary and art criticism falls into line with his political convictions, and reveals how constant the latter have in fact remained over the past twenty years. He is refreshingly forthright: impatient with received opinion and political correctness, always careful to maintain what he refers to here as 'moral independence'" (Griffin 22).

In other words, his dynamism makes it impossible to classify him as a slavish follower of any intellectual master, or *idée fixe*. Emphasizing the importance of Sartre and Camus in the development of his ideas is a critical commonplace, despite the fact that since the early 1980s he has stressed his growing closeness to Camus, as well and his influence on him.

To date the ideological "influences" on such a dynamic intellectual is to limit them to what was the *dernier cri* in the 1950s, ideas that then claimed to universal relevance. Then came Vargas Llosa's break with the socialist ideas that the Cuban government prescribes until now. But his reaction against the ideas that sustain the Cuban revolution was linked to other related pressing preoccupations, such as his concern with José María Arguedas's *indigenismo*, a topic on which he has been writing since 1955, when he published a brief article simply titled "José María Arguedas" in the Peruvian newspaper *El Comercio*. From the mid-1960s to the end of the 1970s, after Vargas Llosa's writings had already become part of the literary canon, his relation with the world of ideas became more complex, as his interests expanded geographically toward transatlantic sociopolitics. During the mid-1980s, due to his still misunderstood "conservative" or "neoliberal" turn, it became the norm to talk about his dependence on the ideas of the philosopher Karl Popper, in particular his notion of the "open society." Again, he placed these influences in perspective and, for instance, has never subscribed to the radicalism of the United States followers of the socioeconomic thought of Friedrich A. von Hayek.[1] Toward the end of the twentieth century and until their deaths, the Peruvian novelist seemed to base his ideological beliefs on Isaiah Berlin's ideas and, more recently, on the writings of Jean-François Revel.

Today Vargas Llosa implicitly identifies with Revel's willingness to take up fights that no one else dared. When, in a brilliant recent essay, he notes that his French role model "wrote with elegance, thought with clarity, and always conserved an alert curiosity to what was happening in the rest of the world" ("Las batallas" 69), it is as if Vargas Llosa were writing about himself. It is more or less the same when he speaks about Revel's skills (74) and positive personality traits (76). This type of identification can also be traced to the first version of his essay on Berlin, revised for *Wellsprings*. Writing about the latter's "fair play," he says, "This is the scrupulous attention with which he analyses, exhibits, summarizes, and quotes the thoughts of his subjects, considering all their arguments, weighing the extenuating circumstances they faced, the constraints of the age, never pushing the words or ideas of others in one direction or another to make them appear similar to his own" (136).

However, the study of influences can be a clumsy analytical tool because a protean prose writer like Vargas Llosa only lets his reader overhear implied conversations at a distance. The intellectual progression sketched earlier can leave the impression that the greatest influences on the Peruvian novelist have been those international readings aligned with a *pensée unique*. In truth, those associations are not what led him to present himself for the Presidency of his country in 1990, as he explains in *A Fish in the Water* (1993, English 1994). Nothing is further from the truth, and the rest of his understudied nonfiction shows a similar progression. He is a barometer for cultural developments during the last five decades not because he introduces attractive foreign ideas, but rather because he represents a sophisticated "Latinamericanism" free from pseudopatriotic essentialisms. For similar albeit not expansive reasons, the ideas of the Venezuelan critic Carlos Rangel—as well as his sources—inform the Latin American context that would define Vargas Llosa's thought since the 1970s. The examination of these attitudes and the underlying ethics have not been the subject of the many conferences or books on him, and this lack cannot be excused by the argument that his ideas are fluid since, as I argue below, he has also been consistently forthright in the corrective measures he takes.[2]

One of the facile accusations against Vargas Llosa is that his "ideology" is more eloquent than his prose, despite the fact that he has stated to Héctor Aguilar Camín (and many others) that ideology is what was responsible for the twentieth century's atrocities. We examine here one of the authors whose vital paradoxes we can see but whose internal human contradictions we can only pretend to understand. However, one cannot help asking why, with the exception of a few literary journalists, no academics criticize the "progressive" ideology opposed to Vargas Llosa, or why there have not been studies critical of the essays or novels written from this politically situated perspective. Why is it then that the gift for the obvious present in politically oriented criticism is applied in a de-contextualized manner only to certain ideological battles? A lack of critical or ethical conscience is mostly responsible for the relativism and hypocrisy found among many proponents of high theory who interpret the Peruvian novelist, especially when it is clear they have not actually read him. They thus produce only discredited rhetoric, critical commonplaces, lapidary clichés and pusillanimous interpretative models or "positionings." When seen against the background of conventional academic leftism, Vargas Llosa can never be accused of being an extremist, as pointed out by the late Mario Benedetti during one of their famous polemics, because few Spanish American writers go into the battle of ideas in such a visceral, tangible, and complex manner. This complexity is nonetheless tacitly acknowledged in all critical anthologies about him, as well that his critics spend more time on his novels that in understanding how they are invariably conditioned by his ideas. Is the transition from one genre to the other this obvious? Yes, but it has received little examination until now.

I further argue that the comparatist approach, which examines his argument against the mental dependence of contemporary Latin American thinkers, has, till now, ignored the influence on Vargas Llosa of earlier thinkers from the region. For example, in an homage to Alfonso Reyes from 1969, he notes that the Mexican polymath "destroyed with his oceanic curiosity the artificial division that had been created between 'Americanism' and 'Eurocentrism;' he showed that both sources constituted the cultural head and tails of [Latin] America" ("Homenaje a Alfonso Reyes" 162). I propose a similar confluence in order to unknot this Moëbius strip, in particular because one can never substitute the contingencies of a lived experience, constituted by the relation of our author with the world of ideas, with technical abstractions. I must reiterate that the book or article that elucidates his ideas has not been written yet, and there are no critics currently interested in doing so. It is necessary to point out that for the author of *La utopía arcaica. José María Arguedas y las ficciones del indigenismo* (Archaic Utopia. José María Arguedas and the Fictions of Indigenism, 1996), perhaps his most polemical and carefully crafted essay, ideas move throughout geographic and social spaces, together with artifacts, structures and institutions present in their original contexts. The ideological context is Latin American, especially when it refers to the intellectual past of *indigenismo* and other related continental topics, and Latin Americans at least are aware of this. Thus the Peruvian anthropologist Juan Ossio traces the presence of the social sciences in his writings and states that "at least for me, as for my colleagues Masao Yamaguchi, Roberto Da Matta and others, Vargas Llosa's writings are related to our own work" (137).

It is a commonplace in certain areas of academia to blame the United States and the West for all world problems and to present activist actors like Subcomandante Marcos and Rigoberta Menchú as the only true [Latin] American thinkers. Roberto Fernández Retamar, a limited intellectual who only holds one idea in mind, has made this argument, for instance. Like the other two, he does not realize that there is a difference between opinion accepted as ideological marching orders and philosophy as an abstract system. Nor does not being tied to a specific locality or locally manifested political cause mean the intellectual is without affiliation. In other words, the fact that Vargas Llosa is writing from cosmopolitan Madrid or London does not mean that his ideas, whether original or received, have been permanently adapted and transformed by a transcultural movement on his part, despite the fact that his prose is translated almost immediately for the most prestigious publications of the West. During his lifetime, the author of *The Storyteller* has experienced something that is indubitable: even before globalization became a 1990s slogan, the world of ideas relocated, adapted, and transformed when it came into a new environment. What he always makes clear is that objects (perhaps the things that are aspirations for art) not ideas or ways of life can be lost. This characteristic has led to his being accused of recycling material for his book on Onetti. However, one must remember that this criticism is limited to his ideas about fiction. Kwame Anthony Appiah correctly asks about the degree to which one can hold on to the idea of being a "citizen of the world," as if one could truly deny one's connections in the name of humanity, that vast abstraction (xv–xvi). I see no reason to deny this interpretation, although there is little reward in believing in it.

These coalescences do not necessarily imply that Vargas Llosa is a hybrid cultural thinker. No matter what is said about his neoliberalism— an opinion that is rarely contextualized, conveniently eliding his conversion from young Peruvian bourgeois into a progressive internationalist committed to the Cuban experiment of the 1960s—the truth is that it is difficult to find texts by him that are not Latin American in spirit. This premise holds even if their Latin Americanism is frequently perceived as enigmatic, due to their distancing from any version of magical realism or local resentment. For him, the circulation and transference of ideas implies the use of traditions and aesthetic forms that never have frontiers. This view used to be known in traditional terms as "universalism" but today is more trendily called "interdisciplinarity." If one had to bet where Vargas Llosa is today when it comes to the cavalcade of ideas, one could argue that he is in the midst of the cultural dynamic that examines how they are appropriated, found and received to create transnational networks and intermediaries. As the *New York Times* points out in a note that supplements Harrison's review of *The Bad Girl*, one can measure the import of an author by the writers who line up to review his books. Hence, between 1982 and 1990, Anglo-American writers of the caliber of William Kennedy, Robert Stone, Julian Barnes, Robert Coover, Ursula K. Le Guin, and the late Anthony Burgess reviewed his books in that newspaper. To these names, one can add the late John Updike's special devotion to the Peruvian author in the *New Yorker*. With this sense of his wide currency, let us move then to an emblematic representation of his ideas as they are collected, fragmented, and actualized in *Diccionario del amante de América Latina*, in order to contextualize them with the previous development that serves as their blueprint.

The word *amante* (lover) is easily associated with our continent, for myriad cultural reasons. Furthermore, authors like Vargas Llosa continuously seem to have lovers' spats with the world. Voltaire, in his own dictionary, said that they are made from dictionaries. Dr. Johnson believed dictionaries are like watches, because they do not work, but it is better to have one. Both nouns—lover and dictionary—can be linked to the Peruvian author because his nonfiction is symbiotic with his fiction. Even if it seems redundant, the current dissemination of his nonfiction can only seem necessary, and not just because his dictionary is the second of his essay books originally published in French (*Dictionnaire amoureux de l'Amérique latine* [2005]—the first was *Un demi-siècle avec Borges*, [Half a Century with Borges, 2004]). In rapid succession, his essays are also (partially) published in English, and *Touchstones* and *Wellsprings* are the two most recent examples, as if the West wants to keep up with the energy of one of the writers who does the most to promote its culture. Because of his energetic vision and kinetic language, in addition to his courage, Vargas Llosa is never boring; a fact that does not imply that every text included in *Diccionario del amante de América Latina* is of similar relevance. After all, every personal dictionary becomes a personal testimony, as he notes in his prologue. This is the dynamic on which permanent romance is built, and it is from there that this book, for now a comprehensive summary of his ideas, ensues.

The entries on writers—and we are aware he knows all those who are of worth and more—have the fearsome critical edge of his books on Flaubert, Arguedas, and the one he has recently resurrected on García Márquez. (The latter was his second full-length study of an author, if one takes into account his thesis on Rubén Darío presented as an undergraduate in Lima). This perception is correct only if one accepts these encyclopedia entries as such, not in the context of the major books he has produced on these four authors, to which one can add *The Temptation of the Impossible* on Victor Hugo, of which he had given a preview in 1983, and now the recent one on Onetti. Personal memories, generous anecdotes, and recognizable episodes of this "alphabetic life" run the gamut from fascinating to superficial, from marvelously entertaining to extremely informative, as we see in the notes, comments, fragments and references to Balzac, Bioy Casares, Eco, Foucault, Monterroso and others. What are "foreigners" doing in a work in which the author attempts to give value to what is Latin American? The answer is not complicated. As he says in a text about his Parisian years (partially and retrospectively fictionalized in *The Bad Girl*) in Paris, "The artist and writers from Latin America met, spent time together, recognized each other as members of the same historical and cultural community. While there [in Latin America], we lived walled inside our countries, paying attention to what was taking place in Paris, London or New York, without having any idea of what was going on in our neighboring countries and, sometimes, even in ours" (*Diccionario* 285). It is obvious that for him and his contemporaries leaving Latin America made it possible to evaluate the differences between the achievements, myths, and flaws of the continent, and its place in the West, as he explains in "Dentro y fuera de América Latina" (Within and out of Latin America) and as he confessed to Cueto (*La vie en mouvement* 93–95).

Due to his resistance to provincialism, when writing about international contexts, Vargas Llosa gravitates to other prose writers of the Latin American continent. The longer entries are for the nomad authors and nationalist politicians with whom he also seems obsessed. This is the case with the entries on Borges, Cortázar, Donoso, Edwards, Mariátegui, Moro, Sartre, and Vallejo, without excluding Castro, Che Guevara and his electoral antagonist Fujimori (compare the brilliant social and personal contextualization that he gives the latter in the entry "Cholo"). These share the "cut and paste" nature that characterizes this type of compilation. Thus in order to provide a wider context or to avoid creating the sensation that previous texts have been recycled, other entries are on "commitment," "country," and "utopia"—the last one presented as a key word. Each entry has footnotes, some unnecessary for a cultured Latin American, and it is clear that they were composed by the editor, not the author. Moreover, as stated in the *Diccionario del amante de América Latina*, almost every human activity (and one can add ideas) creates its celebrities, scandals, paradigm shifts, and gossip. If these do not explain the concepts, they provide conversation topics and, at best, food for thought, because the amplitude and construction of the ideas to which Vargas Llosa refers require more than a volume, if what is desired is strict analysis. As is the case with every author of his caliber, he takes up ideas but never "adapts" them to a specific public or period, instead developing them. This is a trait his detractors refuse to accept, but of which he is aware, as evidenced in the "Acknowledgments" to *Wellsprings* (201–2), where he describes the genesis of those essays.

The *cognoscenti* are aware that the world of letters does not have a good reputation. Since he believes in being direct, Vargas Llosa does not disappoint in the pages he devotes to various literary personalities. Those dedicated to his agent Carmen Balcells and his first publisher Carlos Barral are of particular interest, as are those on his mentor and professor at the University of San Marcos, Raúl Porras Barrenechea. Consequently, the longest entry is on Octavio Paz. Vargas Llosa adds five paragraphs to the beginning of the eponymous text of his anthology *The Language of Passion*, in which he amply praises the mastery of the Mexican poet and cultural commentator. He has not given up on his belief in the responsibility of novelists to be self-critical and consistent in their reach. Among the notable entries on literary topics are those on "Short Stories," "*Indigenismo*," "Literature," and "Novel," supplemented by others on concepts linked specifically to Peruvian popular culture, such as "Humor," "*Huachafería*," "Radio Plays," "Religious Sects," and "*Telurismo*," as well as on the locations of several of his novels: "Lima," "Jungle," "Backlands," and, why not, "Europe."

This representative selection of topics does not exclude some of his works or the objects that inspired them, as with *The Cubs* and *The Green House*, or the characters on which they were based, including "The Counselor" and "Flora Tristán." Vargas Llosa did not write to justify an obvious critical assumption to which interpreters overwhelmed by the power of his work often succumb: that one of the sources of his fiction is "his own experience," or the incredibly naïve belief that his political ideas are only "independent criticism."[3] There is nothing wrong with admiring Vargas Llosa deeply, but a reasonable parricide is a healthy, almost religious, act that those critics closest to him do not want to exercise. Beginning with his often quoted "Literature Is Fire," his acceptance speech upon receiving the Rómulo Gallegos Award in 1967, until now, Vargas Llosa has shown that when dealing with ideas, even if they are philosophical, these are expressed by an author, not by characters talking in dialogues or parables. Critics, especially those who have or seek the author's imprimatur, forget we all contain a multitude of characters and patterns of behavior, and these are bidden by cues we don't even hear. This is why it is useful not to see critical reactions against Vargas Llosa as personal attacks but, instead, as part of an intellectual discussion on concrete issues, an act of which his acolytes never partake.

He is certainly aware that all revolutions structurally require antagonists who frequently become fixed rhetorical adversaries, and among these none is as easy a target as the bourgeoisie, which is contradictorily also a source of support and stimulus. For analogous reasons, he has taken a similarly complex attitude when it comes to his ideas on fiction. Thus, throughout *The Temptation of the Impossible*, Vargas Llosa asks if the world has truly advanced by means of the revolutionary fantasies of the Left and comes to the conclusion that these promises have been as false as fairy tales. In "Literatura y política: dos visiones del mundo" (Literature and Politics: Two Worldviews), he asserts that "with Trujillo political life became literature, that is, pure fiction" (66). In this regard, George Orwell provided one of the best midcentury analyses of the relation between politics and literature. In a 1946 reading of Swift's *Gulliver's Travels*, Orwell—whose *Animal Farm* is studied by Vargas Llosa in *La verdad de las mentiras* (The Truth of Lies)—examines the relationship between agreeing with an author's opinions and enjoying a work of literature (1104). He concludes, "If it seems to you a really pernicious book, likely to influence other people in some undesirable way, then you will probably construct an aesthetic theory to show that it *has* no merits" (1105, emphasis in the original).

Vargas Llosa can only agree. His statement about politics and fiction implies much more than a return to a long-felt passion; it describes a prodigious demon that propels his exploration of the artist's internal world. While he has felt the need to always return to the defense of "the culture of freedom," the unreconstructed Left of the Americas has been unable to abandon its obsession with "dependency," whose pontifications never include any essays dealing with literary culture vis-à-vis politics. In a companion essay titled "Literature and the Left," Orwell states that it is one thing for a writer to dislike politics, another for him to dislike it because it forces one to think (472). Orwell believes that left-wing literary criticism has been correct in emphasizing the importance of politics, but "where it has been wrong is in making what are ostensible literary judgments for political ends" (473). This 1943 acknowledgment has not been heeded by politically committed Latin Americanist criticism, although this political fixation can be determinative for a certain type of thinker or thought. This raises the unavoidable question regarding the audience of both Vargas Llosa and his progressive adversaries (as he says to Boyers and Bell-Villada, "We need both a left and a right if we want real democracy" ["Exhilaration and Completeness" 227]), a question that cannot be answered with the simplistic response that his allies write books about idiots for idiots. The answer does not lie necessarily or exclusively with the readership of both ideological poles. The fact is that on the one hand, intellectual history must be contextualized, but on the other, it must explain why a general theory proposed by a writer like Vargas Llosa is applicable to different circumstances in the future—that is, if it is a theory. In this sense, when criticism of his ideas comes from the Anglo-Saxon world, the distinctions established by late U.S. scholar John P. Diggins among a "Lyrical Left," an "Old Left," and a "New Left," adding, as an anomaly, an "Academic Left," come to mind.

More akin to his combinatory art, his practice as an essayist still gives rise to blank and naive literary interpretations. A recent one is that "when Vargas Llosa writes about his own work as a novelist, and establishes a theory about his own work, he develops an activity that is *interesting and exciting* for the reader and for the student of literature as an *introduction* to his creative method" (Angvik 51, my emphases).[4] In the same manner that in his literary criticism he consistently uses terms like "communicating vessels," "the added element," and "craters," regarding his political ideas, one can ponder why some terms have also become a permanent part of his lexicon, even though he does not seem to have made a conscious selection of these. After being asked by Cueto what he has discovered about himself from his practice, Vargas Llosa replied, "I believe I have discovered time and again my consistencies and some recurring obsessions. These are things that I see clearly now, but that I absolutely did not see at the start" (55). This statement must be seen within the context given by Ricardo A. Setti nearly a quarter of a century ago in *Conversas com Vargas Llosa*, which provided a fairly thorough perspective on Vargas Llosa's political vision (131–80).

Because of reasons like the ones mentioned, it could seem that the entries in his *Diccionario del amante de América Latina* concentrate on subjects excessively close to its author, but this is not the case. Vargas Llosa knows how easy it is for an idea to become a fixed impression or perception, or for an empirical observation to be elevated to an affirmation of principle. Because of this, Latin America and its diversity is at the core of his dictionary. Overall, he exhibits no false concern for political correctness, as can be verified in his entries on the Andes, Brazil and Euclides da Cunha, Chile and Neruda—the latter a personal statement, more an homage than the diatribe against the Chilean poet expected by the novelist's detractors. The same approach is patent in the entry on Havana and Lezama Lima and his *Paradiso*, and Paraguay and Roa Bastos. Similarly, the crisis in painting, artists and dictators is brilliantly captured. But there is no attempt at an amateur psychoanalysis of the region's culture or inhabitants in *Diccionario del amante de América Latina*, even though we know that introspection comes easily to the author, and we have never suspected him of ambivalence regarding fathoming his own inner life. Consequently, in October 2007 Vargas Llosa told an interviewer from the *New York Times* that he was opposed to psychoanalysis because "it's too close to fiction, and I don't need more fiction in my life" ("Questions for Mario Vargas Llosa").

When he concentrates on politics, of which the notes dedicated to Camus, Cuba, and Literature in his dictionary are very good examples, he does not indulge in pessimistic rhetoric on Latin America and Latin Americans. For him, defining oneself as being from that bailiwick does not imply denying our Western character, nor does it mean resorting to essentialisms based on attacks against a neoliberalism that, it must be noted, is no longer the exclusive policy of any current Latin American state. No one has traced or examined this trajectory better than Revel in "Mario Vargas Llosa et la politique," included in the volume the *Cahiers de l'Herne* dedicated to the Peruvian writer. Revel points out the simplifications of European Marxists and U.S. liberals regarding Latin American developments. He notes that they are the specific butt of Vargas Llosa's critiques (366); and reminds us of the connection between his literary criticism and novels such as *The Feast of the Goat*, which provides political lessons that are always shown, never theorized (365), as the novelist himself thoroughly points out to Boyers and Bell-Villada ("Exhilaration and Completeness" 219–26). At the same time, like Berlin (196–97), Vargas Llosa knows that the doctrine whereby the artist is socially responsible has a long and complex history, and like the Latvian thinker, the Peruvian also knows that "art is neither journalism nor moral instruction. But the fact is that art does not absolve the artist from responsibility. Neither is artistic activity a costume that can be put on or taken off without reason: it is the expression of an individual nature or it is nothing" (*Diccionario*, 213). He had qualified this notion in the earlier lecture "Literatura y política," in which he argued that both intellectual fields—literature and politics—are distant for a number of reasons, but it is unavoidable that they merge (62). This is why he affirms that "to believe that literature has nothing to do with politics, and if they get close, literature becomes degraded, is to believe that literature is a game, a distraction, entertainment" (50). Not in vain, he had already said in the same lecture: "In the kind of literature that is called 'light,' and which has become the dominant tendency in contemporary literature, politics has no place" (44). As Orwell states in the previously mentioned 1946 essay,

> We are told that in our age, for instance, any book that has genuine literary merit will also be more or less 'progressive' in tendency. This ignores the fact that throughout history a similar struggle between progress and reaction has been raging, and that the best books of any one age have always been written from several different viewpoints, some of them palpably more false than others. In so far as a writer is a propagandist, the most one can ask of him is that he shall genuinely believe in what he is saying, and that it shall not be something blazingly silly. (1107)

Throughout his recent essays and novels, one can easily verify that Vargas Llosa is not an ideological writer, from Orwell's or any other perspective. To a great degree, this is because he does not write about politics but about the political behavior of all types of individuals. In the best, historically informed reading of *Temptation of the Impossible*, Graham Robb identifies a mirrorlike relationship between Hugo and Vargas Llosa. Robb asks why "an individual who pretends to have an exceptionally clear view of today's political realities spends his time, inasmuch as he is writer, inventing stories" (24).

For Robb the problem resides in the fact that the "real reality" in question is historical and that our perception of it has been strongly influenced by works of fiction, such as *Les Misérables*. According to Robb, Vargas Llosa has an optimistic view of the recent historiography on Hugo and concludes by revealing the manner in which Vargas Llosa's ideas have developed and how this implies an advantage: "The strength of this study resides in the doubts that it raises about the process of literary creation and the awareness that the writer has of his own processes and their provocative effect on the reader. Instead of justifying this with his own method, as it is done by numerous university studies on *Les Misérables*, like the novel itself, Vargas Llosa poses questions that are still inevitably unanswered" (25).

In his worldview, opinion never shapes a person's character, as can be surmised from the arc of fanaticism found from *The War of the End of the*

World to *The Feast of the Goat*, nor does prejudice annul its imperfections. This is why, within the structure of Vargas Llosa's ideas, one can see him as the novelist of personal lives. Following the model set by Hugo, he is concerned with political ideas and events to the degree that they distort, stimulate, or frustrate lives, and these become more vivid than any theory interpreters could concoct to explain them. This vision does not entail presenting himself as a redeemer of humanity by means of ideas that are, perhaps, too grandiose for individual human beings—or by communicating these ideas as merely symbolic, only a cultural good. Throughout his books, Vargas Llosa's readers consistently verify his clear and just evaluation of human reason. This is why his imagination does not generally stray from contemporary topics, even if, on occasion, he attempts to find their roots in the ideas of the nineteenth century, for instance. In addition to the influence of European culture, one must also consider that at the start of his writing career he read the novelists of the "lost generation" (Dos Passos, Faulkner, Fitzgerald, and Hemingway), as he notes in interview after interview. These readings verify the Western geopolitical family relationships always found in his writings.

In the 1969 article in which he praised Reyes, Vargas Llosa notes that the Mexican critic "was a lover of the West," who took charge of this tradition and judged it with rigor and infallible good taste. Once a disciple, now a master; the trajectory that provisionally concludes in *Diccionario del amante de América Latina* shows that good influences are added on, not erased. As he says in "El viaje de Odiseo" ("Odysseus's Voyage"), "There is a constant in Western culture: the fascination with human beings who break limits, who instead of accepting the servitude of what is possible, attempt, against all logic, to achieve what is impossible" (39). The references found in his dictionary show that this statement is broadly applicable to his world of ideas. In the entry "América Latina" (dated 1988), probably the initial expression of the misunderstood neoliberalism with which he is associated, he says, "To be free while poor is to enjoy a precarious and incomplete freedom. True and complete freedom will only flourish in our region when prosperity, which allows men and women to make their dreams reality and to conceive new fantasies, is achieved." (*Diccionario del amante de América Latina* 26). More than a socioeconomic view, his statement expresses another of his obligations as an intellectual and novelist: to unmask official truths. Nevertheless, one cannot find in his novels intellectuals who expound on serious topics, as is the case with what are known as "novels of ideas." The exceptions may be those that have Don Rigoberto as their main character (*In Praise of the Stepmother* and *The Notebooks of Don Rigoberto*). In this relative absence of characters who are practicing intellectuals, Vargas Llosa's novels do not differ from most major Western fiction, with the exception of Dostoyevsky.

The composition of his nonfiction exhibits parallel provisos, and his prologue to *Diccionario del amante de América Latina* states that the book was suggested by some of his collaborators (mainly Albert Bensoussan, his translator into French). However, there is no doubt that the book has his DNA, as one would expect from one that includes "lover" in its title; especially if one understands his "Latin Americanism" as being above and beyond any national atavism. As in his fiction, general conceptual consistency is another ruling thread that erases national borders and aesthetic limits. Still another review of *Touchstones*, a representative sample of his recent shorter essays for journals and magazines, states that Vargas Llosa is "a narrator one can trust," because as a reader he is a liberator. In other words, writing transforms a writer into what reading makes a reader: both become *thinkers*, not merely doers. Thus ideas, texts, sketches, combine in fragments (with the dates of composition indicated between parentheses) that have as their template a concept *of* Latin America. Vargas Llosa does not supply pontifications that proclaim "in this I believe," which are unconvincing due to their being written in accord with the ideological positions the author believes are expected from him. It is true that he has previously analyzed some of these questions in longer essays, studies, and even in articles for journals and other anthologies of his nonfiction writing. Even so, this collection is a sui generis cultural concordance, for an entry titled "Game" is in reality an analysis of Cortázar, and one titled "Kola Real" is a scrutiny of entrepreneurial genius.

Following a conventional alphabetic order in his dictionary does not provide a precise idea of the conditions of production nor of the chronology of the author's ideological development. This lack is heightened by the heterogeneity of his works, which has led his critics to despair. One can imagine that Bensounssan, who edited the original French version, organized the text. However, it would be a mistake to give this too much importance since the order of the text does not change the result. For instance, we already know what Vargas Llosa thinks about Latin American "cut-rate intellectuals" even before he distilled this term definitively in *A Fish in the Water*, since the description was used in the first two volumes of *Contra viento y marea*. Yet the entry on the topic in this dictionary dates back to a text originally published in 1966, in which he distinguishes between creator and intellectual: "If both—vocation and political commitment—coincide, fine, but if they diverge there is tension; a cleavage is produced. We should not avoid, however, this cleavage. We must on the contrary assume it fully and from this cleavage produce literature, create" ("Intelectual" *Diccionario del amante de América Latina* 210). As we also know, the discount mediators of ideas have never accepted their contradictions, while the Peruvian writer has been honest with his, has been tolerant of difference, and has shown no desire to become the spokesperson of any single idea. He thus avoids the essentialist tendency that has characterized more than one progressive intellectual in whose "dictionary" one cannot find any freedom from or tolerance for that which is not "Latin American." Vargas Llosa concludes his compendium by showing that there are more people and things that unite than separate us. This is why we should care for (in an intellectual rather than sentimental sense) the words and things that have always defined us as human beings.

Placing his current thinking—of which his dictionary is just one recent example—in perspective, it is clear that the author is sure that the storm of ideas of the last four decades resists any belief in an end of their history and that, at the same time, he sees them in relation to their different human periods and mythologies. In other words, during uncertain times, in which the arts have returned to the security of sequels and sentimentalism, in a period in which the central idea is to not have any new idea and continue with the tried and true, Vargas Llosa presents himself as a unique voice that recovers the historical uncertainty that has impelled artistic imagination. Not surprisingly, this is what happened in Latin America during the seventies and eighties, when he came into his own as a writer, and is another example of the consistency of his ideas and of his desire to go from theory to action. As I pointed out earlier, temporarily *both* reader and writer are thinkers, not doers. Imagination makes it possible for readers, as well as authors, to rise to the world of ideas and ideals, but it also may make them misconstrue the total meaning of both. This is why, to give surplus value to his activity, he has had to develop a language and value code different from that of the social sciences.[5] No matter the phobias from which his ideas may arise, Vargas Llosa trusts in the language he uses to express them, while hyperspecialized academic language reveals its suspicion that common language is no longer useful or appropriate to eliminate the underlying causes of its ideological terrors.

Thinkers like Vargas Llosa react to intellectual developments, as they acknowledge the professionalization of intellectual fields, because for them conceptual developments cannot become mired in what is politically transient. *Historia secreta de una novela* (Secret History of a Novel, 1971), based on conferences presented in 1968, is his first systematic excursion into the study of nonfiction prose. His ideological progression actually began with *Entre Sartre y Camus* (Between Sartre and Camus,

1981), which served as the basis for the first volume of *Contra viento y marea, 1962–1982* (Against All Odds, 1983), even if it did not strictly wander outside the literary field. Because these beginnings are not part of a totalizing plan, foundational authors like him, despite the safeguarding of their documents in foundations or universities, are always exposed to recuperation or rescue. For instance, one wonders how a holistic view of his prose will change with the recent edition of what are being called his complete works.[6]

It would be easy to attribute his wide-ranging interests to the fluctuating character of his writing and his verbal authenticity as a critic. It is also obvious that we lack interpretations that explain these traits or permit comparing the opinions expressed in countless interviews, journalistic pieces, and reportages. However there is still another guiding characteristic underlying this evolution: his concern with the crisis in the arts and artists, both terms being understood in the most ample sense. Indeed, he explores how art comes from real life and ends up in a book or an exhibit and how ultimately that progression and the market change the nature of art. As can be gleaned from *Touchstones*, for Vargas Llosa, artists are permanent rebels, a consideration that leads to a revealing paradox: he has been the least conservative of the Boom writers. Every time his antagonists criticize him, it is as if they were not hearing what he is truly saying. It is as if they are programmed to ignore what has happened in the world of ideas outside their own. In an exhaustive and timely revision of Latin American literary antimodernism, wisely inserted within the dialectic between "universal and local, cosmopolitanism and nationalism, what is foreign and what is one's own, etc." (76), Claudio Maíz begins with conviction and accuracy from the "the metaphysics of location" (68–72). As Appiah posits in his study of values in our contemporary world of strangers, it is not problematic that we cannot share a lexicon of evaluation, that we can give the same vocabulary different interpretations and assign different importance to the same values. According to Appiah, "Each of these problems seems more likely to arise if the discussion involves people from different societies" (66). The problem, according to Hopenhayn, is that current thought "is primarily consecrated to studying how to study, to protect itself from those who are more methodical. Under the guise of a healthy cautiousness, it has renounced the adventure of thinking. It has become a detective, referee, and a strategy of knowledge. It does not write to provoke but to be refuted" (28).

Unlike the disintegration of the act of thinking, Vargas Llosa wants to show both sides of words and things and does not want to be seen as a "Minister of Culture" of any country or continent. He is aware that any antiestablishment thinker, or any savant professing a doctrine, is open to the accusation of messianism. Precisely because today we live in microwave oven societies in which with the touch of a button, things are ready, the Peruvian novelist has looked for alternative articulations for the speculations of his time, and his position does not imply that he wants to "guide" with unthinking reactions. Rather, he attempts to anchor himself in rationality so as not to get lost while exploring profound topics. Because of this concern, he generally ignored a vocabulary—seen as "ideas" only by its blinded enthusiasts—that includes terms akin to "globalization," "modernity," "multiculturalism," "postcolonialism," and their avatars. He has also never ignored the changes introduced in the configuration of society by science and technology. In other words, by default he has to be more concerned with art, with the weight of bad ideas, and not with the baroque seriousness of the concepts present in Western social thought. Appiah demands "one connection—the one neglected in talk of cultural patrimony—is the connection not *through* identity but *despite* difference. We can respond to art that is not ours; indeed, we can fully respond to 'our' art only if we move beyond thinking of it as ours and start to respond to it as art" (135, his emphasis). Given that Appiah links cosmopolitanism to border crossings, diversity, localism, nationalism, and tolerance, all at a global level, one could also argue that we are facing "freely floating signifiers." Not Vargas Llosa, because he grasps and mines the ambiguities and nuances of a globalized world and its dizzying movement of ideas and people.

The frivolity and apolitical character of the academic marketers of those signifiers, especially those in U.S. universities, frustrate Vargas Llosa. He first mentioned these institutional sources of ephemeral knowledge in *Desafíos a la libertad* (Challenges to Freedom, 1994), a text also composed by articles previously published in his biweekly column "Piedra de toque," whose register has been transferred to his English language recompilations.[7] Those views of Anglo-Saxon academia, which he still maintains, do not mean he does not admit U.S.-based corrections to the "great theory" of the West as applied to Latin America. Within the taxonomy proposed by Diggins for the U.S. Left and his concern with the failure of theory (342–70), Latin American radicalism does not share the radical innocence or the wounded idealism of the former. Latin America's Left's current nostalgia for the movements of 1968 is the most convincing proof of this. As Diggins points out, the Latin American academic Left, like that of the North, inhabits worlds separate from those of the majority of the population (288–91). In its present practice the Latin American

Left still resembles the Lyric Left (251–55), whose exploits have even been parodied by the recent generation of Latin American novelists.

There is not enough space to examine the extensive criticism Vargas Llosa has leveled against nationalism and its close links to populist dictatorships; recently he has extended these criticisms to the problems faced by the Basque country (see "The Challenge of Nationalism" in *Wellsprings*) and to Hugo Chávez. There is little doubt that his analysis is based on reason not sentiment. But what leads to divergent readings of writers like him? Is it that they muddle in political waters or "make waves"? This thinking against the current is consistent with Arthur O. Lovejoy's views. According to this founder of the study of the history of ideas, this discipline is "especially concerned with the manifestations of specific unit-ideas in the collective thought of large groups of persons, not merely in the doctrines or opinions of a small number of profound thinkers or eminent writers" (19). I have concentrated on the Peruvian's nonfiction prose, because his aesthetics are decontextualized even in sympathetic statements: "The Marxist orthodoxy of Latin American intellectuals has come under increasing challenge from writers [sic] like Hernando de Soto, Mario Vargas Llosa, and Carlos Rangel, who have begun to find a significant audience for liberal, market-oriented economic ideas" (Fukuyama 42).

The objection that must be made to comments like Fukuyama's, which may be characteristic of the reception of Vargas Llosa in the anglophone world of ideas, is that they describe Latin American thought monolithically. For instance, even if the political scientist Nikolaus Werz does not present the criticisms made by Octavio Paz, Rangel, and Vargas Llosa against state overreach as contradictory, he makes a necessary distinction among them (227–32). After pointing out that the Venezuelan scholar and the Peruvian writer agree that the decisive factors that have promoted underdevelopment are to be found in the countries of the third world themselves and their intellectuals, Werz adds, "Unlike Rangel, however, he [Vargas Llosa] does not presuppose the incompatibility between capitalism and socialism" (225). The well-known problem is that, no matter who presents it, ideology is never fully coherent, a fact forgotten when dealing with Vargas Llosa's ideas. In the 1978 essay "Yo, un negro" (I, a Black Man), included in *Contra viento y marea* III (19–22), he criticizes the insistence on "ideology," which he sees as the rhetorical usurpation by the Left of notions considered to have universal or self-evident meaning or content. In a brief article that predates the book quoted previously, Appiah mentions that unlike nationalism, cosmopolitanism and patriotism are feelings rather than ideologies.[8] This necessary distinction has never been applied to the ideas of the Peruvian novelist.

According to the author, words, such as "black," do not have an exclusive racist meaning, a Latin American cultural subtlety that nonetheless does not justify their careless use. This distinction would seem obvious to any rational thinker but is not accepted in a politically correct environment, which fosters the reticence and euphemism Vargas Llosa never practices. This is another reason why it is impracticable to summarize his arguments regarding ideology, which, according to his definition, ignores the endless semantic varieties produced by public written and oral language. One of the justifications for this view from 1978 is that "according to Isaiah Berlin, there are two hundred different definitions of 'freedom'" ("Yo, un negro" 22). In "La cultura de la libertad" (The Culture of Freedom), a lecture from 1985, Vargas Llosa presents a robust defense of the notion and practice of freedom as it has developed in the West. According to him, this dynamic would explain how the Western notion grew and spread, despite the fact that there have been attempts at incorporating incompatible meanings into this concept. In his 1985 address, he then reminds his audience that "Isaiah Berlin has detected at least forty different definitions of the concept of freedom" (435). The text of the conference, which is different from the version that appeared in *Making Waves* (1996), has been expanded and brought up to date for *Wellsprings*.

There is no attempt at explaining the difference in the number of meanings of the term freedom ascribed to Berlin in the 1978 version of "Yo, un negro." Although neither figure is mentioned in the English versions of the essay, it is not transcendental to find out whether the decrease in the figure has to do with any change in Berlin's ideas, or if it is a printing mistake. What is essential is to notice the importance that Vargas Llosa ascribes to Berlin in his elaboration of the "common sense" of his own ideas. This is the reason why one must scrutinize his relationship with Berlin and other "real thinkers," as the intellectuals who have influenced him and who form a discernable ideological group he uses as "signs" of identity have been called. In his reading of thinkers classified as "liberal," in the Latin American and European meaning of the word, Vargas Llosa is continuously making ideological connections; as the reader of *Diccionario del amante de América Latina*, or the English language collections of his essays has to do. Some may disagree with him by pointing out that the end of totalitarian regimes does not necessarily lead to democracy and the market economy. Others may argue that the escape from socialism proposed by the "real thinkers" does not necessarily lead to a true liberalism, because the press and prerevolutionary tendencies do not necessarily predict true interest in reform. Revel concurs that prerevolutionary ten-dencies do not predict a true interest in reform. He further explains Vargas Llosa's advantage on this topic: "If those nostalgic for totalitarian socialism (reconverted today into enemies of globalization) deploy such aggression against Vargas Llosa, it is not only because he defends liberal democracy, but because he was a Marxist for a long time" (368).

Vargas Llosa is undeniably interested in liberal thinkers and in the question of liberalism, as can be ascertained in his fullest interviews with Cueto ("La vie en mouvement" 87–90) and Setti. Nevertheless, he has pointed out that he takes many of his ideas from socialism and that, despite this, he vindicates freedom as more important than power. For him, the work of the "true thinkers" is not an invariable matrix, model, or starting point. Instead, it is the frame, the scaffolding, the background to his dynamic and ever evolving current thinking. In addition, there is a sympathy based on their contemporaneity. Just as one could argue that he always returns to his conceptions of lies, demons, or the allegory of the tapeworm to explain his fiction or a writer's vocation, one can point out that he always returns to the previously cited thinkers in order to amplify his ideas, not to set them in stone. One could also argue that even if he repeats for the umpteenth time that all fictions are lies or that we can never be certain of anything, he will have to admit that one can find in his characters, beginning with his first novels, ideas that attract the reader. This attitude links him to three ways of evaluating the efficacy of the adaptation of ideas with reality, summarized by Maíz as "those that are 'misplaced' (Roberto Schwarz), those in 'the space in between' (Sil-viano Santiago), and what we could call 'migrant'" (85). According to this framework Vargas Llosa would, therefore, be the Latin American thinker with the widest influence, a perception that actually started back when he was a progressive's ideal writer.

It is well known that Vargas Llosa's notion of the "demon," which like others in his intellectual arsenal has been consistently present in his writings, became a cause célèbre when he defended its probable political implications from the criticisms of the late Uruguayan critic Angel Rama. Rama began the dialogue with his review of *García Márquez: historia de un deicidio* (García Márquez: History of a Deicide; 1971). Later, together with Julio Cortázar, Vargas Llosa criticized the then young Colombian novelist Oscar Collazos (Collazos et al. 78–93), better known today for the political positions he held than for his novels. The positions expressed by Vargas Llosa are very similar to those found in the seductive story of chapter 5 of *A Fish in the Water*, which narrates his decision of the 1950s to become a novelist. He has also presented this narrative and opinions in various and fragmentary variants, in earlier and even later texts, such as "El viaje a la ficción" (The Voyage into Fiction), now the "Preface" to his book on Onetti (11–32). The one that would become his "unit-idea," or the history of trial and error that according to Lovejoy constitutes the history of ideas (23), continues in his essay about the logistics of writing *The Green House*. There, as occurs in subsequent writings, he corrects the exegesis of his critics: "It is around this period that I discovered that novels were written principally out of obsessions and not convictions, that in the construction of a work of fiction, the contribution of the irrational dimension is, at least, as important as the rational" (*Historia secreta de una novela* 57–58). One may wonder whether this quotation could not be translated as asking "how many facts make up a work of fiction" and, by extension asking "how many constitute a political position."

Nevertheless, what further signals his coherence or insistence regarding any apolitical description of his craft as a novelist is the fact that the English language version of his essay on *The Green House*, included in *A Writer's Reality* (1991), reproduces the original with only one brief, though important, change regarding the "true real." Due to similar reasons, the conspicuously mutable character of his thought must also include his work as a critic of the novel. With cautious nods to various theories, he has continued that work until the present, with the second edition of *La verdad de las mentiras*, the essays dedicated to literature in *Touchstones*, and *El viaje a la ficción*. I say "recent" because Vargas Llosa is always studying other prose writers and until now has kept his word about writing a book about them, consistently returning to ideas that inspired him when he was young, and Flaubert continues being the most notable example. Still, academic critics have not been able to establish whether these relations with his favorite writers have, over the years, changed, stabilized, or deepened. Why? Because those critics generally believe that one should not concentrate on writers but must take into account the ideas of other critics like themselves. But what a good critic must do is concentrate on an author, in the same manner in which a "nonprofessional" reader would.

In his nonfiction Vargas Llosa has never attempted to explore the limits of public tolerance, instead preferring to exemplify it; thus he leaves both liberals and conservatives unsatisfied. In the *New York Times* interview previously mentioned, he asserts, "I am in favor of economic freedom, but I am not a conservative" ("Questions for Mario Vargas Llosa"). No one believes him, especially those who control academic discourse. Here we discover a contradiction: at universities, in principle the institutions committed to the free exchange of ideas, the loudest voices are precisely those that do not let others express themselves. For Vargas Llosa, as for the American pragmatist philosophers, an idea is a rule for action, and the word has not lost its connection with its root, the Greek word for "seeing." If some Latin American prose writers considered his peers have unfortunately become poseurs, Vargas Llosa cannot be accused of being insincere, even if his irrefutable logic irritates many. As a writer he attempts to bring into contact levels of society that are not normally connected, not always sure about how to bring together these differences in his essayistic and novelistic discourse. The authenticity of his prose, the conviction that ideas and their vicissitudes affect all of us, are proof of a precise documentary vision that has never been absorbed by ideology. In this sense, in the twentieth century, only Orwell is comparable as a defender of the West's history of ideas. And Vargas Llosa still has much to say about the century in which he and his readers now live. This is the reason why one can even now present only a preliminary approach to the avatars of his ideas.

NOTES

1. Werz states: "Vargas Llosa expresses admiration for the philosophical contents of Hayek's writings, but adds that a purely liberal economic model would not function in Latin America: (227). For a more general analysis on the free market in a Latin American context, see Steven Topik.

2. See: Mariela A. Gutiérrez, "Mario Vargas Llosa: Essais d'éthique historique (1962–1982)" which deals only with the first volume of *Contra viento y marea*. For the 1980s: Jesús Pindado, "Vargas Llosa: el discurso periodístico-polémico," and Mario Paoletti, "Las ideas políticas del joven Mario Vargas Llosa." Pindado wrongly hypothesizes that Vargas Llosa writes exclusively for the readers of Spain's *El País* (374); while Paoletti limits himself to texts written until 1975. It is as if Vargas Llosa had not written any nonfiction from the 1980s until the 1990s, when one can already examine what he has written during this century.

3. See my "Por qué Vargas Llosa sigue buscando la verdad de sus intérpretes," which discusses a brilliant reading by Mexican novelist Enrique Serna of the lectures collected in *Literatura y política*. In the interview with Jeremías Gamboa and Alonso Rabí do Carmo, "Mario Vargas Llosa critica a los críticos" he criticizes the academic obscurantism, logorrhea and dogmatism that "promotes a self-centered criticism or one that just fulfills an academic routine . . . which is prevalent in the universities of the United States" (2). Also see *La vie en mouvement* 83–85.

4. See Angvik 21–52. The novelist disappoints specialized critics due to his repetitions and the lack of "theory" in his essays, starting with his *Historia secreta de una novela* (1971) through his *Letters to a Young Novelist* (1997, Eng. 2002) and *El viaje a la ficción*. As Robb notes in his review of the French translation of *The Temptation of the Impossible* (2004), academic critics discard the value of his texts on García Márquez, Flaubert, Arguedas and Hugo, or his essays on

individual novelists that he has published in recent years, some included in the most recent edition of *La verdad de las mentiras*.

5. In synthesis, Vargas Llosa's practice is a kind of philosophy of judgment, at the same time that it is a philosophy of freedom. The relationship between both is fully developed in "Alain" (Emile Auguste Chartier), *Les Idées et les Âges* (Paris: Gallimard, 1927), regarding dreams, illusions, stories, games, loves, professions, worship and nature.

6. There is no study of *Textos del joven Vargas Llosa*, ed. Omar Prego (Montevideo: Cuadernos de Marcha/Intendencia Municipal de Montevideo, 1994), or Miguel Angel Rodríguez Rea's *Tras las huellas de un crítico: Mario Vargas Llosa, 1954-1959* (Lima: Pontificia Universidad Católica del Perú, 1996), which is a descriptive study of articles, interviews, and reviews he published during those years, one of which is the previously mentioned "José María Arguedas" (37–39). One also awaits the reaction to his 1958 Bachelor's thesis: *Bases para una interpretación de Rubén Darío*, ed. Américo Mudarra Montoya (Lima: Universidad Nacional Mayor de San Marcos, 2001).

7. It is superfluous to analyze how the reception of his nonfiction in Europe and the United States has always been very positive. The reception responds to his criticism's being at the level of the best ideas proposed by his critical equals. The not exaggerated comparisons with Amis, Coetzee, Kundera, Rushdie, Updike, and Henry James, and the few remaining peers are frequent. Something similar happens with his fiction. In her review of *The Bad Girl*, Harrison calls Vargas Llosa "master" and compares him with Flaubert, arguing that the novel is "splendid, suspenseful and irresistible" (9). According to Harrison, the novel is complete, convincing and does not let the reader close the book.

8. See Appiah's "Cosmopolitan Patriots."

WORKS CITED

Allatson, Paul. "'My Bones Shine in the Dark': AIDS and Chicano Queer Description in the Work of Gil Cuadros." *Aztlán: A Journal of Chicano Studies* 32.1 (Spring 2007): 23–52. Print.

Anderson, Perry. "Balanço do neoliberalismo." *Pós-neoliberalismo: As políticas sociais e o Estado democrático.* Eds. Emir Sader and Pablo Gentili. Rio de Janeiro: Paz e Terra, 1995. 9–23. Print.

Angvik, Birger. *La narración como exorcismo. Mario Vargas Llosa, obras (1963–2003).* Lima: Fondo de cultura económica, 2004. Print.

"Annual Dinner and Lecture." *Aei.org.* American Enterprise Institute, 2005. Web. 9 May 2007. http://www.aei.org/events/seriesID.8/series_detail.asp.

Archard, David. *Children: Rights and Childhood.* New York: Routledge, 2004. Print.

Appiah, Kwame Anthony. *Cosmopolitanism: Ethics in a World of Strangers.* New York: Norton, 2006. Print.

———. "Cosmopolitan Patriots." *For Love of Country: Debating the Limits of Patriotism.* Ed. Joshua Cohen. Boston: Beacon Press. 21–29. Print.

Arguedas, José María. *Formación de una cultura indoamericana.* 2nd ed. México: Siglo XXI 1977. Print.

Armas Marcelo, J. J. *Vargas Llosa. El vicio de escribir.* Madrid: Alfaguara, 2000. Print.

Arnold, Matthew. *Culture and Anarchy: An Essay in Political and Social Criticism.* New York: Macmillan, 1911. Print.

Beebee, Thomas. "Talking Maps: Region and Revolution in Juan Benet's *Volverás a Región* and Euclides da Cunha's *Os Sertões.*" *Comparative Literature* 47.3 (1995): 193–214. Print.

Benson, Elizabeth P., and Anita G. Cook, eds. *Ritual Sacrifice in Ancient Peru.* Austin: U of Texas P, 2001. Print.

Bensoussan, Albert, ed. *Mario Vargas Llosa.* Paris: Editions de l'Herne, 2003. Print.

Berlin, Isaiah. "Artistic Commitment: A Russian Legacy." *The Sense of Reality: Studies in Ideas and Their History.* Ed. Henry Hardy. New York: Farrar, Straus, and Giroux, 1996. 194–231. Print.

Bernucci, Leopoldo M. *Historia de un malentendido: Un estudio transtextual de La guerra del fin del mundo de Mario Vargas Llosa.* New York: Peter Lang, 1989. Print.

Bersani, Leo. "Is the Rectum a Grave?" *AIDS: Cultural Analysis, Cultural Activism.* Ed. Douglas Crimp. Cambridge, MA: MIT, 1988. 197–222. Print.

Boersenverein des Deutschen Buchhandel. 1 Dec 2010. Web. N.d. www.boersenverein.de.

Booker, M. Keith. *Vargas Llosa Among the Postmodernists.* Gainesville: UP of Florida, 1994. Print.

Borón, Atilio. "Vargas Llosa y la democracia: breve historia de una relación infeliz." *Rebelión* 13 June 2006. Web. 6 Jan. 2008. http://www.rebelion.org/noticia .php?id=32985.

Bowles, Samuel, and Herbert Gintis. *Democracy and Capitalism: Property, Community, and the Contradictions of Modern Social Thought.* London: Routledge, 1987. Print.

Browitt, Jeff. "Remembering Futures Past: National Failure in Gabriel García Márquez's *Cien años de soledad* and Mario Vargas Llosa's *La guerra del fin del mundo.*" Diss. Monash University, 1999. Print.

Camus, Albert. *The Myth of Sisyphus and Other Essays.* New York: Knopf, 1983. Print.

Caro, Olga. "Conceptos varguianos y sexualidad." *Coloquio Internacional: Escritura y sexualidad en la literatura hispanoamericanal.* Eds. Alain Sicard and Fernando Moreno. Madrid: Fundamentos, 1990. 167–80. Print.

Castro, Fidel. "Discurso pronunciado por el Comandante Fidel Castro Ruz . . . en la clausura del Primer Congreso Nacional de Educación, efectuado en el Teatro de la CTC, el 30 de Abril de 1971." *Cuba.cu.* Ministerio de Cultura de la República de Cuba. Web. 28 July 2008. http://www.cuba.cu/gobierno/discursos/1971/esp/ f300471e.html.

———. "Palabras a los intelectuales." June 1961. Ministerio de Cultura de la República de Cuba. Web. 28 July 2008. http://www.min.cult.cu/historia/palabras .doc.

Castro-Klarén, Sara. *Understanding Mario Vargas Llosa.* Columbia: U of South Carolina P, 1992. Print.

Christensen, Jerome C. "Rhetoric and Corporate Populism: A Romantic Critique of the Academy in an Age of High Gossip." *Critical Inquiry* 16 (1990): 438–65. Print.

Chrzanowski, Joseph. "Mario Vargas Llosa y la interpolaridad vida-ficción." *La historia en la literatura iberoamericana.* Ed. Raquel Chang-Rodríguez y Gabriella de Beer. New York: City U of New York P, 1989. 317–25. Print.

Collazos, Oscar, et al. *Literatura en la revolución y revolución en la literatura.* Mexico: Siglo XXI, 1970. Print.

Cornejo Polar, Antonio. "La guerra del fin del mundo: Sentido (y sinsentido) de la historia." *Remate de Males: Revista do Departamento de Teoria Literária* 13 (1993) 83–90. Print.

———. "Una heterogeneidad no dialéctica: Sujeto y discurso migrantes en el Perú moderno." *Revista Iberoamericana* 62.176–77 (July–Dec. 1996): 837–44. Print.

Corral, Wilfrido. "Por qué Vargas Llosa sigue buscando la verdad de sus interpretes." *El error del acierto.* Quito: Paradiso Editores, 2006. 179–90. Print.

Da Cunha, Euclides. *Rebellion in the Backlands.* Trans. Samuel Putnam. Chicago: U of Chicago P, 1944. Print.

Degregori, Carlos Iván. "El aprendiz de brujo y el curandero chino." *Elecciones 1990: demonios y redentores en el nuevo Perú, una tragedia en dos vueltas.* Eds. Carlos Iván Degrégori and Romeo Grompone. Lima: IEP ediciones, 1991. 69–136. Print.

De Man, Paul. "Autobiography as De-Facement." *MLN* 94.5 (1979): 919–30. Print.

———. *The Rhetoric of Romanticism.* New York: Columbia UP, 1984. Print.

De Soto, Hernando. *The Other Path: The Invisible Revolution in the Third World.* Trans. June Abbott. New York: Harper, 1989. Print.

"*Diario Granma* 'Vargas Llosa sigue siendo un canalla que escribe bien.'" *Expreso* 9 July 1997. Web. 6 Jan. 2009. http://www.laobradevargasllosa. com/baul07.html.

Diggins, John Patrick. *The Rise and Fall of the American Left.* New York: Norton, 1992. Print.

Diaz, Roberto Ignacio. *Unhomely Rooms: Foreign Tongues and Spanish American Literature.* Lewisburg, PA: Bucknell UP, 2002. Print.

Douglas, Mary. *Purity and Danger: An Analysis of Concepts of Pollution and Taboo.* London: Routledge, 1966. Print.

Dunkerley, James. "Mario Vargas Llosa: Parables and Deceits." *Political Suicide in Latin America and Other Essays.* London: Verso, 1992. 139–52. Print.

Elmore, Peter. "Los duelos de la historia." *ElComercio.com.pe.* El Comercio, 23 June 2007. Web. 12 Jan. 2008. http://elcomercio.pe/EdicionImpresa/Html/2007–06 –23/ImEcDominical0743850.html.

Edelman, Lee. *Homographesis: Essays in Gay Literary and Cultural Theory.* New York: Routledge, 1994. Print.

"El escritor Vargas Llosa acusa a Chávez de 'populista y corrupto." *Eldía.es.* El Día, 11 Oct. 2003. Web. 6 Jan. 2010. http://www.eldia.es/2003–11–10/VENEZUELA/ VENEZUELA1.HTM.

Ellis, Robert Richmond. *They Dream Not of Angels but of Men: Homoeroticisim, Gender, and Race in Latin American Autobiography.* Gainesville: UP of Florida, 2002. Print.

Escárzaga, Fabiola. "La utopía liberal de Vargas Llosa." *Política y Cultura* 17 (2002): 217–39. Print.

Faverón, Gustavo. "'Herbert Morote, extraña costumbre." *Puente AAéreo* 23 July 2006. Web. 9 Jan. 2010. http://puenteareo1.blogspot.com/2006/07/herbert-morote -extraa-costumbre.html.

Flores, Juan. *Divided Borders: Essays on Puerto Rican Identity.* Houston: Arte Público, 1993. Print.

Forgues, Roland. *Mario Vargas Llosa. Ética y creación. Ensayos críticos.* Paris: Mare & Martín, 2006. Print.

———. *Mario Vargas Llosa. Ética y creación.* Lima: Ed. Ricardo Palma, 2009. Print.

Foucault, Michel. "The Subject and Power." Rabinow and Rose. 126–44. Print.

———. "What Is an Author?" Rabinow and Rose. 377–91.

Franco, Jean. *The Modern Culture of Latin America: Society and the Artist.* Harmondsworth: Penguin, 1970. Print.

Friedenspreis des Deutschen Buchhandels 1996. Mario Vargas Llosa. Ansprachen aus Anlassder Verleihung. Frankfurt: Börsenverein des Deutschen Buchhandels, 1996. Print.

Fuentes, Carlos. *La nueva novela hispanoamericana.* Mexico City: Joaquín Mortiz, 1969. Print.

Fukuyama, Francis. *The End of History and the Last Man.* New York: Macmillan, 1992. Print.

Galvão, Walnice Noguera Galvao. "Prólogo." *Los Sertones.* Euclides da Cunha. Trans. Estela Dos Santos. Caracas: Biblioteca Ayacucho, 1980. ix–xxv. Print.

García Berrío, Antonio, and J. Huerta. *Los géneros literarios. Sistema e Historia.* Madrid: Cátedra: 1992. Print.

García Márquez, Gabriel. "Gabriel García Márquez." Interview by Rita Guibert. *Conversations with Gabriel García Márquez.* Ed. Gene H. Bell-Villada. Jackson: U of Mississippi P, 2005. 31–58. Print.

Gerdes, Dick. *Mario Vargas Llosa.* Boston: Twayne, 1985. Print.

Gewecke, Frauke. "*La fiesta del chivo* de Mario Vargas Llosa: Perspectivas de recepción de una novela de éxito." *Iberoamericana* 1.3 (2001): 151–56. Print.

Gilman, Sander L. "Plague in Germany, 1939/1989: Cultural Images of Race, Space and Disease." *Nationalisms and Sexualities.* Ed. Andrew Parker, et al. New York: Routledge, 1992. 175–200. Print.

Gilmore, Leigh. *Autobiographics: A Feminist Theory of Women's Self-Representation.* Ithaca, NY: Cornell UP, 1994. Print.

González Prada, Manuel. *El tonel de Diógenes.* México: Edición Tezontle, 1945. Print.

Grandin, Greg. *Empire's Workshop: Latin America, the United States, and the Rise of the New Imperialism.* New York: Metropolitan, 2006. Print.

Grandis, Rita de. "La problemática del conocimiento histórico en *Historia de Mayta* de M. Vargas Llosa." *Revista de Crítica Literaria Latinoamericana* 19 (1993): 375–82. Print.

Griffin, Clive. "Read for Freedom." *TLS: The Times Literary Supplement* 17 Aug. 2007: 22.

Guzmán, Jorge. "A Reading of Vargas Llosa's *The Real Life of Alejandro Mayta.*" *Latin American Literary Review* 15 (1987): 133–39. Print.

Guillermoprieto, Alma. *Looking for History: Dispatches from Latin America.* New York: Pantheon Books, 2001. Print.

Gutiérrez, Mariela. A. "Mario Vargas Llosa: Essais d'éthique historique (1962–1982)." Bensoussan. 236–242. Print.

Harrison, Kathryn. "Dangerous Obsession." Rev. of *The Bad Girl. New York Times Book Review* October 14, 2007: 1, 9. Print.

Harss, Luis, and Barbara Dohman. *Into the Mainstream: Conversations with Latin American Authors.* New York: Harper & Row, 1967. Print.

Harvey, David. *A Brief History of Neoliberalism.* New York: Oxford UP, 2005. Print.

Heritage Foundation. 6 Jan 2010. Web. 2010. http://www.heritage.org.

Higgins, James. *A History of Peruvian Literature.* Liverpool: Cairns, 1987. Print.

Hopenhayn, Martín. *Así de frágil es la cosa.* Bogotá: Norma, 1999. Print.

Huston, Hollis. "Revolutionary Change in *One Hundred Years of Solitude* and *The Real Life of Alejandro Mayta.*" *Latin American Literary Review* 15 (1987): 105–20. Print.

Hutcheon, Linda. *A Poetics of Postmodernism.* London: Routledge, 1988. Print.

Huntington, Samuel. "The Hispanic Challenge." *Foreign Policy* 141 (Mar./Apr. 2004): 29–45. Print.

Instituto de Cooperación Iberoamericana. *Semana de autor: Mario Vargas Llosa.* Madrid: Ediciones Cultura Hispánica, 1985. Print.

Jameson, Fredric R. "Posmodernism and Consumer Society." *The Cultural Turn: Selected Writings on the Postmodern, 1983–1998.* New York: Verso, 1998. 1–20. Print.

Johnson, Adriana Michele Campos. "Subalternizing Canudos." *MLN* 120.2 (2005): 355–82. Print.

Kam Wen, Siu. *Viaje a Ítaca*. Morrisville, NC: Diana, 2004. Print.

King, John. "Editor's Preface." *Touchstones: Essays in Literature, Art and Politics*. London: Faber & Faber, 2007. Print.

Kokotovic, Misha. *The Colonial Divide in Peruvian Narrative: Social Conflict and Transculturation*. Brighton: Sussex Academic P, 2005. Print.

Köllmann, Sabine. "*La fiesta del chivo*: Cambio y continuidad en la obra de Mario Vargas Llosa." *Iberoamericana* 1.3 (2001): 135–50. Print.

——. *Literatur und Politik—Mario Vargas Llosa*. Bern: Peter Lang, 1996. Print.

——. *Vargas Llosa's Fiction & the Demons of Politics*. New York: Peter Lang, 2002. Print.

Kristal, Efraín. *The Andes Viewed from the City: Literary and Political Discourse on the Indian in Peru, 1848–1930*. New York: Peter Lang, 1987. Print.

——. *Temptation of the Word: The Novels of Mario Vargas Llosa*. Nashville: Vanderbilt UP, 1998. Print.

Kristeva, Julia. *Powers of Horror: An Essay on Abjection*. Trans. Leon S. Roudiez. New York: Columbia UP, 1982. Print.

Kristol, Irving. "The Neoconservative Persuasion." *The Neocon Reader*. Ed. Irwin Steltzer. New York: Grove, 2004. 33–38. Print.

Larsen, Neil. "Mario Vargas Llosa: The Realist as Neo-Liberal." *Journal of Latin American Cultural Studies* 9.2 (2000): 155–79. Print.

Latour, Bruno. "Why Has Critique Run Out of Steam? From Matters of Fact to Matters of Concern." *Critical Inquiry* 30 (2004): 225–48. Print.

Lecarme, Jacques, and Eliane Lecarme-Tabone. *L'autobiographie*. París: Armand Colin, 1999. Print.

Lemus, Rafael. "La novela como arte." *Letras Libres* (Oct. 2007): 46–47.

Lins, Rómulo, and Marcos V. Teixeira. "Latin America: 'Technology in History.'" *Science, Technology, and Society: An Encyclopedia*. Ed. Sal Restivo. New York: Oxford UP, 2005. Print.

López-Calvo, Ignacio. *God and Trujillo: Literary and Cultural Representations of the Dominican Dictator*. Gainesville: UP of Florida, 2005. Print.

Lovejoy, Arthur O. *The Great Chain of Being: A Study of the History of an Idea*. 1936. Cambridge, MA: Harvard UP, 1964. Print.

Loyola, Hernán. "Canudos. Euclides da Cunha y Mario Vargas Llosa frente a Calibán." *Casa de las Americas* 32.185 (1991): 64–80. Print.

Maíz, Claudio. "La 'realidad' como fundamento y la eficacia de las ideas: El caso del antimodernismo literario." *Cuadernos Americanos* 2.120 (2007): 55–86. Print.

Malraux, André. *The Walnut Trees of Altenburg*. Trans. A. W. Fielding. Chicago: U of Chicago P, 1992. Print.

Manrique, Nelson. *La piel y la pluma. Escritos sobre literatura, etnicidad y racismo*. Lima: SUR,1999. Print.

Mariátegui, José Carlos. *Siete ensayos de interpretación de la realidad peruana*. Lima: Amauta, 1968. Print.

Miller, D. A. *The Novel and the Police*. Berkeley: U of California P, 1988. Print.

Monereo, Manuel. "En Perú hay una posibilidad." Interview by Miguel Reira. *El Viejo Topo* 227 (2006): n. pag. Web. 6 Jan. 2010. http://www.revistasculturales.com/articulos/100/elviejo-topo/656/1/entrevista-a-manuel-monereo.html.

Morote, Herbert. *Vargas Llosa, tal cual.* Lima: Jaime Campodónico, 1998. Print.

Muñoz, Braulio. *A Storyteller: Mario Vargas Llosa between Civilization and Barbarism.* New York: Rowman & Littlefield, 2000. Print.

Nealon, Jeffrey. *Foucault Beyond Foucault: Power and Its Intensifications Since 1984.* Stanford: Stanford UP, 2008. Print.

Neuwirth, Robert. *Shadow Cities: A Billion Squatters, A New Urban World.* New York: Routledge, 2005. Print.

Newman, Kathleen. "Historical Knowledge in the Post-Boom Novel." *The Historical Novel in Latin America: A Symposium.* Ed. Daniel Balderston. Gaithersburg, MD: Ediciones Hispamérica, 1986. 209–20. Print.

Nuñez, Ana. "No me arrepiento de mi voto por García." *Larepublica.com.pe.* La Republica, 1 Feb. 2008. Web. 8 Jan. 2010. http://www.larepublica.pe/archive/all/larepublica/20080201/pasadas/15/24105.

O'Bryan-Knight, Jean. *The Story of the Storyteller: La tía Julia y el escribidor, Historia de Mayta, and El Hablador by Mario Vargas Llosa.* Amsterdam: Rodopi, 1995. Print.

Okin, Susan Moller, ed. *Is Multiculturalism Bad for Women?* Princeton, NJ: Princeton UP, 1999. Print.

Omaña, Balmiro. "Ideología y texto en Vargas Llosa: sus diferentes etapas." *Revista de crítica literaria latinoamericana* 12.25 (1987): 137–54. Print.

Orwell, George. *Essays.* Ed. John Carey. New York: Knopf, 2002. Print.

Ossio, Juan. "Vargas Llosa y las ciencias sociales." *Las guerras de este mundo. Sociedad, poder y ficción en la obra de Mario Vargas Llosa.* Ed. Edgar Saba. Lima: Planeta, 2008. 135–45. Print.

Oviedo, José Miguel. *Mario Vargas Llosa. La invención de una realidad.* Barcelona: Seix Barral, 1982. Print.

Paoletti, Mario. "Las ideas políticas del joven Mario Vargas Llosa." *Conversación de otoño: homenaje a Mario Vargas Llosa.* Ed. Victorino Polo García. Murcia: Caja de Ahorros. 95–112. Print.

Página Web Oficial Mario Vargas Llosa. 10 May 2010. Web. 2005. http://www.mvargasllosa.com,

Paz, Octavio. *The Bow and the Lyre: The Poem, Poetic Revelation, Poetry and History.* Trans. Ruth L. Simms. Austin: U of Texas P, 1973. Print.

Pindado, Jesús. "Vargas Llosa: el discurso periodístico-polémico." *Mario Vargas Llosa: opera omnia.* Ed. Ana María Hernández de López. Madrid: Pliegos, 1994. 367–80. Print.

Pope, Randolph D. "Precauciones para la lectura de *Conversación en la catedral.*" *Journal of Spanish Studies: Twentieth Century* 6 (1978): 207–17. Print.

Puertas, Laura. "Vargas Llosa acusa a Toledo de socavar las bases de la democracia en Perú." *El País* 25 Mar. 2004. Web. 6 Jan. 2010. http://www.elpais.com/articulo/internacional/Vargas/Llosa/acusa/Toledo/socavar/bases/democracia/Peru/elpepiint/20040325elpepiint_18/Tes/.

Quijano, Aníbal. "Colonialidad y modernidad/racionalidad." *Los conquistados: 1492 y la población indígena de las Américas*. Ed. Heraclio Bonilla. Bogotá: Tercer Mundo-Libri Mundi, 1992. 437–47. Print.

Quiroz, Alfonso W. *Corrupt Circles: A History of Unbound Graft in Peru*. Baltimore, MD: Johns Hopkins U P, 2008.

Rabinow, Paul and Nikolas Rose, eds. "The Subject and Power." *The Essential Foucault: Selections from the Essential Works of Foucault 1954–1984*. New York: The New Press, 1994. Print.

Rama, Angel. "*La guerra del fin del mundo*: Una obra maestra del fanatismo artístico." *Angel Rama: Crítica literária y utopía en América Latina*. Ed. Carlos Sánchez Lozano. Antioquía, Colombia: Editorial de la U de Antioquía, 2006. 296–43. Print.

Rama, Angel, and Mario Vargas Llosa. *García Márquez y la problemática de la novela*. Buenos Aires: Corregidor-Marcha, 1973. Print.

Reisz de Rivarola, Susana. "La historia como ficción y la ficción como historia: Vargas Llosa y *Mayta*." *Nueva Revista de Filología Hispánica* 35 (1987): 835–53. Print.

Revel, Jean François. "Mario Vargas Llosa et la politique." In Albert Bensoussan, *Mario Vargas Llosa*. Paris: Editions de l'Herne, 2003. PP. 364-70. Print.

Robb, Graham. "Mario Vargas Llosa, Victor Hugo et *Les misérables*." *Le monde diplomatique* 55.650 (May 2008): 24–25. Print.

Rodríguez, Marita. "Mario Vargas Llosa, un escritor con conciencia." Asociación por la tolerancia, 24 Sept. 2007. Web. 6 Jan. 2009. http://www.tolerancia.org/asp/index_g.asp?vengode_g=Premios+Tolerancia&area=area10&tots=SI&port=NO&p4&t=NO&tema_1=NO&resett=SI&bk=NO.

Romero, José Luis. *Situaciones e ideología en Latinoamérica*. Buenos Aires: Editorial Sudamericana, 1986. Print.

Rowe, William. "Liberalism and Authority: The Case of Mario Vargas Llosa." *On Edge: The Crisis of Contemporary Latin American Culture*. Ed. George Yúdice, et al. Minneapolis: U of Minnesota P, 1992. 45–64. Print.

Sartre, Jean-Paul. "An Explication of *The Stranger*." *Camus: A Collection of Critical Essays*. Ed. Germaine Breé. New York: Prentice Hall, 1962. 108–21. Print.

———. *Nausea*. Tr. Lloyd Alexander. New York: New Directions, 1964. Print.

———. *What is Literature and Other Essays*. Ed. Stephen Ungar. Cambridge, MA: Harvard UP, 1988. Print.

Sedgwick, Eve Kosofsky. *Epistemology of the Closet*. Berkeley: U of California P, 1990. Print.

Setti, Ricardo. *Conversas com Vargas Llosa*. Sao Paulo: Ed. Brasiliense, 1986. Print.

———. *Sobre la vida y la política.Diálogo con Vargas Llosa*. Madrid: Intermundo, 1989. Print.

Sontag, Susan. *Illness as Metaphor/AIDS and Its Metaphors*. London: Penguin, 1991. Print.

Souza, Raymond D. *La historia en la novela hispanoamericana moderna*. Bogotá: Tercer Mundo, 1988. Print.

Spitta, Silvia. *Between Two Waters: Narratives of Transculturation in Latin America*. Houston: Rice UP, 1995. Print.

Stone, Robert. "Revolution as Ritual." Rev. of *War of the End of the World*, by Mario Vargas Llosa. *New York Times* 12 Aug. 1984. Web. 8 Jan. 2010. http://www .nytimes.com/books/98/06/28/specials/llosa-war.html.

Topik, Stephen. "Kart Polanyi and the Creation of the 'Market Society.'" *The Other Mirror: Grand Theory Through the Lens of Latin America*. Eds. Miguel Angel and Fernando López-Alves. Princeton: Princeton UP, 2001. 81–104. Print.

Treichler, Paula A. "AIDS, Homophobia, and Biomedical Discourse: An Epidemic of Signification." *AIDS: Cultural Analysis, Cultural Activism*. Ed. Douglas Crimp. Cambridge, MA: MIT, 1988. 31–70. Print.

Ubilluz, Juan Carlos. *Sacred Eroticism: Georges Bataille and Pierre Klossowski in the Latin American Erotic Novel*. Lewisburg, PA: Bucknell UP, 2006. Print.

Updike, John. "An Interview with John Updike." Interview by T. M. McNally and Dean Stover. *Conversations with John Updike*. Ed. James Plath. Jackson: UP of Mississippi, 1994. 192–206. Print.

Vargas Llosa, Álvaro. *El diablo en campaña*. Madrid: El País/Aguilar, 1991. Print.

Vargas Llosa, Mario. *Aunt Julia and the Scriptwriter*. Trans. Helen R. Lane. New York: Farrar, Straus, and Giroux, 1982. Print.

———. *The Bad Girl: A Novel*. Trans. Edith Grossman. New York: Picador, 2007. Print.

———. "Resurreción de Belcebú o la disidencia creadora." *Contra viento y Marea*. Vol. 1. 271–84. Print.

———. "Borges en París." *Caretas* 1571 (10 June 1999): n. pag. Web. 6 Jan. 2010. http://www.caretas.com.pe/1999/1571/mvll/mvll.htm.

———. "Borges, político." *Letras Libres* Nov. 1999: 24–26. Print.

———. "Camus and the Morality of Limits." *Making Waves*. 107–16. Print.

———. "Camus y la literatura." *Contra viento y marea*. Vol. 1. 84–87. Print.

———. *Captain Pantoja and the Special Service*. Trans. Ronald Christ and Gregory Kolovakos. New York: Harper, 1978. Print.

———. "Carta a Fidel Castro." *Contra viento y marea*.Vol. 1. 250–52. Print.

———. "Chronicle of the Cuban Revolution." Vargas Llosa, *Making Waves*. 20–24. Print.

———. "Confessions of a Liberal: 2005 Irving Kristol Lecture." *Aei.org*. American Enterprise Institute. Web. 20 Jun. 2007. http://www.aei.org/publications/pubID.22053,filter.all/pub_detail.asp.

———. "Confessions of an Old-Fashioned Liberal." *The American Enterprise Magazine* June 2005: 40–42.

———.*Contra viento y marea*. Vol. 1. Barcelona: Seix Barral, 1986. Print.

———. *Contra viento y marea*. Vol. 2. Barcelona: Seix Barral, 1986. Print.

———. *Contra viento y marea*. Vol. 3. Barcelona: Seix Barral, 1990. Print.

———. *Conversación en La catedral: I y II*. Barcelona: Seix Barral, 1969. Print.

———. *Conversation in The Cathedral*. Trans. Gregory Rabassa. New York: Harper, 1975. Print.

———. "The Culture of Liberty." *Foreign Policy* 122 (Jan.–Feb. 2001): 66–71. Print.

———. *Death in the Andes*. Trans. Edith Grossman. New York: Farrar, Straus, and Giroux, 1996. Print.

———. "Demons and Lies: Motivation and Form in Mario Vargas Llosa." Interview by Luis Rebasa-Soraluz. *Review of Contemporary Fiction* 17.1 (Spring 1997): 15–24. Print.

———. "Dentro y fuera de América Latina." *Letras Libres* Dec. 2005: 48–52. Print.

———. *Diccionario del amante de América Latina*. Barcelona: Paidós, 2006. Print.

———. "El bueno y el malo." *Caretas* 1540 (29 Oct. 1998): n. pag. Web. 6 Jan. 2010. http://www.caretas.com.pe/1998/1540/mvll/mvll.htm.

———. "El desquite de los pobres." *Caretas* 1498 (8 Jan. 1998): n. pag. Web. 6 Jan. 2010. http://www.caretas.com.pe/1998/1498/1498.htm.

———. "El futuro incierto de América Latina." *El País* 18 Oct. 2004, Internacional 51. Print.

———. "El intelectual, el poder y la política." Interview by Roland Forgues. *Mario Vargas Llosa escritor, ensayista, ciudadano y político*. Ed. Roland Forgues. Lima: Minerva, 2001. 619–50. Print.

———. "El pez vuelve al agua." *Caretas* 1490 (6 Nov. 1997): n. pag. Web. 6 Jan. 2010. http://www.caretas.com.pe/1490/pez/pez.htm.

———. "El PSOE se ha vuelto el caballo de Troya de los nacionalismos." Interview by Tulio Demichelli. *ABC* 20 May 2007, 10+. Print.

———. "El suicidio de una nación." *Caretas* 1580 (12 Aug. 1999): n. pag. Web. 6 Jan. 2010. http://www.caretas.com.pe/1999/1580/mvll/mvll.htm.

———. "El viaje a la ficción." *Letras Libres*, Feb. 2008: 12–18.

———. *El viaje a la ficción. El mundo de Juan Carlos Onetti*. Madrid: Alfaguara, 2008. Print.

———. "El viaje de Odiseo." *Letras Libres* Mar. 2007: 32–39. Print.

———. "Exhilaration and Completeness: an Interview with Mario Vargas Llosa." Interview by Robert Boyers and Gene H. Bell-Villada. *Salmagundi* 155–56 (Summer–Fall 2007): 212–40. Print.

———. *The Feast of the Goat*. Trans. Edith Grossman. New York: Farrar, Straus, and Giroux, 2001. Print.

———. *A Fish in the Water: A Memoir*. New York: Farrar, Straus, and Giroux, 1994. Print.

———. "A Fish Out of Water." *Granta* 36 (1991): 17–75. Print.

———. "Foreword." *The Other Path: The Invisible Revolution in the Third World*. By Hernando de Soto. xiii–xxii. Print.

———. "Ganar batallas, no la guerra." *Contra viento y marea*. Vol. 2. 92–106. Print.

———. *The Green House*. Trans. Gregory Rabassa. New York: Harper, 1968. Print.

———. "Gunter Grass en la picota." *El País* 27 Aug. 2006. Web. 6 Jan. 2010. http://www.elpais.com/articulo/opinion/Gunter/Grass/picota/elpporopi/20060827elpepopi_5/Tes.

———. *Historia de un deicidio*. Barcelona: Barral, 1971. Print.

———. *Historia de Mayta*. Madrid: Punto de lectura, 2008. Print.

———. *Historia secreta de una novela*. Barcelona: Tusquets, 1971. Print.

———. "Homenaje a Alfonso Reyes." *Presencia de Alfonso Reyes. Homenaje en el X aniversario de su muerte (1959–1969)*. Ed. Alicia Reyes, et al. Mexico City: Fondo de Cultura Económica, 1969. 162–63. Print.

——. *In Praise of the Stepmother*. Trans. Helen Lane. New York: Farrar, Straus, and Giroux, 1990. Print.

——. "La amenaza de los nacionalismos." *Letras Libres* Oct. 2001. Web. 6 Jan. 2010. http://www.letraslibres.com/index.php?art=7001&rev=2.

——. "La cultura de la libertad." *Contra viento y marea*. Vol. 2. 425–42. Print.

——. "La falacia del tercermundismo." *Contra viento y marea*. Vol. 2. 334–39. Print.

——. "La insurrección permanente." *Contra viento y marea*. Vol. 1. 107–10. Print.

——. "La literatura y la vida." *Vargas Llosa escritor, ensayista, ciudadano y político*. Ed. Roland Forgues. Lima: Minerva, 2001. 29–40. Print.

——. *La utopía arcaica. José María Arguedas y las ficciones del indigenismo*. México: Fondo de Cultura Económica, 1996. Print.

——. "Las batallas de Jean-François Revel." *Letras Libres* Nov. 2007: 67–76. Print.

——. "Latin America from the Inside Out." Trans. Gerald B. Whelan. *Salgamundi* 153–54 (2007): 32–41. Print.

——. "The Latin American Novel Today." Trans. Nick Mills. *Books Abroad* 44.1 (1970 Winter): 7–16. Print.

——. *La vie en mouvement. Entretiens avec Alonso Cueto*. Trans. Albert Bensoussan. Paris: Gallimard, 2006. Print.

——. "Letter to Haydée Santamaría." Vargas Llosa, *Making Waves*. 105–6. Print.

——. *Letters to a Young Novelist*. Trans. Natasha Winner. New York: Picador, 2002. Print.

——. "Literatura y política: dos visiones del mundo". *Literatura y política*. 2nd. ed. Madrid: Instituto Tecnológico y de Estudios Superiores de Monterrey/Fondo de Cultura Económica, 2003. 39–66. Print.

——. *Literature and Freedom:CIS Occasional Paper 48*. St. Leonards, NSW, Australia: Centre for Independent Studies, 1994.

——. "Literature and Life." *Touchstones*. London: Faber & Faber, 2007. Print.

——. "Literature Is Fire." Vargas Llosa, *Making Waves*. 70–74. Print.

——. "Los Añaños." *Caretas* 1799 (20 Nov. 2003): n. pag. Web. 10 Jan. 2010. http://www.caretas.com.pe/2003/1799/columnas/mvll.html.

——. "Luzbel, Europa y otras conspiraciones." *Literatura en la revolución y revolución en la literatura*. Oscar Collazos, Julio Cortázar, and Mario Vargas Llosa. Mexico: City Siglo XXI, 1970. 78–93. Print.

——. "Los próximos cuatro años." *La Nación* 20 Nov. 2004. Opinión 20. Print.

——. *Making Waves: Essays*. Ed. and trans. John King. New York: Penguin, 1996. Print.

——. "Mario Vargas Llosa critica a los críticos." Interview by Jeremías Gamboa and Alonso Rabí do Carmo. *La Nación, Cultura* (8 July 2007): 1–2. Print.

——. "'Nos mató la ideología.' Una entrevista con Mario Vargas Llosa." Interview by Héctor Aguilar Camín. *Nexos* 23.271 (July 2000): 42–55. Print.

——. *The Notebooks of Don Rigoberto*. New York: Penguin, 1999. Print.

——. "Obama en los infiernos." *El Comercio* 18 May 2008: A4. Print.

——. "Obama y el sueño americano." *El Comercio* 15 July 2007: A4. Print.

——. "Obama y las primarias." *El Comercio* 13 Jan. 2008: A4. Print.

———. "¿Otro país?" *La Nación* 1 July 2007. Web. 6 Jan. 2010. http://www.lanacion.com.ar/nota.asp?nota_id=923582.

———. *The Perpetual Orgy: Flaubert and Madame Bovary.* Trans. Helen Lane. New York: Farrar, Straus, and Giroux, 1987. Print.

———. "Perú en llamas." *Desafíos a la libertad.* Madrid: El País/Aguilar, 1994. 37–41. Print.

———. "Prólogo." *El otro sendero.* By Hernando de Soto. Buenos Aires: Editorial Sudamericana, 1987. xvii–xxxvi. Print.

———. "Queremos ser pobres." *Caretas* 1739 (11 July 2002): n. pag. Web. 6 Jan. 2010. http://www.caretas.com.pe/2002/1729/columnas/mvll.phtml.

———. "Questions for Mario Vargas Llosa: The Storyteller." Interview by Deborah Solomon. *New York Times Magazine* 7 Oct. 2007. Web. 9 Jan. 2010. http://www.nytimes.com/2007/10/07/magazine/07wwln-q4–t.html?_r=1.

———. "Questions of Conquest and Culture." *The Centre for Independent Studies,* 1993. Web. 1 Jan. 2009. http://www.cis.org.au/events/jbl/ifr_llosa.html.

———. "Questions of Conquest: What Columbus Brought and What He Did Not." *Harper's Magazine* 281 (Dec. 1990): 45–53. Print.

———. "Raza, botas y nacionalismo." *El Comercio.* 15 Jan. 2006. A4. Print.

———. "Razones contra la excepción cultural." *Caretas* 1834 (5 Aug. 2004): n. pag. Web. 6 Jan. 2010. http://www.caretas.com.pe/2004/1834/columnas/mvll.html.

———. "Razones para una alianza." *El País* 23 Apr. 2006. Web. 6 Jan. 2010. http://www.elpais.com/articulo/opinion/Razones/alianza/elpepiopi/20060423elpepiopi5/Tes/.

———. *The Real Life of Alejandro Mayta.* Trans. Alfred Mac Adam. New York: Noonday, 1998. Print.

———. "Sabio, discreto y liberal." *Caretas* 1492 (20 Nov. 1997): n. pag. Web. 6 Jan. 2010. http://www.caretas.com.pe/1492/mvll/mvll.htm.

———. "Socialismo del siglo XXI." *El País* 16 June 2007. Web. 8 Jan. 2010. http://www.elpais.com/articulo/opinion/Socialismo/siglo/XXI/elpepiopi/20070617elpepiopi_4/Tes.

———. "Tambores de guerra." *El Comercio.* 9 Mar. 2008. A4. Print.

———. "The Sign of the Cross." *The Language of Passion: Selected Commentary.* Trans. Natasha Winner. New York: Farrar, Straus, and Giroux, 2000. 82–86. Print.

———. *The Storyteller.* Trans. Helen Lane. New York: Farrar, Straus, and Giroux, 1989. Print.

———. "The Truth of Lies." Vargas Llosa, *Making Waves.* 320–30. Print.

———. *The Time of the Hero.* Trans. Lysander Kemp. New York: Noonday, 1966. Print.

———. *Touchstones: Essays on Literature, Art and Politics.* Ed. and trans. John King. London, 2007. Print.

———. "¿Una Luz en el Túnel?" *Caretas* 1613 (7 Apr. 2000): n. pag. Web. 6 Jan. 2010. http://www.caretas.com.pe/2000/1613/columnas/mvll.phtml.

———. "Una montaña de cadáveres (carta abierta a Alan García)." *Contra viento y marea.* Vol. 3. 389–93. Print.

———. "Una visita a Lurigancho." *Contra viento y marea.* Vol. 2. 303–7. Print.

———. "Un mundo sin novelas." *Letras Libres* Oct. 2000: 38–44. Print.

———. "Vargas Llosa: 'Alan García es el mal menor.'" *AgenciaPerú* 24 May 2006. Web. 6 Jan. 2010. http://agenciaperu.com/sociedad/2006/may/vargas_llosa.html.

———. "Vargas Llosa: 'se cancela la dictadura." Interview by Luis del Valle. *BBC-mundo* 9 Apr. 2001. Web. 6 Jan. 2010. http://news.bbc.co.uk/hi/spanish/latin _america/newsid_1268000/1268059.stm.

———. *The War of the End of the World*. Ed. Helen Lane. New York: Farrar, Straus, and Giroux. 1984. Print.

———. *The Way to Paradise*. Trans. Natasha Wimmer. New York: Picador, 2003. Print.

———. *Wellsprings*. Cambridge, MA: Harvard UP, 2008.

———. "The Writer in Latin America." *Index on Censorship* 7.6 (1978): 34–40. Print.

———. *A Writer's Reality*. Ed. Myron I. Lichtblau. Syracuse, NY: Syracuse UP, 1991. Print.

———. "Yo, un negro." *Contra viento y marea*. Vol. 3. 19–22. Print.

"Vargas Llosa afirma que los peruanos se arrepentirán si eligen a Humala." *El Diario Exterior* 24 Mar. 2006. Web. 6 Jan. 2010. http://www.eldiarioexterior.com/vargas -llosaafirma-que-los–9296.htm.

"Vargas Llosa: 'El derecho asiste al Perú en la demanda marítima con Chile." *Andina*. 31 Jan. 2008. 8 Jan. 2010. http://www.andina.com.pe/Espanol/Noticia .aspx?id=lUfCTFS5aXk.

"Vargas Llama a García Márquez 'Cortesano de Fidel Castro.'" *ABC*. 3 May 2003. 27. Print.

"Vargas Llosa pide lucidez a los venezolanos." *El Comercio* 25 Nov. 1999. Web. 6 Jan. 2010. http://www.laobradevargasllosa.com/articulos/art23.html.

Vázquez Montalbán, Manuel. "Yo no ve voy a poner a juzgar la novela de Vargas Llosa . . ." Interview by Thomas Bodenmüller. *Iberoamericana* 1.3 (2001): 173– 180. Print.

Venkatesh, Sudhir Aladi. *Off the Books: The Underground Economy of the Urban Poor*. Cambridge, MA: Harvard UP, 2006. Print.

Vich, Victor. "Desobediencia simbólica. Performance, participación y política al final de la dictadura fujimorista." *Hemispheric Institute Journal* 1.1 (Fall 2004). Web. 10 May 2010. http://hemisphericinstitute.org/journal/1_1/vich.html.

Vidal, Hernán. *Literatura hispanoamericana e ideología liberal; surgimiento y crisis: (Una problemática sobre la dependencia en torno a la narrativa del boom)*. Buenos Aires: Ediciones Hispamérica, 1976. Print.

Wasserman, Renata R. Mautner. "Mario Vargas Llosa, Euclides da Cunha, and the Strategy of Intertexuality." *PMLA* 108.3 (May 1993): 460–73. Print.

Werz, Nikolaus. *Pensamiento sociopolítico moderno en América Latina*. Trans. Gustavo Ortiz. Caracas: Editorial Nueva Sociedad, 1995. Print.

Williams, Raymond L. *Mario Vargas Llosa*. New York: Ungar, 1986. Print.

———. *Otra historia de un deicidio*. Mexico: Taurus-UNAM, 2001. Print.

Williamson, Judith. "Every Virus Tells a Story: The Meanings of HIV and AIDS." *Taking Liberties: AIDS and Cultural Politics*. Eds. Erica Carter and Simon Watney. London: Serpent's Tail, 1989. 69–80. Print.

Zapata, Roger A. "Las trampas de la ficción en la *Historia de Mayta*." *La historia en la literatura iberoamericana*. Eds. Raquel Chang-Rodríguez and Gabriella de Beer. New York: City U of New York P, 1989. 189–97. Print.

Contributors

Paul Allatson is the head of the International Studies Program at the University of Technology, Sydney; author of *Latino Dreams: Transcultural Traffic and the U.S. National Imaginary* (Rodopi, 2002) and *Key Terms in Latino/a Cultural and Literary Studies* (Blackwell, 2007); and coeditor of *Exile Cultures, Misplaced Identities* (Rodopi, 2008).

Gene H. Bell-Villada, a professor at Williams College, has authored or edited ten books. Among them are *García Márquez: The Man and his Work* (U of North Carolina P, 1990, revised 2010), *Art for Art's Sake & Literary Life* (U of Nebraska P, 1996), two books of fiction, and a memoir: *Overseas American: Growing Up Gringo in the Tropics* (UP of Mississippi, 2005).

Nicholas Birns teaches at the New School; his books include *Understanding Anthony Powell* (U of South Carolina P, 2004) and *Theory After Theory: An Intellectual History of Literary Theory Since 1950* (Broadview, 2010).

Will H. Corral's most recent books are *El error del acierto (contra ciertos dogmas latinoamericanistas)* (Paradiso, 2006) and *Cartografía occidental de la novela hispanoamericana* (Centro Cultural Benjamín Carrión, 2010). With Daphne Patai he coedited *Theory's Empire* (Columbia UP, 2005).

Juan E. De Castro teaches at Eugene Lang College, the New School for Liberal Arts. His books are *Mestizo Nations: Culture, Race, and Conformity in Latin American Literature* (U of Arizona P, 2002) and *The Spaces of Latin American Literature: Tradition, Globalization and Cultural Production* (Palgrave Macmillan, 2008).

The author of numerous essays on Latin American indigeneity and politics, **Fabiola Escárzaga** is a professor at the Universidad Autónoma Metropolitana Unidad Xochimilco. She is the coeditor of *Movimiento indígena en América Latina: resistencia y proyecto alternativo*, volumes 1 and 2 (Juan Pablos, 2005, 2006), and *Sobre la marcha: análisis sobre el movimiento zapatista* (UAM, 2001).

One of the most prolific European scholars of Peruvian and Latin American literature, Professor Emeritus **Roland Forgues** (Université de Pau) is the author most recently of *Mario Vargas Llosa: ética y creación* (Universidad de Ricardo Palma, 2009) and *Gregorio Martínez, danzante de tijeras* (Universidad de San Marcos, 2009).

Professor of Spanish and Portuguese at Temple University, **Sergio R. Franco** is the author of *A favor de la esfinge. La novelística de Jorge Eduardo Eielson* (Universidad de San Marcos, 2000) and the editor of *José María Arguedas: Hacia una poética migrante* (IILI, 2006).

Jean O'Bryan-Knight teaches at the University of Pennsylvania. Her publications on Andean authors include the book *The Story of the Storyteller: La tía Julia y el escribidor, Historia de Mayta and El hablador by Mario Vargas Llosa* (Rodopi, 1995).

Sabine Köllmann is an independent researcher and translator in London. Her publications include *Literatur und Politik—Mario Vargas Llosa* (Peter Lang, 1996), *Vargas Llosa's Fiction & the Demons of Politics* (Peter Lang, 2002), and coauthored with Brian Vickers, *Mächtige Worte—Antike Rhetorik und europäische Literatur* (LIT, 2008).

Ignacio López-Calvo is a professor of literature at the University of California, Merced. He is the author of *Written in Exile. Chilean Fiction from 1973–Present* (Routledge, 2001); *Religión y militarismo en la obra de Marcos Aguinis 1963–2000* (Edwin Mellen, 2002); *"God and Trujillo": Literary and Cultural Representations of the Dominican Dictator* (UP of Florida, 2005); and *Imaging the Chinese in Cuban Literature and Culture"* (UP of Florida, 2007).

INDEX

CPSIA information can be obtained at www.ICGtesting.com
Printed in the USA
LVOW081606170112

264296LV00005B/5/P